WHEN THE RIVERS RUN DRY

WHEN THE

RIVERS RUN DRY

JOURNEYS INTO THE HEART OF THE
WORLD'S WATER CRISIS

FRED PEARCE

Foreword by DAVID SUZUKI

KEY PORTER BOOKS

Library and Archives Canada Cataloguing in Publication

Pearce, Fred

When the rivers run dry : journeys into the heart of the world's water crisis / Fred Pearce ; introduction by David Suzuki.

Includes index.

ISBN 1-55263-741-7

1. Water-supply.   2. Water-supply—Economic aspects.   3. Water-supply—Political aspects.   4. Water resources development.   I. Title.

HD1691.P433 2006   333.91   C2005-906549-4

The publisher gratefully acknowledges the support of the Canada Council for the Arts and the Ontario Arts Council for its publishing program. We acknowledge the support of the Government of Ontario through the Ontario Media Development Corporation's Ontario Book Initiative.

We acknowledge the financial support of the Government of Canada through the Book Publishing Industry Development Program (BPIDP) for our publishing activities.

This book is printed on acid-free paper that is Ancient Forest Friendy (100% post-consumer recycled paper).

Key Porter Books Limited
Six Adelaide Street East, Tenth Floor
Toronto, Ontario
Canada M5C 1H6

www.keyporter.com

Text design: Marijke Friesen
Electronic formatting: Jean Lightfoot Peters

Printed and bound in Canada

06 07 08 09 10 5 4 3 2 1

ACKNOWLEDGEMENTS

*For Joe, another river who
died before his time*

This book's gestation goes back more than a decade and many hundreds of people helped at various stages. There are too many to name, even if I could remember them all. But I would like to say thank you to those who helped during the field work that brought the book to fruition. Many of them are quoted or otherwise acknowledged in the text, and I hope that will suffice. But some require special mention for guiding me in directions I would never have thought to go, and often for providing the cars, guides and other help necessary to get me there.

In particular I thank Patrick Fuller and the staff of the International Water Management Institute in Colombo, Sri Lanka, who came up with a travel grant that got me to China, Uzbekistan and Stockholm. In India, I am greatly indebted to Tushaar Shah and his staff at IWMI in Anand, Gujarat, and to Kuppannan Palanisami and his students at the Tamil Nadu state university's Water Technology Centre in Coimbatore. In Bangladesh and West Bengal, Dipankar Chakraborti has been indispensable in unravelling the mysteries of the arsenic disaster, while Oxfam guided me to fluoride afflicted villages. Oxfam's Geoff Graves took me to villages in Palestine, while Arie Issar proved to me again that there is decency to be found on the other side of the divide there. In Cambodia, Eric Baran of WorldFish took me up the Tonle Sap. IWMI's Iskandar Abdullaev drove me the length of Uzbekistan and introduced me to many brave and stoical people. On the Rio Grande, Mary Kelly of Environmental Defence guided me well, and in China, Xue Yunpeng and many others at the Yellow River Conservancy Commission proved candid and optimistic on a long and fruitful journey.

At the Eden Project and Transworld in the UK, and at Key Porter in Canada, thanks are due especially to Tim Smit, Susanna Wadeson, Sarah Emsley and Meg Taylor for their faith in the project. Unknowingly, many commissioning editors for numerous magazines and newspaper have helped my travels for this book. Notable among them are Bill O'Neill during his time at the *Guardian* and the innumerable editors I have worked for over the years at *New Scientist*. To them all, thanks again.

TABLE OF CONTENTS

WHEN THE RIVERS RUN DRY

An extragalactic explorer upon discovering our solar system would certainly name the third planet from the Sun, Water. Covering 70 per cent of Earth's surface, water shrouds the globe in atmospheric cloud and vapour. The oceans are where life was born and the salty fluid that courses through our veins is a reminder of our aqueous origins. Space probes to our moon, Mars, and the moons of Saturn search for water as a pre-condition for life as we know it. On Earth, "waterfront" defines our most highly prized esthetic quality of the places where humans live. Small wonder, then, that water has been central to cultures, religions, and rituals; acknowledgement of its life-giving properties.

Although most water is salty or locked away in great sheets of ice, the hydrologic cycle constantly showers us with the freshwater we all need, replenishing lakes and rivers, and recharging water tables and aquifers. Life itself is an integral part of this water cycle: forests suck vast quantities of water from the soil and thrust it skyward through transpiration; plant roots, soil fungi, bacteria, and other micro-organisms filter and cleanse water; and all organisms are inflated by water as it passes through the skin of living things before returning to the biosphere.

Over the past century, the conjunction of exploding human numbers, increased technological prowess, and an expanding global economy have increased the pressures on and demand for this priceless material.

Sky-rocketing consumption of water-intensive food and manufactured products, large dams for hydroelectricity and irrigation, massive discharge of industrial effluent into lakes and rivers, and the drilling and pumping of increasingly deeper wells, have in sum made water an increasingly limited and expensive resource.

Homo sapiens was born in Africa some 150,000 years ago, surrounded by a vast array of impressive animals. Our deficits in physical and sensory prowess were more than compensated by a large, complex brain that endowed us with foresight, the ability to look ahead, recognize opportunities and dangers, and then act to avoid hazards, exploit benefits and maximize survival. It is ironic that today with all of the amplified predictive capacity conferred by scientists, computers, and telecommunications we no longer take advantage by looking ahead and avoiding catastrophe.

Fred Pearce is a renowned science writer who has exhaustively explored the way we are attempting to domesticate and exploit rivers, often with catastrophic consequences. This is an urgent warning and a call for action that we must not ignore. Our rising thirst for water now seems to be slaked with heroic measures that ultimately degrade life's liquid necessity.

Human technology is crude but very powerful so that we create an illusion of control that is temporary and doomed because our knowledge of nature's complexity and interconnectedness, of which water is a part, is so paltry. I believe we have to re-examine our relationship with water, learning from ancient insights that it is not simply a commodity for commerce but a sacred substance that maintains all life on the planet. We don't treat something we revere the way we are treating water. And we must be much more humble about our knowledge; impressive as twentieth-century science and technology have been, our understanding of how the world works remains minuscule and fragmentary. Instead of attempting to overwhelm Nature by bludgeoning her with the power of our technological interventions, we would do far better to mimic what we can see of the way she works. Fred Pearce's work is a timely and urgent message for all of humankind.

A NOTE ON MEASURING WATER

I'd like to introduce you to the cubic kilometre. It is the main unit I'll use throughout this book. It is rather a lot of water, but it measures well what runs down a river in a year—from measly rivers like London's Thames, which manages between two and three cubic kilometres, to the mighty River Amazon, which handles some 6,000 cubic kilometres between its banks. I find it hard to imagine a cubic kilometre, so from time to time I'll refer instead to handy units such as the annual flow of the River Nile, which at least is a real river and has a natural flow of about 50 cubic kilometres.

When we are talking about things smaller than river flows, there is the cubic metre. That I can see in front of me. It weighs a tonne. It is the same as a thousand litres. It is enough water to fill about three bathtubs. You need 3,125 of them to fill an Olympic swimming pool. And there are a billion of them in a cubic kilometre. (So, if it helps, that means there are just over 300,000 Olympic swimming pools in a cubic kilometre.)

I was tempted to use a rather handy American measure for water: the acre-foot. I like it because it is big but imaginable. Flood an acre of land to a depth of a foot and you have it. I decided against, however, because I wanted to stick with metric measures. But if you like it, then there are just over a thousand cubic metres in an acre-foot. Or a bit under a million acre-feet in a cubic kilometre.

13

In the cause of metrication, I have avoided the acre when describing land areas in favour of the hectare, which is two and a half times as much and a bit bigger than a soccer pitch. There are 100,000 square metres in a hectare, and a hundred hectares in a square kilometre.

INTRODUCTION

It would be wrong to say that I have been obsessed with rivers all my life. But, much as when taking a drive down a long river valley, I can't seem to avoid coming back to them. They have a hold.

I was brought up in a village in southeast England where two small rivers began their journey to the sea. One, the River Len, flowed west to the Medway and the Thames estuary. It powered a mill, I remember, and filled a lake in a park. Then one day it flooded and I couldn't get to school. That struck me: the power of a river unleashed.

The other river, the Stour, flowed east through the cathedral city of Canterbury, took in some extra water bubbling up from the bowels of the East Kent coal mines and finished in a marshy mess called Pegwell Bay. It's currently in the news for almost the first time, because my childhood backwater of Kent is to spawn a New Town, and there are plans to dam the Stour to fill the taps. I am amazed that it's believed such a little river can provide enough water to make it worthwhile. But when you are trying to water the driest corner of England, needs must, apparently. And even the smallest river can fill the oceans if it flows for long enough.

Rivers so often define our world. Is there a better book about America than Huckleberry Finn's journey on the Mississippi? Is there a better way of seeing London than taking a boat down the Thames to Greenwich? Some of the greatest human adventures have been along rivers: up the Orinoco to find El Dorado; or the search for the source of the Nile. Millions of Indians keep bottles of Ganges water in their homes, like holy water. We romance on the Blue Danube and the Seine; and fight over the Jordan and the rivers of Babylon.

And yet something disturbing has been happening. I only slowly became aware of it: just a news story here and there seeped through. But the maps in my atlas no longer seemed to accord with reality. Inland seas and lakes were disappearing. The old geography lessons about how rivers emerged from mountains, gathered water from tributaries and finally disgorged their bloated flows into the oceans were now fiction. Many rivers were dying as they went on, not growing.

Because I am a journalist, I assembled a small file of press clippings. The Nile in Egypt, the Yellow River in China, the Indus in Pakistan, the Colorado and Rio Grande in the USA—all were reported to be trickling into the sand, sometimes hundreds of miles from the sea. Individually, these were interesting stories. Taken together, they seemed to me to be something more. Some kind of cataclysm was striking the world's rivers. And so began the idea for this book.

I soon learned more. The Murray in Australia was stopped by a sandbank within sight of the ocean. Israel was draining the River Jordan into pipes before it reaches the country that bears its name. There was drought on the Ganges because India had sucked up the holy river's entire dry season flow. The great Oxus, the Nile of Central Asia, was diverted into the desert, leaving the Aral Sea to dry out. This was a real shocker; the shoreline shown on most maps of what was once the world's fourth largest inland sea was hundreds of kilometres distant from the reality. Even the chalk streams of my Kentish childhood were disappearing.

The wells have been drying up too. Half a century of pumping on the High Plains of the USA has removed water that will take two thousand years of rain to replace. In India, farmers whose fathers lifted water from wells with a bucket now sink boreholes more than a kilometre into the rocks—and still they find no water.

My book is a journey of discovery on the world's rivers: to find out why we face this crisis, what happens when great rivers die, where we could be headed—and how we can restore the rivers' health and our hydrological future.

While it is mainly about rivers, it is also about how we use water: about the quite staggering amount that it takes to feed and clothe us; about how the world trade in food and cotton and much more is also a trade in "virtual water"—the water it takes to grow those crops; and now that implicates Western consumers directly in the emptying of many of the world's great rivers.

Along the way, I met men in overcoats huddled in drafty offices trying to keep the Ruritanian badlands of Karakalpakstan from turning to desert. I marched with a man who used to run the world's largest dam-building organization and now campaigns to tear down dams. I drank with Chinese bureaucrats who say droughts on the Yellow River will one day trigger a flood disaster on a par with the one half a century ago that they try not to talk about—it was man-made and killed almost a million people. I met Indian rainwater harvesters, and the last man alive with the secrets of divining water from underground Cyprus.

Here too are the stories of Colonel Gadaffi's great man-made river, pumping the world's greatest reservoir of fresh water from beneath the Sahara; of the world's third tallest dam, which any day could be ripped apart by either an earthquake or a civil war; of the river that flows backwards to feed ten million people; of the extraordinary ancient water tunnels beneath Iran that could stretch to the moon three times over; of the British-built irrigation project that is one hundred kilometres from the nearest water; of the Australian farm that grabs more water than there is in Sydney Harbour; and the secret truth of the world's biggest-ever water-poisoning scandal.

I hope to answer some pressing questions. Can we fill the world's taps without emptying its rivers? Do we need megaprojects to divert the Great Lakes into the American West, the River Congo into the Sahara, or the torrents of Siberia into the deserts of Central Asia? Or should we think small, catching the rain from our roofs or irrigating crops with bicycle inner tubes or plastic sheaths bought from ice-cream salesmen?

Nothing, perhaps not even climate change, will matter more to humanity's future on this planet over the next century than the fate of our rivers. Plenty of explorers have sought the source of the world's great rivers. This is a journey to chart their deaths. But it is a hopeful journey nonetheless. I am an optimist. Water, after all, is the ultimate renewable resource.

1

THE HUMAN SPONGE

Few of us realize how much water it takes to get us through the day. On average, we drink no more than five litres of the stuff. Including water for washing and for flushing the toilet we use only about 150 litres each. In some countries suburban lawn sprinklers, swimming pools and sundry outdoor uses can double that figure. Typical per-capita water use in suburban Australia is 350 litres and in the USA around 400 litres. There are exceptions, though. One suburban household in Orange County, Florida, was billed for 15.9 million litres in a single year—or more than 40,000 litres a day. Nobody knows how they got through that much.

We can all save water in the home. But laudable though it is to take a shower rather than a bath, put a brick in the lavatory cistern and turn off the tap while brushing our teeth, we shouldn't get hold of the idea that regular domestic water use is what is really emptying the world's rivers. Manufacturing the goods that we fill our homes with consumes a certain amount, but that's not the real story either. It is only when we add in the water needed to grow what we eat and drink that the numbers really begin to soar.

Get your head around a few of these numbers, if you can. They are mind-boggling. It takes between 2,000 and 5,000 litres of water to grow one kilo of rice. That is more water than many households use in a week. For just a bag of rice. Keep going. It takes 1,000 litres to grow a kilo of wheat, and 500 litres for a kilo of potatoes. And when you start feeding grain to livestock for animal products such as meat and milk, the numbers become yet more startling. It takes 11,000 litres to grow the feed for enough cow to make a quarter-pound hamburger; and between 2,000 and 4,000 litres for that cow to fill its udders with a litre of milk. Cheese? That takes about 5,000 litres for a kilo of cheddar or brie or camembert.

And if you think your shopping basket is getting a trifle bulky at this point, maybe you should leave that kilo bag of sugar on the shelf. It took up to 3,000 litres to produce. And the kilo jar of coffee tips the scales at 20,000 litres—or 20 tonnes—of water. Imagine taking that lot home from the supermarket.

Turn those stats into meal portions and you come up with more than 100 litres for a portion of rice, 150 litres for the bread in a sandwich or a round of toast, 500 litres for a two-egg omelette or a mixed salad, 1,000 litres for a glass of milk, 1,500 litres for an ice cream, 2,000 litres for a pork chop, 3,000 litres for a hamburger and 5,000 litres for a small steak. And if you have a sweet tooth, so much the worse: every teaspoonful of sugar in your coffee requires 50 cups of water to grow it. Which is a lot, but not as much as the 140 litres of water (or 1,120 cups) needed to grow the coffee itself. Prefer alcohol? A glass of wine or pint of beer with dinner requires about another 250 litres, and a glass of brandy afterwards takes a staggering 2,000 litres.

We are all used to reading detailed technical information about the nutritional content on most food packaging. Maybe it is time that we were given some clues as to how much water it took to grow and process the food. As the world's rivers run dry, it matters.

I reckon that, as a typical meat-eating, beer-swilling, milk-guzzling Westerner, I consume in this way as much as a hundred times my own weight in water every day. Hats off, then, to my vegetarian daughter, who gets by with about half that. And time, surely, to go out and preach the gospel of water conservation. But don't buy one of those jokey T-shirts advertised on the Internet with slogans like "Save water, bath with a friend." Good message, but you could fill roughly twenty-five bathtubs with the water needed to grow the 250 grams needed to make the shirt. It gives a whole new meaning to the wet T-shirt contest.

Let's do the annual audit. I probably drink only about a thousand litres of water—that's one tonne or a cubic metre—in a whole year. Around the home I probably use between 50 and 100 tonnes. But growing the crops to feed and clothe me for a year must take between 1,500 and 2,000 tonnes—rather more than half the contents of an Olympic-sized swimming pool.

Where does all that water come from? In England, where I live, most home-grown crops are watered by rain. So the water is at least cheap. But remember that a lot of the food consumed in Britain, and all the cotton, is imported. And when, as in much of the world, the water to grow crops is collected from rivers or pumped from underground, it is increasingly expensive and its diversion to fields is increasingly likely to deprive someone else of water and to empty rivers and underground water reserves. And when the rivers are running low, it is ever more likely that the water simply will not be there to grow the crops at all.

The water "footprint" of Western countries on the rest of the world deserves to become a serious issue. Whenever you buy a T-shirt made of Pakistani cotton, eat Thai rice or drink coffee from Central America, you are influencing the hydrology of those regions—taking a share of the River Indus, the Mekong or the Costa Rican rains. You may be helping rivers run dry.

Economists call the water involved in the growing and manufacture of products traded round the world "virtual water." In this terminology, every tonne of wheat arriving at a dockside carries with it in virtual form the thousand tonnes of water needed to grow it. The global virtual water trade is estimated to be around a thousand cubic kilometres a year, or twenty River Niles. Of that, two-thirds is in a huge range of crops from grains to vegetable oil, sugar to cotton; a quarter is in meat and dairy products; and just a tenth in industrial products. That means that nearly a tenth of all the water used in raising crops goes into the international virtual-water trade. This trade "moves water in volumes and over distances beyond the wildest imaginings of water engineers," says Tony Allan of the School of Oriental and African Studies in London, who invented the term "virtual water."

The biggest net exporter of virtual water is the USA. It exports around a third of all the water it withdraws from the natural environment. Much of that is in grains, either directly or via meat. The USA is emptying critical underground water reserves, such as those beneath the High Plains, to grow grain for export. It also exports an amazing 100 cubic kilometres of virtual water in beef. Other major exporters of virtual water include Canada (grain), Australia (cotton and sugar), Argentina (beef) and Thailand (rice).

Major importers of virtual water include Japan and the European Union. None of these countries is short of water, so there are ethical questions about how much they should be doing this. But for other importers virtual water is a vital lifeline. Iran, Egypt and Algeria could starve otherwise; likewise, water-stressed Jordan, which effectively imports between 80 and 90 per cent of its water in the form of food. "The Middle East ran out of water some years ago. It is the first major region of the world to do so in the history of the world," says Allan. He estimates that more water flows into the Middle East each year as a result of imports of "virtual water" than flows down the River Nile.

While many nations relieve their water shortages by importing virtual water, some exacerbate their problems by exporting it. Israel and arid southern Spain both export water in tomatoes; Ethiopia, in coffee. Mexico's virtual-water exports are emptying its largest water body, Lake Chapala, which is the main source of water for its second city, Guadalajara.

Many cotton-growing countries provide a vivid example of this perverse water trade. Cotton grows best in hot lands with virtually year-round sun. Deserts, in other words. Old European colonies and protectorates such as Egypt, Sudan and Pakistan still empty the Nile and the Indus for cotton-growing, as they did when Britain ruled and Lancashire cotton mills had to be supplied. Australia does much the same on the River Murray, which is drying up as a result. When Russia transformed the deserts of Central Asia into a vast cotton plantation, it sowed the seeds of the destruction of the Aral Sea. Most of the missing water for the shrivelling sea has, in effect, been exported over the past half-century in the form of virtual water that continues to clothe the countries of the former Soviet Union.

Some analysts say that, globally, the virtual-water trade significantly reduces water demand for growing crops. It allows crops to be grown where water requirements are less, they say. But this is mainly because the biggest trade in virtual water is the export of wheat and corn from temperate lands like the USA and Canada to hotter lands where the same crops would require more water. But for many other crops, such as cotton and sugar, the trade in virtual water looks like terribly bad business for the exporters.

Pakistan consumes more than fifty cubic kilometres of water a year from the River Indus—almost a third of the river's total flow and enough to prevent any water reaching the Arabian Sea—in order to grow cotton. How much sense does that make? And what logic is there in Australians emptying the Murray River to grow sugar and cotton? Or for the US to pump out the High Plains aquifer to add to a global grain glut? Whatever the virtues of the global trade in virtual water, the practice lies at the heart of some of the most intractable hydrological crises on the planet.

2

CANADA: A SPRING
BREAKUP

It starts with a crack: a small imperceptible shiver in a huge mass of ice. Then a groan and a shift in the mighty white plates. Small streams of barely liquid water begin to lubricate the movement. The thaw has begun and the great rivers are returning to life, building up their force until the ice can no longer hold them back. The spring breakup, one of the great natural sights of the Canadian north, has begun. For months, as the ice gives way, rivers like the MacKenzie and the Yukon, the Liard and Back, are among the greatest rivers on the planet, before the freeze again puts the Arctic hydrology into cold storage.

The Canadian north is one of the great water towers of the planet. Frozen in winter and then raging towards the ocean in summer, or stored for millennia in the Great Lakes, there is more water in Canada than anywhere else on Earth, bar Brazil and Russia. A tenth of the country is covered by lakes and rivers, and as much again by wetlands. It sustains three of the world's top twenty rivers—the Mackenzie, Yukon and St. Lawrence. At any one time during the spring melt, roughly a tenth of all the water in all world's rivers is flowing from the Canadian West into the Pacific and Arctic Oceans. And if that wasn't enough, a fifth of all the surface freshwater in the world sit in the Great Lakes, a stupendous 23,000 cubic kilometres of it.

So, I wondered, as a bemused Englishman, why on Earth do Canadians go crazy at the idea of letting one drop of their water go south to lubricate the lives of Americans? Why do they baulk at the idea of selling a little of their most abundant resource to their near-est neighbour and closest ally? Partly, I concluded, it is a matter of birthright. "It's like the flag; it's very sensitive," Monte Hummel, president of wwf Canada, told me. Water is not like any other commodity. It is, most Canadians believe, not a commodity at all. It is a human right. And human rights are not for sale.

But partly too it is pragmatism. The Great Lakes may be a vast water bank, but they are a bank that contains a deposit that everybody fears drawing on. Much of the water, especially in the great, deep Lake Superior, dates back to the melting of the great ice sheets at the end of the last ice age; it is only naturally replen-ished at a rate of 1 per cent every year—roughly a 75-centimetre skim across the surface. As the Canadian government's water guru Frank Quinn put it: "The Great Lakes are a gift of melting glaciers and cannot be given again."

And some regions of Canada are, amazing though it seems to an outsider, running short of water. Eighty-five per cent of the Canadian population lives in the south, which has only 10 per cent of the country's replenishable water. A quarter of all Canada's municipalities have faced water shortages in the past decade. In 2001 and 2002, the prairie provinces of Saskatchewan, Alberta and Manitoba suffered record droughts that left the prairies looking like a rerun of the thirties dustbowl. Meandering through the provinces, the South Saskatchewan River, the coun-try's most dammed and stressed waterway, ran dry as allocations exceeded supply. Even in British Columbia, just weeks after the spring melt, the people of Vancouver were knuckling down to lawn-watering restrictions for the eighth straight year. By 2004, water tables were so low that, according to provincial water offi-cial, "as the snow melted, it just disappeared and didn't make it into streams."

Canada's water is the world's water in miniature. There is abundance and scarcity; drought and flood; waste and want. And it is going to get worse. Run the global climate models ahead a few decades for Canada and they predict that it will likely get wetter in the north, where the great Arctic rivers will garner more rainfall from their catchments and take more to the sea. But in the water-stressed south, the rains will fail, the prairies will dry out some more, rivers will dry up and rising evaporation rates will rake an extra surcharge from the Great Lakes. Dave Schindler at the University of Alberta, one of the country's most respected ecologists, says global warming could drop lake levels by a metre and reduce outflow over Niagara Falls and down the St. Lawrence by a third.

How does Canada respond to this new uncertainty? By allowing its water infrastructure to fall into disrepair, and its municipal water policies to flounder. Canadians waste more water than most people—even their southern neighbours. In cities like Montreal, 40 per cent and more of the water in the municipal mains leaks away into the ground unused because nobody is keeping up with repairs of the pipes. And many cities have no policies in place to encourage consumers to save water. Despite the years of shortages, Vancouver's domestic water supplies are not metered, despairing government officials told me.

For years, Canadians have been embarrassed to be told that they are the second biggest per-capita user of water in the home in the world, right behind the US—but at least they were better than the US. In recent years, however, the US has got tough by insisting, for instance, on water closets that deliver a six-litre flush. Not so Canada. "You can still go to Home Depot and buy 13-litre toilets; the US manufacturers are dumping their old stock here," says Liz Lefrancois of Environment Canada. And so, in the early years of the twenty-first century, Canada has taken over the mantle of the world's biggest per-capita user of water. Americans use 282 litres per person per day; Canadians use 335 litres per day, says Lefrancois. That's more than twice the tap flow of Canada's European cousins, incidentally. Britons get by on 150 litres.

There we have it. Canadians at home are caught between regarding water as a precious national resource not on any account to be given to their neighbours, and flushing it down their 13-litre toilets. But if there is a symbol of this dysfunctional attitude to water that is greater than the toilet flush, then it is the hydroelectric flush. On the great northern frontier—where tradition has it that land and water are unlimited—dam-builders on James Bay in Quebec have for decades been concreting wilderness, flooding hunting grounds and flushing mercury from the soil to generate cheap power, much of it for sale to the US. I find this odd. The Yankees cannot have Canadian water, it seems; but they can have electricity generated by taming to death Canada's wild rivers.

I had written before about the rows over the James Bay hydro projects. A decade ago, I interviewed at length Cree Grand Chief and charismatic anti-dams campaigner Matthew Coon-Come, who spoke in impassioned terms about how Quebec had taken over their lands and rivers for dams. "The world must realize that environmental disasters don't happen only in the Brazilian rainforest," he said. But he has had a change if heart. The Cree nation and the Quebec government signed an agreement in 2001 that guaranteed the Cree royalties in return for an end to their opposition to proposed dams on the Eastmain-Rupert river system.

The deal seemed to meet the terms of a new international consensus that large dam projects required the active agreement of the communities they will invade. But the wider issues have not gone away. According to local environment group Rupert Reverence, which includes dissident Cree members, the planned weirs on the Rupert River will divert 90 per cent of the water from Quebec's most southerly wild river into its neighbour, the Eastmain, flooding yet more land and destroying sturgeon spawning grounds.

But today, with Quebec hydropolitics in abeyance, there are two cockpits for dispute about Canada's hydrological future: the MacKenzie River and the Great Lakes. The MacKenzie is now globally unique. The huge wild north-flowing Arctic river is the fifth longest river on the planet and drains a sixth of Canada, it is entirely undammed and its valley unroaded. There is no other river like it anywhere in the world, not even in Siberia, where Soviet engineers dammed most of the big Arctic rivers in their upper reaches. The Mackenzie flows through largely pristine boreal forest and tundra, watering the domains of the caribou and grizzly, the beaver and the polar bears, to its Arctic delta. But the plan now is to run a $7-billion pipeline to take natural gas from the delta to the existing gas pipe networks of Alberta. It will be the largest-ever infrastructure project in the Arctic, and will open up for exploitation dozens of potential natural gas fields along the river valley, bringing with it access roads and industrial development.

Most First Nations in the valley now support the plan, believing that they can grow rich while safeguarding their key natural and sacred areas. But the stakes are high, and whatever protection is granted to core areas, the totality of the wild landscape and its wild river will inevitably be lost. But Canadians seemed to me surprisingly unconcerned. Coon-Come was perhaps right when he observed back in the early 1990s that Canadians are better able to see threats to a world treasure when it is abroad, like the Amazon rainforest, than when it is on their doorstep, like the MacKenzie. That is a shame.

The Great Lakes, on the other hand, do attract concern because...well, perhaps because the Americans want the water. The government in Ottawa has for the moment turned down overtures from the US government and its water capitalists to sell bulk water out of the lakes to arid lands in the western states of the US. But if the old saw that "water flows uphill to money" still counts for anything, then one day such schemes could happen.

The granddaddy of all the water export projects was the GRAND Canal scheme. Back in the 1980s, this scheme had big backers. It would have turned James Bay into a giant freshwater holding tank for the rivers of northern Quebec, delivering their flow by canal to Lake Huron. This would in turn have allowed massive diversions of water into the US from Lake Michigan into the Mississippi, and from Lake Superior to the West. GRAND stood for Great Recycling and Northern Development—a rather misleading title which intimated that water was being somehow "recycled" for the good of the north, rather than being exported wholesale to the US. The $100-billion scheme was "visceral... but nuts," as Donald Gamble, head of the Rawson Academy of Aquatic Sciences in Ottawa, put it at the time. But it was nonetheless for a good while the officially supported policy of the province of Quebec.

The GRAND project was seen off. And its successors have been altogether smaller. But they keep coming. In the 1990s, Ontario initially approved private plans to export water from Lake Superior to Asia, before changing its mind in the face of a fusillade of criticism. Then Newfoundland premier Roger Grimes had plans to exported water from Gisborne Lake to the US scuppered by equally widespread opposition. A tiny California corporation did a deal with British Columbia to allow it to buy BC water and ship it south, and claims compensation because the deal was aborted.

Now, opponents of water exports are alarmed that a community in Wisconsin just a few kilometres outside the Great Lakes basin wants to pump water over the watershed to fill its taps. Waukesha is running on empty after its wells sucked in so much water from beneath the surrounding countryside that most have all but given out. Part of Waukesha's plan is to create a new spa town for tourists. It hopes to get rich like the nearby village of Pleasant Prairie, which became a boomtown in the 1990s after gaining access to Great Lakes water, growing its population by a third and doubling property values.

Some say Canada doesn't need to be too concerned about these lesser schemes. Even a big splash for Waukesha won't empty the Great Lakes, after all. But Sara Ehrhardt of the Council for Canadians says the risk lies precisely with such small schemes that could slip beneath the net of public vigilance. The problem is NAFTA, the North America Free Trade Agreement. Lawyers say that once one community is allowed to take water out of the lakes' basin, it will be illegal under NAFTA to prevent other water trades—whatever the size and whether it is trade within the Great Lakes basin or to another part of the continent.

"If Canada permits the sale of bulk water, it becomes a tradeable commodity. Once water is a commodity, a giant water valve will be turned on and stuck in that position," as the *Ottawa Citizen* put it. "Our fear is one small community will drive the exceptions to the rule that will extend to neighbouring Jefferson County to Illinois and eventually open the door all the way to the lawns of Las Vegas and the golf courses of California," says Ehrhardt. Lots of people on the road south and west would like Waukesha to succeed, she says.

Right now, all agree the economics don't add up for long-distance water transfer into the West. But taking water out of the Lakes to refill the Mississippi would be cheap, because nature can take the water a long way simply by gravity. And with the continent's biggest river catchment so close to the continent's biggest water tank, the ultimate potential for such a transfer is huge. And I discovered an alarming truth that seems little understood in Canada. Water is already heading south out of the Great Lakes into the Mississippi on a substantial scale. The US has been doing it for just over a century.

It happened this way. In the late nineteenth century, cholera and typhoid were endemic in Chicago, a city that took its water from Lake Michigan and poured its sewage back into the lake down the River Chicago. The disease was spread by sewage ponding up along the shore of Lake Michigan and in the river, which had become an open sewer. So the city's engineers had the idea of getting rid of the sewage by reversing the river's flow, taking the sewage south and away from the city and the lake. This was surprisingly easy. The watershed between rivers draining into the Great Lakes and those draining south into the Mississippi was just 20 kilometres from the lakeshore and was marked by a ridge just 3 metres high. It was no big deal in engineering terms to cut through the ridge and reverse the River Chicago south into the Mississippi—nor to speed the sewage on its way with extra water poured into the river from the lake.

The job was completed in 1900. The north-flowing River Chicago became the south-flowing Chicago Sanitary and Ship

Canal. And ever since, flow down the canal out of Lake Michigan and into the Mississippi has averaged 91 cubic metres a second, or almost 3 cubic kilometres a year—more than flows down the River Thames in London.

And from time to time there has been pressure to increase that flow. It last happened in 1988, when drought wracked the US, and the Mississippi River dropped to its lowest level on record. As barges ran aground on the river, calls grew for the river to be replenished from the Great Lakes. The US Corps of Engineers drew up plans to triple the flow down the Chicago canal to 280 cubic metres a second. It would, its hydrologists said, have increased the depth of the mighty Mississippi by 10 centimetres as far south as Memphis, Tennessee. But it would also have reduced the level of the Great Lakes by 2 centimetres for every three months that the increased flow operated. Canada railed against the plan. The US argued that, since Lake Michigan alone among the Great Lakes is entirely within its jurisdiction, it could do what it liked. The lawyers argued; the Corps stalled; the drought ended and the political crisis passed. But the legal issue was never concluded. "When the Mississippi gets low again, they may want the water again," says Elizabeth May, director of Sierra Club in Canada.

Water leaks out of the lakes in another way, too—from the "sixth lake," the underground waters beneath and around the lakes. There may be 5,000 cubic kilometres of water down there, but nobody is keeping track of where it goes. Some of it feeds the springs that form the rivers that flow into the lakes. The US Geological Survey estimates that underground water contributes half of all the water entering the lakes. But an estimated eight million people round the lake pump up that underground water to drink it. And, after they have finished with it, much of that water eventually finds its way into rivers that drain away from the lakes. How much? Nobody knows for sure. The USGS thinks as much as 2 cubic kilometres a year—much of it abstracted from sands and gravels beneath Chicago—disappears from the basin. That is almost as much as flows down the Sanitary Canal.

And there is a third threat to the hydrological integrity of the Great Lakes. In early 2005 a small local NGO called the Georgian Bay Association stumbled on a previously unknown (or at any rate undisclosed) cause of a mysterious slump in lake levels in Huron and Michigan. The bottom of the St. Clair River, the outlet from Huron, has been eroding since new shipping lanes were dredged in the river in the 1960s. The dredging scoured the river to a depth of 9 metres, but the dredging destabilized the channel and since then, nature has eroded the channel to a depth of 18 metres. "Water is leaving faster than had been recognized," said association president John Pepperell. The result had been a decline in lake levels of 32 centimetres since the 1960s and of 80 centimetres since the channel was first dredged in the mid-nineteenth century. That is a total loss so far of around a year's flow into the lakes. Gone for good. And unless something is done it will only get worse.

No country on Earth has such contrasts of drought and water plenty as Canada. None has so much water ready and available for use. But Canada is learning that national statistics do not begin to portray the complexity of its relationship with its most vital resource. On the MacKenzie and the Rupert and the South Saskatchewan; in the leaking water mains of Montreal and the emptying reservoirs of Vancouver; down Canada's turbines and toilets, a new reality is emerging. It is a reality in which water is in increasingly short supply in some places at some times, where water suddenly has real value rather than being an unlimited resource—and where the rivers truly can run dry.

3

ENGLAND: THE HILLS
·   ARE EMPTY

When Roger de Vere's children were young, they caught eels by the hundred along the banks of the River Kennet in Wiltshire. "Our house was full of eels in jars," he remembers. "But now you hardly ever see any along the river. The river's flow is reduced and there are very, very few wild fish left. Seeing the state of the river today is like seeing an old friend die of a terrible wasting disease."

The Kennet is fed by springs in the chalk hills that make up most of the county of Wiltshire. It flows over water meadows where students play lacrosse in front of Marlborough College, and past the huge neolithic earthworks of Silbury Hill. Nothing is more English than this. But if the water level in the hills drops too low, the stream fails. And it has. The local water company has been pumping millions of litres of water from the hills each day to supply the county's distant boom town of Swindon, which for a while claimed to be the fastest-growing town in Europe. The river now virtually dies in late summer and its gravel beds, where fish spawn, become clogged with mud and algae.

Roger's tale from the riverbank is a story of ecological decline and a sign of impending water crisis across much of England, one of the driest but most densely populated parts of Europe. The Kennet is but one of dozens of small English rivers that run dry most summers as water companies empty the hills of water. Wessex Water draws a billion litres a month out of the little River Wylye, a trout stream in Wiltshire, and pumps it to Somerset, for instance. And as the country's demand for water continues to rise, the number of these part-time rivers is likely to grow.

The hills of England, the green and pleasant land, are being sucked dry. At least forty chalk streams out of about 160 in lowland England are under threat, according to scientists at the government's Environment Agency, which is in charge of rivers. From the Piddle in Dorset to the Darent in Kent, and the Hampshire Avon to the Frome in Somerset, gravel beds are clogged, reeds are dying and fish are gasping for air. As the river banks dry out, water voles leave their holes—and get eaten by marauding mink.

Sometimes, when the political heat is on, the water companies offer a solution. They respond to summer crises by pumping yet more water out of the hills to refill the rivers. It is a quick fix in which their pumps replace nature's springs. But the result is even lower water tables and even less water to sustain natural flows the next year. Wessex Water now wants to spend £100 million to install a pipe to pump water from the River Avon to "save" the Wylye. Another company repaired the Misbourne in Berkshire by taking water from the River Colne. Engineers have sunk new boreholes into the North Downs in a last-ditch effort to save the River Darent, hoping for a return of fish like the grayling and brown trout.

English chalk streams were the birthplace of fly-fishing; they watered the meadows painted by Constable in front of Salisbury Cathedral; they inflamed passions in the works of Thomas Hardy. They harbour water-crowfoot and watercress, mayflies and crayfish, brown trout and salmon, otters and lapwings. "Present abstractions are not sustainable," said the Environment Agency in its first-ever report on the country's chalk rivers. The rivers are, it said, "a unique and irreplaceable part of our cultural heritage and the landscape of England. They face mounting pressure which threatens to damage them forever." But the Agency is often helpless to defend such Englishness because of long-standing licences for water abstraction that it has no power to overturn. If the pumps keep going, one day there will be no water for humans either.

It is more than twenty years since a large reservoir was built in Britain. We built too many in the 1960s and 1970s, flooding valleys and drowning villages, often for water that is rarely used. But that is about to change. The dam-builders are back. The most dramatic scheme is earmarked for less than twenty kilometres from Roger de Vere's home in Whiltshire. There Thames Water, the water company that supplies London, wants to spend £700 million building a giant new reservoir. Most reservoirs flood valley bottoms, but this one will rise above the Vale of the White Horse near Abingdon. It will be Britain's biggest man-made structure and visible for miles. Its earth bank, as high as a church tower, will surround ten square kilometres of flat countryside. "We could end up under forty feet of water," says farmer Neil Walker, whose fields and farm buildings would all be submerged.

The reservoir would take heavy winter flows out of the River Thames and store them to top up the river in summer. The alternative, claims the company, is regular water shortages for twelve million Londoners and the risk of standpipes in the streets of the capital. As the announcement was made, in October 2003, the main reservoirs on the Thames were just 40 per cent full. The company was pumping fourteen million litres of water a day from chalk aquifers set aside for use only in emergencies. That meant more dry rivers. Not least the Kennet.

So is that the choice: a new reservoir or dry rivers? Well, no. Campaigners against the new dam say London loses more than 30 per cent of its water supply in leaks from water mains—a million cubic metres a year. "Thames Water should be encouraging water efficiency, not grandiose plans for dams," says Friends of the Earth boss Tony Juniper. Conservative Wiltshire MP Robert Key says years of reducing water prices have encouraged greater water demand, while failing to provide the cash for action against leaks in the water distribution system. "What sort of economics of the madhouse is it that assumes it is all right for Wessex Water to lose more than two billion litres a month in leaks, at the same time as a billion litres are being taken out of the headwaters of a sensitive chalk stream on Salisbury Plain?"

Baroness Young, the head of the Environment Agency, agrees: "Most companies that put forward proposals for reservoirs are not thinking about how they can reduce customers' demand and manage their leakage effectively." Indeed, as Thames Water launched its reservoir plan, her agency had just uncovered a 6 per cent rise in leakage rates across Britain in 2003. "Enough water leaks from mains pipes to supply half the households in England," says Young. The row hit the headlines in the dry summer of 2005, when Thames Water pleaded with customers to reduce their demand while being forced to admit that it had failed to meet its leakage reduction targets for three years running and was losing 100 litres a day for every home it supplied.

The stakes are high. The country has less water available per head than Afghanistan. Southeast England has less than Ethiopia, Syria or Somalia. But, by and large, England has been spared water shortages because it has got by without having to irrigate crops. The rain has done the job. So per-capita water demand from public supply systems has been a fraction of that in many poorer but hotter countries—a fifth of that in Egypt, for example. But hotter summers, longer droughts, more farm irrigation, a domestic medley of dishwashers and lawn sprinklers and the government's desire to build new homes in the arid Southeast is raising demand, especially in places where, and at times when, water is in shortest supply.

A few years ago, Wales had so much water it wanted to sell large quantities to Saudi Arabia. Now any spare water is more likely to be shipped round the coast of England. To Kent, maybe. Kent, my home county, is already the driest in England. And if global warming has the effect currently predicted, flows of rivers such as the Stour and Medway—scene of the first drought order in 2005—will fall by 50 per cent within fifty years. At Kent's arid heart is a small town called Ashford, and this is the place where the government plans to build 31,000 new homes by 2030—catering for a population increase of 76 per cent. Did nobody tell the deputy prime minister John Prescott, a former environment minister whose brainchild this was, that it might be a mistake? It seems not.

In a hole, the local Mid-Kent Water Company says the only solution is to build a giant new reservoir just east of Canterbury. The Broad Oak reservoir will be almost three kilometres long and cost £100 million. Its water will come from the tiny and diminishing River Stour, which rises in the village of my childhood. The Broad Oak project was first proposed back in the 1970s, but was thrown out at a public inquiry because it would remove 70 per cent of the flow of the Stour. Now it is back. Is the river any bigger? No, it is not.

And Broad Oak isn't the only revival. The idea for a giant reservoir on the Thames near Abingdon also dates back to the 1970s. It was dropped then in favour of boreholes in the Wiltshire Downs, even though an economic study done for Thames Water at the time showed that plugging leaks or buying water-saving valves for every toilet cistern in London would be the most cost-effective solution to the expected water shortages.

If these two old and dodgy dam projects are rising from the grave, what else could be in the works? A survey in 2004 found at least seven new reservoirs planned that would flood thousands of hectares of crowded southeast England. There are schemes in Essex, Sussex and Hampshire, as well as in the Southwest, Yorkshire and northwest England. And that's not all. Water planners are ready to dust off schemes for a national water grid that could bring water from Wales to London, from Cumbria to Bristol and from Northumbria to East Anglia.

One long-discussed link in the grid would involve building a new dam in Wales to discharge water down the River Severn for piping over the Cotswold hills to top up the headwaters of the River Thames. Others foresee using the Thames Barrier to pond up fresh water in the Thames estuary, building a reservoir on

Otmoor, a nature reserve near Oxford—and even putting barrages across the Wash and Morecambe Bay to turn them into giant freshwater reservoirs.

The water crisis across Britain is getting serious. We are using more water; and it is raining less, especially in summer when we need the water most. In the past twenty-five years large parts of Britain have had three droughts of an intensity that, say government scientists, we should expect only once in two hundred years. We are in all probability moving towards a climate more like Spain. In parts of southeast England, summer rainfall is expected to halve by mid-century, and evaporation rates from reservoirs could rise by a third. Meanwhile farmers are expected to increase massively their use of irrigation in summer. So are gardeners. During 2005 planning permission was being sought for the first desalination plant on the Thames estuary. The echoes of Ethiopia and Sudan suddenly seem not so fanciful.

Britons have grown used to always having water in our taps. But will we always be able to take that for granted? During the last major drought, in the mid-1990s, West Yorkshire came within days of running out of water altogether. Secret plans were drawn up to evacuate as many as a million people from Bradford and Halifax as their taps ran dry. The plans came close to being carried out. They remain in place.

PART ONE

WHEN THE RIVERS RUN DRY ...
THE CROPS FAIL

4

RIDING THE WATER CYCLE

Earth is the water planet. It contains an unimaginable 1.4 billion cubic kilometres of the stuff. But more than 97 per cent of it is sea water that we cannot drink and cannot, except in very local circumstances, afford to purify; "Water, water, everywhere, Nor any drop to drink," as Coleridge's ancient mariner put it. Of the remaining 35 million cubic kilometres of fresh water on and near the planet's surface, two-thirds is locked up in ice caps and glaciers and one-third, about 12 million cubic kilometres, is in liquid form. The greater part of it is in the pores of rocks. These reservoirs of underground water, known as aquifers, vary hugely in their accessibility and drinkability. But the water is there, beneath our feet.

The remaining smidgeon of the world's liquid fresh water—we are now down to a mere 200,000 cubic kilometres or so—is above ground. The biggest volumes, around 90,000 cubic kilometres, are in lakes and there are probably another 90,000 cubic kilometres in soils and permafrost. Next comes atmospheric water vapour, which contains another 13,000 cubic kilometres, or about a thousandth of 1 per cent of all the water on Earth. After that come swamps and wetlands at 11,000 cubic kilometres; rivers, which contain around 2,000 cubic kilometres at any one time; and living organisms, from rainforests to you and me, with about 1,000 cubic kilometres.

But this is a static picture: where the water is at any one moment in time. And water is not a static resource. It is constantly on the move: through soils and into ancient geological formations, down rivers, into the ocean depths, freezing and melting, evaporating into the air and forming clouds to fall again as rain. If we are concerned about how much water is available to us in a form that we can keep on using, the static figures for water don't tell us much. It is the dimensions of these movements, known as the water cycle, that are critical.

Take aquifers. The crude statistics suggest that they should be easily our number one resource. And, yes, the volume of water down there is huge, dependable and ready to be pumped to the surface. With current technology perhaps a tenth of the known resource could be extracted. Sink a well and away you go. But as everyone knows, wells run dry. Pumping out an aquifer will empty it for ever—unless that aquifer is being refilled. So a more useful measure of the water available to us underground, year in and year out, is how much of that water is replenished by rain.

Looked at this way, underground water shrinks in importance. By some perversity of nature, many of the biggest aquifers are beneath deserts and get virtually no recharge because there is no rain. The largest quantities sit in the pores of sandstone rocks beneath the Sahara and the Arabian peninsula. Other big reserves are beneath the Australian outback and the arid High Plains of the American Midwest. We can and do pump this water; but, as we do, the water level falls, pumping costs rise and quite often water quality deteriorates too. Probably about a tenth of 1 per cent of the fresh water in the world's aquifers is replaced each year by rains. So, while the amount of time that water spends in underground rocks varies from a few months to millions of years, on average it is getting on for a thousand years.

Water in the other big reservoirs, the oceans and ice caps, has a similar long residence time. But if most of the water in what we might call the "slow" water cycle moves at a snail's pace, water in other parts of the water cycle—generally the parts with smaller volumes at any one time—moves around much more quickly.

There is a "fast" water cycle, too—a constant rapid flow of water evaporating from land and sea, forming water vapour and then clouds, raining to the Earth and then evaporating again.

Of course some water from the fast cycle disappears into the slow cycle. Rain percolates into rocks or gets frozen on glaciers or trapped in inland seas or tied up in plants and animals. And some water moves from the slow to the fast cycle—in meltwater from glaciers, or bubbling from rocks in springs, for instance. But in a year, about 500,000 cubic kilometres of water flows through the fast water cycle. In practice, there is much less water; it just circulates several times. But if this entire annual cycle were collected together, it would cover the entire Earth's surface to a depth of almost a metre.

Because most of the planet is covered in ocean, the larger part of this fast cycle is again not much use to us. It comprises water evaporating from the sea and falling back onto the sea in rain. But, for the rest, we are beginning to home in on the bit of the cycle from which we get most of our water.

First there is the water that falls as rain onto the land and then evaporates from the land again. This involves about 60,000 cubic kilometres each year. Some evaporates from soils; some is taken up by plants as they grow and then released from leaves in a process called transpiration; some evaporates from bodies of water, including man-made reservoirs. Second, there is a constant flow of water from the land, where rainfall exceeds evaporation, to the sea, where evaporation exceeds rainfall. Some of this flows directly off the land, some shoots down gullies that form when it rains, and some flows down permanent rivers. Most of the water we use round the world today comes from this part of the water cycle. There is about 40,000 cubic kilometres of water making the journey from the land to the sea every year. Or there was before we started diverting it.

So how much of this runoff do we use? Of those 40,000 cubic kilometres a year, much hurtles off the land in occasional floods or flows away from permanent rivers. Of the rest, hydrologists reckon the maximum that might reasonably be caught and used by humans employing current technology is 14,000 cubic kilo-metres. But nature has played one more trick on us. Many of the world's greatest rivers are in regions where few people can or want to live. The three rivers with the biggest flows—the Amazon, Congo and Orinoco—all pass through inhospitable jungle for most of their journey from headwaters to the sea. Those three alone carry almost a quarter of the water we have to survive on. And two more of the top ten—the Lena and Yenisei in Siberia—run mostly through Arctic wastes. A tenth of the world's river waters flow into the Arctic. Take out these and we are left with around 9,000 cubic kilometres of river water for our needs.

That still amounts to about 1,400 cubic metres a year for every citizen on the planet. Not bad, but in chapter one I calcu-lated my own annual water use at between 1,500 and 2,000 cubic metres a year. I imagine most of the world would like to live as well as I do; so we have a problem.

Water is heavy stuff. It's not easy to move around unless gravity is with you, as anyone who has carried a bucket of it any distance will agree. So all these global numbers can still give a misleading impression of how much water we can really get our hands on. The water business, like the property business, comes down to a matter of "location, location, location." So where is the water?

Just six countries have half of the world's total renewable freshwater supply on their territory—Brazil, Russia, Canada, Indonesia, China and Colombia. But some smaller countries do even better if we measure the amount of water available per head of population. Greenland's 60,000 citizens have more water than anyone else. Each of them could make use of 30,000 cubic metres of it every day without having to defrost a single piece of ice. But, having no crops to irrigate, they need little. Alaskans have avail-able 4,500 cubic metres a day each. Also weighing in above 500 cubic metres each a day are the citizens of the Congo, Iceland and the three neighbouring South American rainforest states of Guyana, Suriname and French Guiana.

Meanwhile people in the driest countries have by far the greatest need—to irrigate crops as well as to quench their thirst. The Palestinian desert enclave of the Gaza Strip is the most water-starved political unit on Earth, with just 140 litres of brackish underground water a day for each inhabitant. Others at the bottom of the hydrological heap include small desert states such as Kuwait and the United Arab Emirates, and island states like the Bahamas, the Maldives and Malta.

Even at the continental level there are clear haves and have-nots. Europe and North America are well served—especially considering that irrigation demands are mostly fairly low—though both continents generally have a surplus in the north and shortages in the south. Australia is the driest continent, but has a low population. Asia, by contrast, has almost two-thirds of the world's population but only a third of its runoff, 80 per cent of which is concentrated in the short monsoon season.

Africa's continent-wide allocation isn't too bad, but a third of the continent's runoff goes down a single river, the Congo. South America has only 5 per cent of the world's population but glories in three of the world's top ten rivers—the Amazon, Orinoco and Parana. Fully a quarter of the world's runoff occurs here, but little of this water is near to people. The vast and wet Amazon basin, with 15 per cent of the entire world's runoff, has just 0.4 per cent of the world's population.

Even within countries, water can be inconveniently distributed in time and place. Most of India gets all its rain in a hundred hours during a hundred days. Parts of Ethiopia suffer perennially from drought and famine, even though 84 per cent of the flow of the River Nile begins within the country's borders. Canada has 90 per cent of its water where 10 per cent of its people are, and vice versa. If northern China were a separate country, it would be one of the most water-stressed in the world. All this has come to matter a very great deal because of two changes over the past half-century: the soaring world population, and the manner in which the world went about trying to feed that population.

———

Around forty years ago, the world was gripped by Malthusian nightmares of mass starvation. The world's women were having an average of more than five children each. The world's population was set to double in a generation. Billions, it was said, would die of famine. In his influential book, *The Population Bomb*, biologist Paul Ehrlich declared that "in the 1970s hundreds of millions of people are going to starve to death...the battle to feed all of humanity is over." And, as famines spread through Africa in the early 1970s, he was not alone in holding such apocalyptic views. A crude computer model projection of ecological Armageddon called *Limits to Growth* became a worldwide best-seller.

But it didn't happen that way. The world's population has since doubled, but scientists defied the doomsayers by breeding new high-yielding varieties of rice, wheat and maize that kept the granaries full. And Henry Kissinger was proved right when he got up at a World Food Conference in 1974 and declared that "for the first time, we may have the technical capacity to free mankind from the scourge of hunger." He rather overestimated the world's ability to get food to those who needed it, however, so his follow-up that "within a decade no child will go to bed hungry" was sadly wide of the mark. Africa in particular has missed out. But, averaged globally, the "green revolution" has ever since kept growth in food production ahead of growth in population.

It is an impressive achievement. But those new high-yielding crop varieties needed water, huge amounts of it. So the world embarked on a vast investment program, first in dams and then in irrigation canals to deliver that water to fields. With a typical bill for supplying water from rivers to fields of between $1,000 and $10,000 per hectare, the financial cost has been huge. But today, poor developing countries like India, China and Pakistan have three-quarters of all the world's irrigated farmland. And many of them have defied the doomsayers by moving from famine to self-sufficiency in their staple grains.

The problem now is escalating shortages of water. Today,

some 70 per cent of all the water abstracted from rivers and underground reserves is being spread onto the 270 million hectares of irrigated land that grows a third of the world's food. This massive global undertaking has kept the world's granaries full, but it has emptied the rivers. Back in the 1960s and 1970s, neither the green revolution scientists nor the doomsayers fully appreciated that while the new crops were indeed very "efficient" at delivering more crop per hectare, they were often extremely inefficienct when measured against water use. They often produced less "crop per drop" than the varieties they replaced.

As a result, the United Nations' food and agriculture agency says that on at least a third of the world's fields today, "water rather than land is the binding constraint" on production. Perhaps the most telling statistic of all is this: the world grows twice as much food as it did a generation ago, but it abstracts three times more water from rivers and underground aquifers to do it.

In arid countries such as Egypt, Mexico, Pakistan and Australia and across Central Asia, 90 per cent or more of the water abstracted from the environment is for irrigation. In the green revolution countries, water consumption per head of population is several times that of European countries. Pakistan abstracts five times more water per head than does Ireland; Egypt five times more than Britain; and Mexico five times more than Denmark. No wonder their rivers are emptying.

One straw in the wind: the Mexican valley that once described itself as "the home of the green revolution," because its farmers pioneered the use of new high-yielding wheat varieties half a century ago, has run out of water. Reservoirs on the Yaqui River in the Sonora desert of northwest Mexico have dried up since the mid-1990s as farmers' demand exceeded supply in the rivers. Today, fields are being abandoned and farmers are leaving the valley.

The Yaqui valley is far from alone. Since the 1970s, Egypt, for instance, has had to import growing amounts of food because there is not enough water to sustain the new high-yielding varieties. And other countries are living on borrowed time. In some cases the water is running out. Thus, a quarter of India's crops are being grown using underground water that is not being replaced by the rains. In others, salt from the irrigation water is invading their fields and rendering large areas sterile and useless. Each year, ten million hectares of fields round the world are lost to its toxic embrace. Projects that initially greened the desert are now creating desert.

It is dangerous to predict doom when it didn't happen last time. Science may come up trumps again. But without a second agricultural revolution that targets water, a "blue revolution," then the gains of the past generation could be wiped out as rivers run dry, underground water reserves are exhausted and fields are caked in salt.

5

PAKISTAN: THE UNHAPPY VALLEY

I f any country sums up the profits and perils of the overuse of water for irrigation, it is Pakistan. The saga began with British colonial engineers. When they first surveyed the Indus valley in the nineteenth century, they saw with delight a near-replica of the Nile, yet three times the size. The snow melting each spring in the Himalayas provided a vast volume of water all down the Indus to its delta on the Arabian Sea. The river could, they decided, be engineered to irrigate its wide desert plain: a land of fertile soils but no rain.

Like the land by the Nile, the Indus valley had a long indigenous tradition of irrigating fields along the banks of the river. The Harappa civilization had prospered in this way five thousand years before, diverting the summer monsoon flows through the river's banks and onto their fields. The practice of raising temporary earth dams to force the river and its tributaries to flood bankside fields continued right into the nineteenth century, when the British decided that they could do things better. They wanted to trap the summer floodwaters permanently behind massive barrages to provide year-round irrigation that could sustain two or even three annual crops. The British were dreaming of imperial splendour, but they were driven at least as much by the prospect of financial gain. They saw full granaries across the Indus valley as a source of tax revenues for the Treasury in London.

In the words of imperial historian James Morris, they would "create a new country out of a gloomy wasteland," turning a land peopled only by "disputatious nomads who made a living by cattle-thieving" into something more like home. The first and greatest creation was to transform the Sikh state of Punjab. To do this, after sending in the soldiers to subjugate the locals the engineers built a succession of barrages across the great river and its tributaries where they emerged from the Himalayas, and extended canals for hundreds of kilometres through the wide flat plain. In 1892 they completed the largest of the canals, Lower Chenab Canal, which carried six times the flow of the River Thames back home, and irrigated an area the size of Yorkshire.

They were remaking the social landscape, too. The British threw the by now understandably disputatious nomads off their land and marched farmers in from central India. They dotted the plain with villages and established market towns at regular intervals along the canals. At the heart of the new Punjab they laid out a new city in the pattern of the Union Jack, naming it Lyallpur after the local governor. (After Independence it was renamed Faisalabad). There they built what remains to this day the largest agricultural university in Asia.

No Stalinist social engineer could have ordered things more tidily, though the British added their own element. The city's new geography reflected clear ethnic divisions, with Sikhs in one area, Muslims in another and Hindus in a third—but also British class sensibilities, with the imported settlers divided between peasants, yeomen and gentry. The last group, the officer class, got the biggest plots and were expected to be natural leaders.

By its own lights, it was a huge success, turning the backward province into one of the most productive in the Indian empire. But there was still water in the river, flowing past the barrages and through the desert of Sindh province to the rich and green delta and the Arabian Sea. And by now the British had a new market they wanted to supply: the cotton mills in Lancashire. So in 1932 they finally, and probably somewhat reluctantly, trekked south into the Sindh desert, which they had called "the unhappy valley," and began building new hydraulic works. At their heart was the Sukkur barrage, which strode across the Indus in sixty-six arches and diverted most of the river's remaining flow into the desert, where they established what amounted to one giant cotton farm.

British engineering endeavour in the unhappy valley eventually produced what remains the largest unbroken irrigated area on the planet. Even California cannot compete. And it was just one part of Britain's grand plan to irrigate its great Indian Empire, the "jewel" in Queen Victoria's crown. Engineers like Sir Arthur Cotton—who had sailed for India as a callow youth of sixteen intent on making his way in the empire and became the architect of the greatest irrigation network the world had ever seen—thought nothing of damming rivers far bigger than any they knew back home in England.

With the help of countless "coolies" carrying soil in baskets on their backs, they turned the muddy flats of the Cauvery delta in Tamil Nadu into a vast rice paddy covering some 2,500 square kilometres. They created a dam near Bombay that was, they claimed, the largest piece of masonry erected since classical times. They dug canals the length of the great northern plain of the Ganges, channelling most of the river's winter flow to fields. "Great tracts of country once desert and without inhabitants are now filled with people," declared John Colvin, governor of the northwest provinces, one morning as he opened the largest brick aqueduct in the world, over the River Solani at Roorkee. In these great works, says technology historian Daniel Headrick, "they laid the foundations of modern hydraulic engineering."

The British-built railways of India are more famous, but the empire spent far more on digging canals than laying railways. Britain ended its rule in 1947 with 100,000 kilometres of canals carrying water the length of the subcontinent, and with more land irrigated than there was in the whole of England. As the sun went down on the British Empire in India, one in every eight formally irrigated fields round the world was in India. And the greatest irrigated expanse of them all was on the Indus.

But the engineers were not done. The newly independent Pakistan, funded by the World Bank and other agencies set up after the Second World War, strove to enhance its control over the Indus yet further, by building on the upper reaches of the river in the foothills of the Himalayas a series of giant dams. One such was the Tarbela, which when it was completed in 1974 was the world's largest. These upstream dams were intended both to generate electricity and to store water in wet years, so drought-proofing the country in dry years. And Pakistan has since also built two more barrages in Sindh to divert more Indus water into the desert and to increase its irrigated land further—to around 160,000 square kilometres in all.

Today, no other country bar Egypt on the Nile is as dependent on one river as Pakistan is on the Indus. Just as the Greek geographer Herodotus two thousand years ago called Egypt "the gift of the Nile," so modern Pakistan, a country of 140 million people, is "the gift of the Indus." Without the river, most of the country would be desert. Besides watering about 90 per cent of its crops, the river produces nearly half of its electricity. Thanks to irrigation, the country is one of the world's leading exporters of cotton and manufacturers of textiles. The Pakistani Water and Power Development Authority is the country's largest civilian organization.

But there are escalating problems, made more critical by the country's huge dependence on the river. The hydraulic regime created over the past 150 years contains the seeds of its own downfall, and they are multiplying fast. The barrages in Sindh and Punjab have diverted so much water onto the flat Indus plains that the soils are becoming waterlogged. And salt brought down by the river is accumulating in the fields, poisoning crops.

By one calculation, the river delivers 22 million tonnes of salt onto the plain each year, but removes only 11 million tonnes to the Arabian Sea. The rest, almost a tonne a year for every irrigated hectare, stays on the fields. Farmers have responded in the only way they can, by pouring on every available drop of water to wash away the salt before they plant crops. But with water in short supply, that is increasingly difficult to achieve. When it cannot be done, the salt forms a white crust on the surface of the soil and the fields die.

In recent years, farmers have been abandoning salt-encrusted land at a rate of 40,000 hectares a year. A tenth of the fields have been lost so far; of the remainder, a fifth are badly waterlogged and a quarter produce only meagre crops. The situation is worst in Sindh province, where four out of five fields are waterlogged. In some parts, more than half the land is barren, with a few clumps of grass poking through the white crust of salt. Hugely expensive programs to install drains across Sindh in an effort to empty fields of the salt have been only partially successful.

Meanwhile, the country's population is soaring. It has quadrupled since Independence and is projected to reach 250 million by 2025. These people all need feeding. Nationally, despite the lost land, food output has so far kept pace with the rising population, thanks to new high-yielding crop varieties. But this seems unlikely to continue. As salt builds up, it takes ever more water to enable fields to produce. And there is no more water to be had in the country.

Typically, 70 cubic kilometres of the Indus's water is used to grow rice and a further 50 cubic kilometres each to grow wheat and cotton. That is a total of 170 cubic kilometres—out of an average flow of 180 cubic kilometres. And in the majority of recent years, the average has not been reached. The gloomy prognosis is that as Pakistan's population continues to soar, the country will have less and less land and water capable of producing the crops with which to sustain itself.

Politicians in the capital, Islamabad, want to build more dams to secure more water. Top of the list is the Kalabagh dam downstream of the Tarbela dam. It would, they say, extend irrigated farming into the unploughed west. But there are even grander plans. They want to flood the city of Skardu, capital of an area known as Baltistan, or Little Tibet, to create a huge dam in the distant Karakum mountains on the northwest frontier. It would store the waters that occasionally rush out of the mountains in "superfloods" and which other dams cannot contain. But downstream in Sindh, farmers believe the scheme will simply empty yet more of their irrigation canals. Punjab and Sindh often seem on the brink of a water war. Back in 1998, Sindh leader Benazir Bhutto led tens of thousands of farmers in demonstrations against the Kalabagh project. Three years later, two people died in riots during a political rally to protest water shortages, and bombs exploded in Karachi during strikes against water shortages. "The word Kalabagh has become synonymous with Punjabi chauvinism," says local commentator Ayaz Amir. If there is ever a war between the provinces, Kalabagh is the likely spark.

Whatever the politics, and however the water is shared, it is abundantly clear that the Indus is in deep trouble. In the first years of the twenty-first century, the river was largely dry for its final few hundred kilometres to the sea. The Indus delta was once a rich expanse of mangrove swamps stretching for hundreds of kilometres, interspersed with pastures and creeks where river dolphins swam and fish spawned. Even half a century ago, it got water for several months a year. But years of meagre flows since have killed half the mangrove swamps. Many of the fish have vanished. One economic assessment puts the loss of fish alone at $20 million a year. Even drinking water has become scarce.

With little silt or fresh water reaching the delta, the sea is advancing inland. At least half a million hectares of mangroves and farmland have disappeared beneath the waves. Life is becoming intolerable, says Mohammed Tahir Qureshi, an ecologist with the World Conservation Union. "More than three-quarters of the local population depend on these products for their livelihoods, so there has been a mass migration out of the area."

As the irrigation systems fail and the natural resources of the Indus and its delta expire, the social cohesion that the British once so deliberately sought to create in Pakistan is also fast breaking down. The farms of Sindh could once employ everyone. But today gangs of unemployed bandits stalk the country-side, exacting protection money from those farmers still in business. And millions of people have left the fields and moved to Karachi. This former colonial port near the mouth of the Indus became, during the 1990s, the fastest-growing city on Earth. Swelled by disgruntled environmental refugees, it now has more than ten million inhabitants. Most live in the city's vast lawless slums, which are a breeding ground for Al-Qaeida and other terrorist groups.

Irrigation has made, but it has also destroyed. Sindh is once again, as the British called it before they marched south to remake its hydrology, the unhappy valley.

6

NORTH AMERICA: CROSSING THE RIO GRANDE

They serve a strong brew at the Alamo coffee house in Presidio, a small farming town near the US–Mexican border. They need to. Times are tough, says Terry Bishop, looking up from his second mugful. This land, next to the Rio Grande in Texas, has probably been continuously farmed for longer than anywhere in America, he says. Six hundred years minimum. It's been home to scalp-hunters and a penal colony; it's seen Comanche raids, Spanish missionaries, marauding Mexican revolutionaries and a population boom during a recent aliens amnesty. All that time, it has been farmed. But soon it will be back to sagebrush and salt cedar.

Climbing the levee by the river at the end of his last field, Bishop shows me the problem. The once mighty Rio Grande is now reduced to a sluggish brown trickle. In its middle stretches, the river often dries up entirely in the summer. All the water has been taken out by cities and farmers upstream. "The river's been disappearing since the fifties," says Bishop, who has farmed here virtually all that time. There hasn't been a flood worthy of the name since 1978. For three hundred kilometres upstream of Presidio, there is no proper channel anymore, he says. They call it the forgotten river.

Bishop's land brings with it legal rights to 10 million cubic metres of water a year from the river—enough to flood his fields to a depth of more than a metre, enough to grow almost any crop he wants. But in recent years he has taken only a quarter of that. Even when he gets water, "it's too salty to grow anything much except alfalfa." But that's all a bit academic now. Yields got so low, the farm went bust. Bishop lets some fields to tenants, but most of them are idle these days. The land is gradually returning to desert. And Bishop drinks a lot of coffee.

This is the way of things in Presidio. The town was once a major farming centre. It used to ship in thousands of Mexican workers to harvest its crops. Bishop's farm alone once employed a thousand people. But that's all ended and the unemployment rate among the town's permanent residents is almost 40 per cent. About the only profitable businesses is desert tourism. An old silver mine a few miles up the road has been turned into a "ghost town," and a fort at Cibolo creek is now an upmarket resort where Mick Jagger once stayed. Harvesting tourists, that's the game now, says Bishop.

On the map, the Rio Grande is the fifth longest river in North America and among the twenty longest in the world. Its main stem stretches 3,000 kilometres from the snowfields of the Colorado Rockies to the Gulf of Mexico, via New Mexico and Texas. It drains a tenth of continental USA and more than two-fifths of Mexico. The hub of human exploitation of the Rio Grande is the Elephant Butte reservoir just upstream of El Paso in Texas. It was built in 1915 and changed the river forever. The wild, untamed flow—which obliterated villages and once rode right through downtown Albuquerque—was ended for good and its waters were corralled for irrigation.

Today, Elephant Butte and its downstream sister, the Caballo, all but empty the river to supply El Paso and nearby farmers. Downstream the river is partly renewed with water from two tributaries, the Pecos out of Texas and the Rio Conchos, which comes in from Mexico and joins the main stem at Presidio, right by Bishop's farm. But this new water doesn't last long before being taken out to fill other reservoirs supplying farms in the lower basin. More than nine million people in the basin rely on the Rio Grande's waters. But it is the farmers who make most use of it. Four-fifths of the water in the river is taken for irrigation—most of it to grow two of the thirstiest crops in the world: cotton and alfalfa, a grain that is fed to cattle. And the wastage is huge. Only about 40 per cent of the water reaches the crops, and evaporation in the hot sun takes more than two metres of water a year from the reservoirs—a total of around 300 million cubic metres from Elephant Butte alone.

Usually a trickle of water gets through to the sea. But since the mid-1990s, a decade during which drought has gripped the basin, the flow has been at record lows. It should have come as no surprise when, on February 8, 2001, Cameron county agent Tony Reisinger took a photograph of the mouth of the Rio Grande in the delta at Boca Chica. The flow had ceased. A sand bar a hundred metres wide had completely blocked off the river from the Gulf of Mexico. The bar lasted for five months before summer flows washed it away. And for much of the next two years it returned. You could drive a car across the beach between the USA and Mexico. And though a couple of storms raised the flow in 2004, nobody doubts that the river is in serious trouble.

My exploration of the strange death of the Rio Grande started in El Paso at the Chamizal national memorial, which commemorates a treaty that fixed the boundary between the US city of El Paso and its Mexican twin, Juarez, by forcing the meandering river to pass down an unchanging concrete canal. This brutal carve-up may have underlined the river's geographical importance, but it hardly accorded it respect. Today, the river is virtually invisible from the memorial behind a high chain-link fence designed to keep out the Mexican wetbacks. Only up on the ugly, heavily guarded border bridge can you see it—a fetid trickle in an absurdly wide concrete canal flanked by a six-lane highway and a container dump. There is so little flow that, as I watched, the wind ripping upstream was blowing the water back towards its source in distant Colorado.

El Paso is in hydrological trouble. With its river now trickling through the town virtually empty and upstream reservoirs scarcely any fuller, the *El Paso Times* regularly alerts readers to the days when they can use public water on lawns, and the days they can't. Jittery suburbanites are repairing old wells in the hope of capturing some private water from beneath their land. And in the unplanned shantytown colonias, where Mexicans usually end up after crossing the river, thousands of people live without access to piped water at all—and that is a shock to find in the US, even in the desert.

Across the border in Juarez, things are worse, of course. People there are so short of water that sewage effluent and salty underground water have become major resources. I visited a gleaming new works that treats half the city's sewage and sends the cleaned-up effluent forty kilometres downstream to irrigate crops. And I went to Anapra, one of the city's more notorious colonias, where migrant Raphael Valarez told of his delight that he could now walk down the street to collect water from a new desalination plant. He had so much water his young daughter could paddle in a big washing tub.

Meanwhile, El Paso is buying up properties from local farmers to bag their rights to underground water reserves. Its "water ranches" are dotted all along the highway to Presidio. Tiny cattle towns like Valentine and Dell City could in future provide half El Paso's water. But water-ranching is only a temporary solution. The major aquifer here—which underlies six million hectares of Texas, New Mexico and the Mexican Chihuahua desert—is rapidly running dry because there isn't enough rain to replace what is pumped out.

As we drove east, Mary Kelly, a leading environmentalist campaigning to save the river, said she feared that pumping out this underground water will trigger the final and irreversible desiccation of the landscape. "Most of the recharge for the aquifer comes from seepage from the canals supplying the farms—which ultimately means it comes from the Rio Grande." Now the government wants to line the canals to save water. So the seepage will stop and the aquifer will die even faster. "That is not a good plan," she said. But, as I discovered on my subsequent journey round the world, it is exactly the kind of thing that happens when rivers run dry.

Downstream of El Paso and Juarez, the "forgotten river" was worthy of the name—a dribble of sewage effluent that disappears into remote scrub most of the way to Presidio. An invasion of salt cedar has taken over the channel, sucking up what liquid remains. Salt cedar, also known as tamarisk, is a nasty and extremely tough shrub, able to withstand fire and drought, flood and searing desert heat. A single plant can suck up more than a thousand litres of water a day.

Hydrologically speaking, the Rio Grande pretty much ends here. The river that rolls out of the Colorado snowpack and once ransacked Albuquerque dies now amid the salt cedars and saline pools of the forgotten river. The only water for the channel comes from Mexico. Back in Presidio, standing on the levee on Terry Bishop's land, I could see the empty Rio Grande bed being filled from the south by the Rio Conchos. For all practical purposes, the Rio Grande downstream of Presidio is in fact the Rio Conchos.

Beyond Presidio the river winds through dramatic canyons in the Big Bend National Park. But the flow is small and muddy. "We get about a sixth of the historical flow here," Dave Elkovitz of the park authority told me. A couple of weeks before my visit, the river dried up here for the first time in more than fifty years. Stagnant pools of water evaporated, leaving dry gravel beds and thousands of dead catfish. Starved of food, a troop of black bears headed back to Mexico. Border patrols drove up the riverbed, pursuing Mexicans heading in the other direction—people who once merited the description "wetbacks" but who could now simply walk across the border without wetting their feet.

"We have treaties for the river," said Elkovitz. "But they allocate more water than actually exists. What good is that?" The main treaty, signed back in 1944 when northern Mexico was much emptier than today, certainly sounded one-sided to me. It might have been fine half a century ago when the rains could be relied upon, but it puts a bullet to the head of Mexican farmers in modern times of drought. The treaty requires that one-third of the water flowing into the Rio Grande from six Mexican tributaries, much the largest of which is the Rio Conchos, is allocated to the US. Worse, however low the tributaries flow, and however little the rainfall in the deserts of northern Mexico, the Mexicans are still required to deliver annually for US use a minimum of 430 million cubic metres, averaged over five years. The US can dry up the Rio Grande at El Paso as much as it wants, but, come hell or low water, the Mexicans have to deliver that quota.

That, at any rate, is the theory. Drought and the demands of their own farmers had by 2003 left Mexico more than four years in arrears. Some good rains south of the border in early 2004 relieved things a little, and Mexico reduced its water debt to three years. But by late 2004, Texas farmers were back on the warpath, demanding reparations of a billion dollars for crop losses over the previous decade. "We want to be good neighbours, but it's hard to do when you are losing money," said citrus farmer Jimmie Steidinger, who reckoned he personally lost a quarter-million dollars. A debt is a debt, even in water flowing down a river.

Thunder clapped in the canyons and it started to rain as I headed over the border for Presidio's twin town, Ojinaga, on the Rio Conchos. Long before the arrival of Europeans, native Americans lived along this river, hunting the animals that congregated beside its waters. Early Spanish explorers came north up the Conchos before moving on into Texas and New Mexico. A century ago, Ojinaga was the headquarters for Pancho Villa's Mexican revolution.

The Ojinaga irrigation district has been a source of prosperity here for a generation, taking water from the Rio Conchos. The district covers 9,000 hectares, growing cotton and corn in the Chihuahua desert. But here, as in Presidio, farming seems to be on its last legs. Under the shade of cottonwood trees on his small-holding, I met sixty-eight-year-old Rito Guerrero. He came down from the Sierra hills to farm here when he was young and the irrigation canals were new. "Once, the water came right up from the river. All my land would be watered." He still gets water some-times from the canals that run right past his gate. But a combination of water shortages and falling prices for crops is forcing him out. "It's six years since I planted corn. I tried water-melons two years ago, but I lost everything. Cotton had a good market, but there isn't enough water. I could be living in the USA with my son." One day soon, he will probably join the diaspora.

Farmer-cum-teacher Humberto Lujan took me round the irri-gation district. Most of the canals were dry and their sluice gates closed and rusting. Three-quarters of the fields were abandoned. The sagebrush was returning. "Virtually nothing comes down the river any more," said Humberto as we peered into the town's empty reservoir and spotted the invasion of salt cedar along the riverbank. The town has lost a quarter of its population. "The young have gone north to the USA, and the old are selling up," said Humberto.

As Humberto sees it, northern Mexico has been living an impossible dream for too long. For thirty years, people flocked here from across the country to grow water-guzzling crops. Before they dug the irrigation canals, he remembers, "There was a traditional irrigation system here—a few small dams on the streams made with the branches of trees. It was a lot more effi-cient. It had less water but served more acres." They grew onions and melons and corn for the local markets. "Every *campesino* had chillies and tomatoes and a few cows for milk." Then they built the dams and canals to grow cotton. They ripped up all the existing vegetation, destroyed the soils, which became salty. Then the water ran out. "Before, we had irrigation here and good soils. But we have ended up creating desert."

Northern Mexico is littered with irrigation areas living on borrowed time and water they owe to Texas. I took the bus south through the desert to the Delicias irrigation district, which stretches for more than a hundred kilometres east of Chihuahua town. It is the largest irrigation district on the Rio Conchos. Its glory days were in the 1960s and 1970s, when farmers became rich growing cotton, which they called "white gold." Today it is the cornerstone of a big dairy industry. The cattle feed on alfalfa grown on its irrigated fields. This is madness. Alfalfa is an extremely thirsty crop. Out here in the desert, where water shortages are critical, they use more than 2,000 litres of irrigation water to produce a litre of milk.

Most of the fields are fed from the river's Boquilla and Madero dams. The Madero dam is decorated with two statues, one carrying corn and the other cotton. It has a recreation area with water slides and advertises itself as a fishing resort. The initial effect was impressive but misleading. The reservoir was at a third of capacity. Beneath a bridge over the 400-metre-wide riverbed, the stream of water was only about two metres wide. The reservoir was shutting off the river's entire flow. It turns out that of the district's 10,000 farms, only about a third can be sure of getting any water most years. And none now get water in winter as they once did. "Some areas have not been irrigated for ten years," said district engineer Ezequil Bueno Torres. The farmers complain that the government gives away all their water to Texans. One, Rogelia Bejarano, was standing in the upcoming local elections. He had a simple campaign pitch: "I won't give away the water; I'll give it to the farmers here."

Meanwhile, the district is engaged in a big modernization process to save water. But its efforts are likely to prove just one more step in an escalating hydrological tragedy. The engineers like Ezequil are lining canals to prevent water seeping out of their porous bottoms. And they are installing perforated rubber piping to get water right to the plant roots rather than flooding fields. The $130-million modernization is mostly paid for by the US government, and the aim is to save 350 million cubic metres of water a year. That volume is close to the amount that Mexico should be sending down the Rio Conchos into the Rio Grande each year. "The Americans will get what we save," said officials at the dam.

It sounds like a win-win situation, and almost everyone I spoke to considered it a great idea. The Mexican farmers, I was told, would get greater water security, while the US gets its missing water. But there is a fallacy here, just as there is a fallacy in lining the canals round El Paso. The modernization won't actually make any more water, and most of the savings are not real savings. As the canal water has failed in recent years, many farmers have come to rely on pumping underground water. It already accounts for about a fifth of all the irrigation in Delicias. Farmers have dug holes up to forty metres wide that fill with underground water. One of the pioneers, Marcial Marquez, said he could pump from the holes dug on his land every day without them emptying. But most of the underground water in the wells comes from seepage from the canals and fields—the supposedly wasted water. If the seepage is cut, Marcial's wells will dry up.

The local irrigation engineers, and the people funding their work, seemed unconcerned by this prospect. But the tragedy is that to meet their immediate obligations to deliver water to Texas farmers, the Mexicans are imperilling the future of their own underground water reserves. The win-win could quickly turn into a lose-lose as the ratchet emptying the Rio Grande is given another turn, this time in the name of efficiency.

PART TWO

WHEN THE RIVERS RUN DRY...
WE MINE OUR CHILDREN'S
WATER

7

INDIA: A COLOSSAL ANARCHY

A generation ago, Indians were starving. Their grain stores were empty and the doomsayers were gathering with the vultures. Today the stores are full and the fear of famine has receded—thanks to a "green revolution" built largely on irrigation. India, like many of its Asian neighbours, has kept bellies full while its population has doubled. This has come about as a result of a new generation of high-yielding varieties of staple crops such as rice, wheat and maize. The key to the success of these super-crops has been abundant supplies of irrigation water. Most other Asian countries have achieved agricultural self-sufficiency by emptying their rivers into irrigation canals. But India's green revolution is increasingly being watered by plundering the country's underground water. More than twenty-one million farmers now tap underground reserves to water their fields.

This self-reliance is born partly of the administrative failure and technical inefficiency of many surface irrigation schemes built by India in the early years of the green revolution. The then–prime minister Rajiv Gandhi effectively wrote their obituary in 1986 when he complained that only a quarter of the 246 large surface irrigation projects begun in the previous thirty years had been completed. "Perhaps we can safely say that almost no benefit has come to the people from these projects. For sixteen years, we have poured money out. The people have got nothing back: no irrigation, no water, no increase in production and no help in their daily life."

He was exaggerating. But his diagnosis that "the drama of harnessing a major river may be more exciting than the prosaic task of getting a steady trickle of water to a parched hectare" was spot on. Indian engineers liked building dams and canals more than the fiddly works needed to get the expensively collected water to farms and fields or to ensure that that water was used efficiently. And their political masters liked grand openings of large structures—often festooned with plaques with their names on—more than the actual business of feeding their people.

But the failure of surface irrigation projects is not just about administrative indolence. India's rivers just do not contain enough water to sustain the demands being made on them. So, millions of farmers have taken things into their own hands. They are hiring drilling rigs and buying $600 electric pumps to mine water that has lain undisturbed beneath their land for millennia. Most of the water goes onto the fields, though some enters India's burgeoning private-water market.

India's farmers have spent in the region of $12 billion on pumps and boreholes in the past two decades. In many ways they should be congratulated for their enterprise and investment. They have kept India fed. And there is plenty of evidence that farmers tapping their own underground water use it more efficiently than their neighbours relying on canal water. Typically they get twice the yield, mostly because the water is there *when* they want it and *where* they want it.

But how long will there be water underground? I went to see Tushaar Shah, the director of the International Water Management Institute groundwater research station, based in the Indian state of Gujarat. He has spent more than a decade following India's groundwater revolution. And at present, he says, Indian farmers are living in a fool's paradise. They are draining their water reserves with reckless abandon, growing thirsty crops like rice, sugar cane, alfalfa and cotton with no thought for the future. "It's a colossal anarchy," he said. The farmers are certainly destroying their children's future, if not their own.

The business is a free-for-all. "Regulation is virtually impossible," said Shah. "Nobody knows where the pumps are, or who owns them. There is no way anyone can control what happens to them." There are no reliable statistics on how much water the farmers pump from beneath the ground, but recent estimates put the annual abstraction for irrigation at about 250 cubic kilometres of water a year. That is about 100 cubic kilometres more than the rains replace. This underground water irrigates at least two-thirds of India's crops. It feeds India—while it lasts. But as every year passes, the underground reserves become emptier. The pumps have to work ever harder. The boreholes have to be replaced or sunk to ever greater depths.

"This has all just exploded in the past decade, since the arrival in India of cheap pumps. And the juggernaut is still accelerating. There are a million more pumps every year," says Shah. "We are only just beginning to see the consequences. But I must say it looks like a one-way trip to disaster." Shah estimates that at least a quarter of Indian farmers are mining underground water that nature will not replace. That is 200 million people facing a water-less future. The groundwater boom is turning to bust and, for some, the "green revolution" is over.

Fifty years ago in northern Gujarat, circling yoked bullocks could lift water in leather buckets from open wells dug to about ten metres. Now tubewells are sunk to 400 metres, but still run dry. Half the traditional hand-dug wells and millions of tubewells have dried up across western India. In the south, two-thirds of Tamil Nadu's hand-dug wells have failed already, and only half as much of the state's land is irrigated as a decade ago. There are 15,000 abandoned wells around Coimbatore, the state capital. Whole districts in arid states like Tamil Nadu and Gujarat are emptying of people. There have been thousands of suicides among farmers. Many more farmers are joining the millions crowding into urban slums or the gangs of construction workers and labourers travelling the roads of India.

As the water tables fall, some states find that half their heavily subsidized electricity is being used by farmers to pump water to the surface. Shah estimates than the total energy subsidy to Indian farmers to pump up underground water amounts to some $5 billion a year, more than 1 per cent of gross domestic product (GDP). There is no easy way out. "If the electricity sold to farmers for pumping were charged at its full market price in northern Gujarat, nothing would grow except what the rains can sustain," he says. But the grids cannot take the strain and there are widespread blackouts—the only effective limit on pumping, as Shah ruefully points out.

Why have Gujarat and so many other parts of India reached such a dangerous hydrological state? This is not a case of bad people doing bad things. Far from it, as I discovered when I visited Jitbhai Chowdhury, farming on the edge of a village called Kushkal in northern Gujarat. He is, by conventional measures, a model farmer. That's why Shah's researchers took me to see him: they rated him the most efficient farmer for miles around. He is ecologically minded, too. He uses organic manure and natural pesticides made on his farm by soaking wayside weeds in water. He grows fruit trees round the edge of his fields and tends his cattle with care. I met him early one morning as the sun burnt off the mist over his fields. He was milking his cattle, emptying their udders into a milk churn, which he took twice daily to a village collection point, from where trucks transported the milk to the state dairy. It seemed a perfect organic dairy farm.

But probe a little deeper and Jitbhai's very efficiency suggests the madness of the water economics being played out here. Milking done, Jitbhai described for me how his farm works. He has just two hectares of land—land that, but for underground water, would be virtual desert. He has a small pump that brings to the surface 12 cubic metres of water an hour. It takes him 64 hours to irrigate his fields—a task that he carries out 24 times a year, mostly to grow alfalfa to feed his cows. His farm's main output is 25 litres of milk a day.

I did the math. He uses 18,000 cubic metres of water a year to grow the fodder to produce just over 9,000 litres of milk. That's 2,000 litres of water for every litre of milk. According to Shah that is better than the local average, which varies between 3,000 and 4,600 litres. Even so, calculated over the year, it means he pumps from under his fields twice as much water as falls on the land in rain.

No wonder the water table in the village is 150 metres down and falling by about six metres a year. What looks at first sight like an extremely efficient local economy, making milk in the desert for a dairy that trades across India, is in fact hydrological suicide. Some have called the dairy industry here a "white revolution." But, says Shah, "The dairy industry is one of the major reasons for the water crisis in Gujarat." He reckons two districts alone are exporting from the state 1.5 cubic kilometres of "virtual water" a year in the form of milk.

And Jitbhai, the dairy farmer, understands all too well the bind that he and his fellow water plunderers find themselves in. "Yes, I'm worried that the water will disappear. But what can I do? I have to live, and if I don't pump it up, my neighbours will." As we gave him a lift into the village to deliver his milk churn, he added: "I don't want my son to do farming. I want him to get a job in the city." No wonder.

Suresh Ponnusami sat back on his large wooden veranda by the road south of the Indian textile town of Tirupur. He was not rich, but for the owner of a one-hectare farm he was doing well. He had a phone and a television. His traditional white Indian robes were freshly laundered that morning. As we chatted, I notice an improbably large water reservoir at the side of his house. And then a tanker drew up on the road. The driver hauled a large pipe over the hedge and dropped it into the reservoir. I fully expected the tanker to start filling the reservoir with water. This was a drought region, after all. But instead the pump was working in the other direction. The contents of the reservoir began to empty into the tanker.

Ponnusami explained: "I no longer grow crops, I farm water." He has sunk boreholes deep into the rocks beneath his fields and brings water to the surface twenty-four hours a day. He used to grow rice, but apart from cultivating a little fodder for his beloved cattle he doesn't bother any more. He doesn't need to. "The tankers come about ten times a day," he said. "I don't have to do anything except keep my reservoir full."

Actually, he doesn't so much farm water as mine it—from ever deeper below ground. The mine will probably soon be exhausted. The water table was 300 metres underground and falling fast, said Ponnusami as his wife poured us a cold lime drink. "Before the trade in water got going here a decade ago, you could tap water at about 15 metres, so it's going down by about thirty metres a year." How much water is left? He didn't know, but he reckoned he had a bit to go yet. In Mandaba, the village down the road, they had drilled to 500 metres. "But they are starting to run out of water there."

When I visited Ponnusami in late 2003, around five hundred water tankers drove each day to this small area in the southern Indian state of Tamil Nadu. Day and night they came, adding their roar to the constant whine of the farmers' Japanese pumps. Ponnusami showed me the books. He sold his water for 200 rupees, about four dollars, for a single tanker load. Of that, he spent about 50 rupees on the highly subsidized electricity available here to farmers for pumping water. There were also bills for deepening his boreholes each time they ran dry. "But it's a good living, and it's risk free," he said. No risk of failed crops. Well, at least not until the water runs out. For this crop will one day fail for good.

I asked where all the water went. Who round here wanted five hundred tankers of water every day? He named two companies with whom he had contracts. They both manufacture textile dyes in the nearby town of Tirupur. This area is part of a region known as "the Manchester of India," because of the huge cotton-growing and knitwear industry set up by local entrepreneurs in the 1950s. They don't grow so much cotton now because they can't compete with cheap imports from China and Bangladesh. But the processing business is still booming. Town billboards advertise industrial sewing machines and computerized embroidery, peroxide bleaching, dyeing and the spinning of local silks.

And all these factories need water—the hundreds of backyard dyeing and bleaching factories most of all. They once got their water from a giant reservoir 100 kilometres away on Tamil Nadu's biggest river, the Cauvery. But not much water flows down that river now. Like many Indian rivers these days, the Cauvery has been reduced to a trickle and Tamil Nadu's main reservoir is nearly empty most of the year. So the factories have taken to buying up underground water from local farmers. It is a trade that is growing all over India. But, as we shall see, there is a twist in the tak, here among the sari mills.

Round the corner from Ponnusami's farm, I came across a drilling rig by the road. His neighbour was probing ever deeper into the earth to keep the water flowing for the tankers. The neighbour had a nice two-storey house that clearly hadn't been paid for from anything growing in the stony land around it. And sure enough, soon another tanker driver was loading up from a big concrete-lined reservoir that was itself being filled from two boreholes. The driver, who collected water from several local farms, said he sold the water in town for 400 rupees—a clear 100 per cent profit.

He sold mostly to the textile factories. But sometimes he toured the streets, filling householders' pots for a rupee each. Public water supplies to houses are as fitful as those to the mills, and many people rely on water from tankers to drink, cook their rice and wash. As we talked, another tanker drove up the track to the next farm. That was three tankers pumping from three farms within a hundred metres of each other on one morning in the middle of the Indian countryside.

The farmer's wife came out to survey the scene. The water trade here was probably on its last legs, she agreed. "Every day the water is reducing. We drilled two new boreholes a few weeks ago and one has already failed. But we will keep drilling till we only have enough water for drinking." Surely this is madness, I suggested. Why not get back to farming before the wells finally run dry? "If everybody did that, it would be well and good," she agreed. "But they don't. We are all trying to make as much money before the water runs out. If we stopped pumping just on this farm it wouldn't affect the outcome."

It is a classic case of what environmentalists call "the tragedy of the commons." Everybody chases short-term wealth even at the cost of destroying their long-term collective future. Nobody can afford to miss out on the boom because they will all share in the eventual bust. Some think it is what we are doing to the planet. It is certainly what is happening to India's underground water.

But the reckless plunder of the water around Tirupur is only the start of this particular tragedy of the commons. I had taken these byways at the suggestion of a local academic, the director of the state university's Water Technology Centre, Kuppannan Palanisami. "For the real tragedy," he told me, "you have to follow what happens to the water that these farmers sell to the factories." So I followed. The two hundred or so dyeing and bleaching factories that take the farmers' water stretch almost thirty kilometres from Tirupur along the banks of the River Noyal, a tributary of the Cauvery. The Noyal should be completely dry for most of the year because, owing to all the pumping, there are no springs to sustain its flow through the eight-month dry season. But it was not entirely dry. It ran with the stinking, brightly coloured efflu-ent pouring from the factories. This is what had become of the farmers' water after it has served its purpose in the textile works.

I did what Palanisami said and followed the foul, untreated effluent down the river. It eventually ended up in a big water-supply reservoir that had been built by the Tamil Nadu authorities a decade before, at a time when there was still clean water in the Noyal. The reservoir is in the shadow of a famous temple on a hilltop at Avanashi. It had been dug to help farmers in a wide area around Avanashi to grow crops all year round. I climbed onto the bank surrounding the reservoir. But one whiff, one look at the chemical encrustation on its shoreline, made clear that its contents were poison. Almost since it opened, I later learned, the reservoir had been little more than an industrial sump in the middle of the countryside.

And a very leaky sump, at that. The reservoir has no lining and, year by year, the poison in its waters has been seeping into the local soils and down into the underground water reserves. So far, said farmers, the poison has spread for two kilometres either side of the reservoir, and for about ten kilometres downstream along the river. All around the dam, I found derelict houses. The fields were barren and empty. No crops would grow, nor even weeds. Only old plantations of coconut trees kept going, and they looked sick and stunted.

The only functioning village I could find in this wasteland survived by processing the coconuts to make oil. "Before the dam we had good profitable crops, like turmeric and banana. We thought the dam would help us grow more; but it turned out to be the opposite," said the village head woman, Kittusami Manonmani. "Now we only have coconuts, and even then new trees don't grow."

Surrounded by coconut shells, she warmed to her theme. The reservoir had polluted the underground water for miles around, she said. "Our wells are full of salt now. It is not natural salt; it comes from the chemicals in the reservoir. You can't even bathe in it, let alone drink it. If we wash our clothes in it, they get holes and we come out in rashes and start itching. At the start, we let the cattle drink the water; but they died." She brought me a pot of well water that had been sitting in the yard all day so that the salts would settle out. There was a thick sludge at the bottom, but the water still tasted bitter. We spat it out quickly. The local hospital in Tirupur later confirmed there are high rates of skin disease and lung disorders in the area as a result of the waste chemicals. The villagers said they had made numerous protests about their water. "Politicians used to come here and make promises to stop this. But they don't even make promises now. We think the textile companies have got to them," said Kittusami.

I can't confirm that, but during the 1990s there were inconclusive legal actions against the Tirupur factories, which at one point promised to build treatment plants. But the effluent has kept coming. During 2002, the controversy revived when local press reports caused a flurry of concern at the State Pollution Control Board. Officials revealed that 80,000 cubic metres of dyeing and bleaching effluents entered the River Noyal each day. Sodium in the effluent was making the local soils infertile. Scientists took some water samples from the villagers. They found peroxide, hypochlorite and benzidine, a cancer-causing chemical used in manufacturing many dyes. But nobody told the villagers the results.

And when I visited, eighteen months after the reports, nothing had changed. With no sign of a clean-up, more and more villagers were leaving the area. Even in the coconut village, more than half of the men had left to get jobs. Inevitably, perhaps, that meant knocking on the doors of the textile factories of Tirupur, the cause of their misery.

How do the villagers left behind live? I asked Kittusami where they got clean water to drink and wash. "We have to buy the water from tankers," she told me. "They come from that way." She pointed west and south. "About fifteen kilometres, I think." And then it dawned on me: the tanker drivers who sold water to these villagers were the same tanker drivers who bought the water from the water-mining farmers on the other side of town.

These villagers in this toxic wilderness were buying their water, at a price of a rupee a pot, from the people who sucked dry the precious underground reserves of Mandaba. The same people who were keeping the dye factories in business, producing the effluent that poisoned their fields and wells for miles around, were making a further tidy profit out of the misery caused by their pollution. The tragedy of Tamil Nadu's disappearing water supplies was complete.

Water disputes in one village in Kerala in the far southwest of India became an international news story in 2003, when angry farmers accused the local Coca-Cola factory of drying up their fields to fill its bottles. The village of Plachimara took the company's biggest bottling plant in Asia to the state high court on a charge of destroying their coconut groves and paddy fields. Since it opened in 1998, the plant had taken around half a million litres a day from a series of boreholes on its sixteen-hectare site.

The story got taken up by the international media. You can see why. The amount pumped sounds a lot and a global corporation like Coca-Cola is an easy target. But the truth is that even half a million litres of water a day is not large on the scale of rural Indian water use. A single local rice farmer with ten hectares of paddy could easily be using as much water as the Coca-Cola bottling plant. The villagers who complained that Coca-Cola was emptying their wells were almost certainly collectively using more water to irrigate their crops than the company was taking to fill its bottles.

In late 2003, the Kerala court told Coca-Cola to stop pumping out the local waters and to find an alternative source. The plant subsequently shut. The decision was later reversed, but the village council claims that it has the final say, and the case went to the Indian Supreme Court. At the time of writing, the plant remains shut. Beyond the legal issues the key hydrological question is: will the water come back? If, as seems likely, it does not, then it will underline a frightening truth: that the state of Plachimara's wells is not a gross example of a global corporation riding roughshod over locals, but simply a typical story of what India is doing itself to its most precious resource.

MEDITERRANEAN SEA

EGYPT

Al Jaghhbub

Tubru

Darnah

Banghazi

Sarir
Wellfield

Al Khufrah

Tazirbu

Tazirbu
Wellfields

L I B Y A

Sirte

400 km

250 m

0

F E Z Z A N

CHAD

MURZUQ BASIN

Sabha

Jebel Hasouna
Wellfields

HAMMDA BASIN

TRIPOLI

Ghadamis
Wellfields

JEFARA PLAIN

Ghadamis

TUNISIA

ALGERIA

Reservoirs

Completed pipelines

Plans for future pipelines

8

HALLIBURTON'S JOB FOR GADAFFI

Some say ancient underground water that will not be replaced by the rains should never be pumped except in dire emergencies. It should be maintained as a precious back-up reserve. Others argue that new water reserves will always be found. Just as shortages of fossil fuels and precious minerals have encouraged geologists to locate new sources, they say, so it will be with water. The problem with this argument is that water does not command the kind of prices that allow it to be transported round the world in the way that other commodities are. Water still needs to be local. Unless you are Colonel Gadaffi, that is.

For Libya, the driest nation of its size on Earth, has a river at last. To be precise, it has two rivers, though they go by the singular name Great Man-made River. Neither are rivers you could go fishing in, or watch flow by as you eat a picnic on their banks. They don't have banks, or fish. The rivers comprise a 3,500-kilometre network of pipes, all of them wide enough to drive an underground train through. Their water comes from hundreds of boreholes sunk up to half a kilometre into the sand in the middle of the Sahara Desert.

The giant Nubian sandstone aquifer is the largest liquid freshwater source on Earth, containing around 60,000 cubic kilometres of water in a series of basins whose only outlet till recently had been a handful of oases in the desert. Some of the water, according to recent radiocarbon dating, is more than a million years old. Most if comes from a more recent wet era when the Sahara was crocodile-infested swamp. But that era ended abruptly some five thousand years ago, when the desert formed. And since then it has sat undisturbed for thousands of years. Until now.

Geologists have eyed this water ever since discovering it in the 1960s while prospecting for oil. Libyan leader Colonel Gadaffi, who seized power in 1969, decided to spend his oil revenues bringing the water to the surface. At first, he tried to persuade Libyans to move to his desert boreholes and grow wheat. But they wouldn't go. They preferred their fields along the Mediterranean coast, even though the aquifers that watered them were emptying fast. The remains of Gadaffi's giant desert farms can still be seen from aircraft crossing the desert.

So the eccentric colonel decided instead to bring the water to the people. The first phase of the Great Man-made River opened back in 1991, carrying three-quarters of a cubic kilometre of "fossil water" each year from well-fields around the oases of Sarir and Tazirbu on a nine-day journey across a thousand kilometres of desert so dry that even camel trains didn't cross it until the nineteenth century.

There was a huge ceremony back on the coast near Sirte to greet the first water. Fellow leaders from Africa and the Middle East gathered in the cool desert night to hear the colonel compare his great work to the pyramids of Ancient Egypt, and watch him unleash the water into a reservoir. It had cost Gadaffi $14 billion to deliver that water. No wonder a thousand Libyans rushed forward to take ecstatic sips. Gadaffi boasted that day how his new river was a revolutionary triumph against the tyrants of the US and Britain, who had bombed Tripoli just five years before. He forgot to mention that the project was being masterminded by the enemy.

The project's headquarters was an office on the fourth floor of a high-security tower block near the railway station at Hampton Wick, in the leafy suburbs of southwest London. There, through the bombings and kidnappings and sieges and murders that characterized Anglo–Libyan relations in the 1980s, and a US embargo on trade with Libya, a European subsidiary of the American engineering combine Halliburton called Brown & Root was legitimately able to work with Gadaffi's staff to make the colonel's pipe dream come true. When I visited Bashir ElSaleh, the colonel's US–trained head man in Hampton Wick, he said, "This is the best investment we have ever made. Hopefully we will be able to depend on it for hundreds of years."

Since then, a second phase of the "river" has been completed along with a series of coastal connections. The second phase is of a similar size to the first, but had to cross mountains and canyons to link the capital Tripoli with the western well-fields at Fezzan. It proved more difficult and has reportedly been delivering only a fifth of its intended flow since coming on stream in the late 1990s.

The project, for some years the world's largest civil engineering project, has used some 5 million tonnes of cement (enough to pave a road from Tripoli to Bombay, say the engineers proudly) and 25 million tonnes of aggregate. So far, half a million concrete pipe sections, each four metres wide, seven metres long and painted Islamic green, have been assembled. Three more phases are planned that will link up the two completed "rivers" and extend the first out to Kufra.

But progress has slowed since Halliburton's collaborator, a giant South Korean steel combine called Dong Ah responsible for making the pipes, went bust in the aftermath of the Asian financial crisis in the late 1990s. And several times, corrosion has caused the partially buried pipes to burst, flinging pieces of pipe a hundred metres across the desert, killing any passing camels and forcing the pipe's closure for months of repairs.

So far, Gadaffi has spent about $27 billion on the project. It has drained Libyan oil revenues for more than two decades. So is this a fantasy born of oil money and the megalomaniac dreams of Colonel Gadaffi? Or could this be the future? Could the twenty-first century see the construction of many more artificial rivers to tap new reserves of water and take them to where the people are?

The project is certainly shot through with fantasy on all sides. The Libyan authorities see it as an "eighth wonder of the world," and a source of "everlasting prosperity" (a term first coined by another colonel, Egypt's Abdul Nasser, to describe his own engineering wonder of the world, the High Aswan dam). Meanwhile, conspiracy-minded foreigners have developed their own bizarre notions. The *New York Times* and the *Guardian* in 1997 splashed a story quoting defence analysts who claimed that the pipes were not intended to carry water at all. They had been built, it said, to provide camouflage for Libyan tanks in some future invasion of its neighbours, and to provide Gadaffi with "somewhere to store chemical and biological weapons."

But Gadaffi does have a serious purpose in all this. The aim is to deliver two cubic kilometres of water a year to help Libya feed its people. The country has more than half a million hectares of irrigated fields. But most are on the coast, where overpumping and an invasion of sea water into aquifers has left irrigated soils so salty that many wheat fields have perished. Oranges are said to grow no bigger than ping-pong balls. Partly as a result, Libya currently imports half its grain. But unlike neighbours such as Egypt, it persists in a goal of agricultural self-sufficiency. No virtual water for Colonel Gadaffi.

The trouble is, the numbers simply do not add up. The embarrassing truth is that, with $27 billion spent on bringing desert water to the coast, most of Libya's irrigation water still comes from the saline coastal aquifers. Irrigating the existing farmland at current standards of efficiency requires around five cubic kilometres, more than twice the intended output of the man-made rivers. The flow down Gadaffi's pipes is actually rather puny. For all the talk of a "New Nile," phase one delivered about as much water as England's River Mersey, and all five phases together will deliver roughly the flow of the River Thames through London. "We would need two or three times more to be self-sufficient in food," says Abou Fayed, who is responsible for allocating the water to farms.

Gadaffi's reach seems to have exceeded his grasp. The vast capital cost and the growing bills for pumping water from ever greater depths beneath the desert make wheat grown with the Saharan water among the most expensive on Earth. "It is madness to use this water for agriculture," says Tony Allan, a British specialist on Middle East water. In future, as Libya begins the painful process of integrating itself into the global economy, pressure is likely to grow for it to import more wheat rather than less, and to reduce rather than increase its irrigation. It seems unlikely now that the great man-made rivers will ever be fully utilized. In the end, they may be left to rust in the desert.

9

THE WORLD'S LARGEST MASS POISONING

I met ten-year-old Shatap on a muddy lane in Hirapur, a village in central India. He had a gait straight out of *Monty Python*'s silly walks. I hope that is not an offensive remark, but it is how it struck me at the time. The diminutive figure was not playing games as he waddled up the lane, his knees locked together and his stunted and misshapen lower legs splayed wide almost like flippers. His disability was permanent. He had been poisoned by the water in the well at the village school. His bones were grossly deformed by fluoride dissolved in the water.

The school tubewell at Hirapur was one of tens of millions sunk round the world in a highly publicized race to provide the world's poor with "safe" drinking water. It was planned and part-funded by the UN children's fund Unicef during the International Water Decade of the 1980s. The decade worked on a simple premise. Millions of the rural poor drank water taken untreated from surface water sources like rivers, ponds and canals. This water was polluted, often with sewage that spread lethal diseases such as cholera, typhoid and diarrhea. But while surface water was often polluted, underground water, because it had not come into contact with man-made pollution, was almost universally safe. So sure of this were the engineers and public health professions behind the campaign that they often didn't even run basic tests for poison in the waters as the wells were sunk.

Such folly. They forgot that nature can poison water too. And now the truth is dawning. Shatap is one of perhaps millions of drinkers from the wells sunk by the UN and other aid agencies who are suffering the symptoms of fluoride poisoning. Next door to Shatap, I met fourteen-year-old bowlegged Krishna Chudaman and her sister Kamala. Both had similar symptoms. Krishna had given up education because, after being poisoned at her primary school, she couldn't walk to the secondary school in the next village. But almost every child in the village had some symptoms. Hirapur is one village among dozens to suffer in Mandla district, a small corner of Madhya Pradesh.

I visited nearby Tilaipani where a young researcher uncovered the mass poisoning in Mandla after querying whether doctors were right to diagnose an epidemic of knock-knees among children as rickets. Unicef funded the wells, said Ravi Shankar Tiwary, director of the local medical centre. Government engineers claimed to have tested the water but "I know they didn't; they didn't have the right equipment." He showed me a file full of X-rays of the limbs of young children, bent like bows. "As they grow it becomes worse and they are crippled," he said.

Fluoride is a common component of the granite rocks that underlie much of India. It slowly dissolves into the underground water in the pores of rocks above it. Usually, the fluoride doesn't spread far from the granite. So, wells that tap water near the surface are generally safe enough. But as water tables across India fall, villagers sink their wells ever deeper and ever closer to the bedrock. As they do, the chances of bringing up toxic water dramatically increase.

A lot of misery gets overlooked in rural India, a country of a million villages. Nobody knows how many suffer from fluoride poisoning. But Andezhath Susheela of the Indian government's Fluorosis and Rural Development Foundation in Delhi told me she guesses that sixty million could suffer to some degree. Unless public health people show much greater vigilance in testing well water and finding alternatives supplies when fluoride is found, then the crisis is bound to worsen as the groundwater crisis itself deteriorates, she said.

"It's a huge time bomb," agreed Tushaar Shah at the International Water Management Institute in Gujarat, a state badly hit. "And in many areas there is really no solution. Going back to polluted surface water would be even worse. We are looking into developing a fluoride filter, but the practicalities of using these in small villages where they can't get the chemicals are huge."

From Assam in the east to Gujarat in the west, Tamil Nadu in the south to Kashmir in the north, doctors are starting to blame outbreaks of anemia, stiff joints, kidney failure, muscle degeneration and cancer on fluoride in the water. In two districts in Rajasthan more than half the population has symptoms. The greatest risks seem to be among the young and old. The young suffer damage to their limbs as they grow; the old have the highest accumulations in their bodies. In western Gujarat, I met elderly hunchbacks and cripples whose problems were almost certainly due to fluoride.

And India is not alone. China is reckoned to have more than a million victims. And from Chile to Ethiopia to Uzbekistan, similar stories are probably waiting to be told in tiny villages where simple hand-pumped tubewells have been installed to provide "safe" drinking water.

But, amazing as it may seem, there is an even bigger scandal that has been created by the trend to drink water from underground sources. Arsenic. Tens of millions of people across Bangladesh and western India are drinking well water laced with concentrations of arsenic that are likely to kill them eventually. The World Health Organization (WHO) calls it "the largest mass poisoning of a population in history." At least half of Bangladesh's estimated twelve million backyard tubewells are thought to be poisoned. Many deliver water with hundreds of times the WHO limit for arsenic in water supplies.

The arsenic began in the rocks of the Himalaya Mountains, but was eroded by great rivers like the Ganges and Brahmaputra and washed downstream, probably over thousands or millions of years. The toxic metal gradually accumulated in the thick muds of the floodplains and deltas that make up most of Bangladesh. And there it stayed undisturbed, until humans in the past thirty years began to pump up water out of the muds for drinking. The water brought the arsenic with it. Tubewells sunk to depths of between 20 and 100 metres contain the most. Catastrophically, that is just the level to which most tubewells have been sunk.

This is a silent epidemic that is stalking the majority of Bangladesh's 68,000 villages. Arsenic, like fluoride, is a cumulative poison. It typically takes a decade of drinking arsenic-laced water before the first symptoms appear. And nobody knows who is at risk. Virtually every backyard has a tubewell and seemingly small differences in location and depth can make big differences in the arsenic content of the water. Almost any tubewell could be delivering lethal concentrations. To be sure, each well has to be tested. Very few have been. Today, tens of thousands of Bangladeshis have already developed skin lesions, cancers and other symptoms. Many have died, and a quarter-million could succumb in the coming decade, says Allan Smith, a US doctor who first alerted the WHO to the scale of the scourge.

The tubewells were installed in Bangladesh and elsewhere to reduce the heavy death toll from sewage bacteria and other water-borne diseases spread in contaminated surface waters. In the 1970s, these diseases were killing an estimated quarter-million people a year in Bangladesh. Many people are alive today as a result of the sinking of the tubewells. But the arsenic epidemic could have been prevented if the risks had been realized in time. Tubewells could have been sunk deeper, to a depth where the water is generally free of the poison, or been tested before being used for drinking.

The true scale of the disaster only emerged slowly during the 1990s. But tragically, ever since then, efforts to undo the damage have been foiled by indolent local bureaucracy. It emerged in

2003 that efforts to find and replace the estimated five million poisoned tubewells were making little headway. The Bangladeshi government had spent less than $7 million of the $32 million given by the World Bank in 1998 for an immediate clean-up. But it is too easy to blame Bangladeshi bureaucrats. The truth is that thousands of people are still being poisoned by tubewells sunk with aid money from the British and other governments, from charities and from UN agencies like Unicef, which itself sunk the first 900,000 wells.

I went out on a survey expedition to find poisoned wells. We had chosen our first village at random. Like thousands of others across Bangladesh, Dipordi, a couple of minutes out of Sonargaon, the ancient capital of Bengal, had never had its water tested for arsenic. And none of its inhabitants had been screened for the debilitating skin diseases that are its first symptoms. Like a travelling medicine man, Akhtar Ahmad of the National Institute of Preventive Social Medicine walked unannounced into the village. He called for a tumbler of water from each well and set out his test kit on a hastily erected trestle table.

Within half an hour, before an enthusiastic crowd, he had analyzed samples from nine wells for arsenic, using test tubes, four chemical reagents, a clamp and test papers which darkened from yellow to brown as the arsenic level rose. It was part circus and part science. But it revealed seven poisoned wells and only two that were safe. One was off the scale with more than 500 parts per billion of arsenic, fifty times the recommended WHO limit and ten times the Bangladesh government's own limit.

The results announced, Akhtar lined up the crowd to check their palms, chest and gums for signs of the sores typical of arsenic poisoning. These fifteen-second consultations yielded five cases: a small hit-rate by local standards, but Akhtar was worried. Villagers said the first tubewell had been installed here only seven years before. Symptoms of arsenic poisoning typically took ten years to show up. Yet, he said, "Already we find symptoms. This is the first phase of something big." One villager was angry, and he asked about installing a deeper well to bypass the arsenic-bearing water. "I am rich; I can afford it," he said.

But it was too late for Abdul Kasem, who we met a few miles away in Barai Kandi village. Abdul had turned up at a clinic a week before with a gruesome carcinoma on one hand and a flask of well water in the other, asking for checks on both. His medical diagnosis had been instant, but we were returning to give Abdul the test results on his well water. And, sure enough, the well from which he had drunk for twenty years contained a lethal 500 parts per billion of arsenic.

Abdul, his carcinoma covered by a leaf from the field, took us to meet his wife and five children. All six, along with another twelve villagers living in houses close by, had warts and other growths characteristic of arsenic poisoning. Akhtar gave them prescriptions for vitamins A, C and E. "It might help, and it's all I can do," he said. Meanwhile, these villagers assembled water samples from thirteen wells, and joined in the testing: 600 ppb, 300 ppb, 30 ppb, 1,000 ppb. Only two samples passed the Bangladeshi limit and none the WHO limit. Before we left, an impromptu village meeting had arm-twisted the owner of the two cleanest wells to let his neighbours take drinking water from him.

Akhtar's work was the first evidence I had seen, after nearly a week in the country, that there were people in the Bangladeshi government's service who possessed the will and skills to tackle an epidemic of arsenic pouring from millions of wells in thousands of villages like Barai Kandi and Dipordi. "We have to act ourselves to find the safe wells in each village," Akhtar said. "We don't need international loans to do this, just commitment." His test kit was cheap and crude and far from accurate by laboratory standards, he admitted. "But we can test a sample for seven thaka [about fifteen cents] and give the results instantly to the village," he said.

This is barefoot science. You couldn't publish scientific papers using such "dirty data." But it is probably the only practical way that villagers will be able to take back some control of their health from the public health professionals who have so damaged it. Akhtar told me he wanted the kit mass-produced so every village could have one. "It is very simple to use. Everything is colour coded so they don't even need to read," he said. "Our work is about empowerment. We want the villagers to be able to say: this is our problem, we will solve it." The difficulty in making that happen was that the kit was so cheap and simple that no company wanted to manufacture it. There were no profits to be made.

The arsenic epidemic keeps growing. High levels of arsenic in ground water were once believed to be confined to an area around the river's delta in Bangladesh and West Bengal. But new studies in 2003 suggested that water laced with arsenic might be lurking in underground waters near the Ganges all the way to the Himalayas—across a region where 800 million people drink underground water.

The new focus of concern was the state of Bihar, home to 83 million people. There, Kuneshwar Ojha, a schoolteacher living in a tiny village called Semria Ojha Patti close to the Ganges, had become concerned after his wife and mother had both died of liver cancer. He noticed that other family members had developed skin lesions, and he thought they looked like symptoms of arsenic poisoning. He took water samples from the family tubewell to Dipankar Chakraborti, director of environmental studies at Jadavpur University in Calcutta, who had originally uncovered the mass arsenic poisoning in West Bengal.

Chakraborti confirmed high concentrations of arsenic in the sample. And it quickly emerged that eighteen young people had died from apparently arsenic-related illnesses in the village in the previous five years, and a hundred more were sick with early symptoms. The only fit people were the Dalits, or untouchables, who because of their lowly status were not allowed to drink water from village tubewells.

Since then, hundreds of similar cases have emerged in the surrounding villages in this part of Bihar, and the authorities have banned people from using many tubewells. Parts of Semria Ojha Patti village were abandoned because there were no safe wells. Chakraborti surveyed wells across a wide area of the state and found that 40 per cent contained arsenic above the government limit—a proportion very similar to that in Bangladesh. More than half of the adults examined in the study showed symptoms of arsenic poisoning.

A few months later, similar findings began to emerge from neighbouring Uttar Pradesh. "The same pattern we saw in Bangladesh is being repeated," Chakraborti said. "There, we began with the discovery of it in three villages. Now thousands are known to be affected and more are being discovered all the time. Our early warnings were ignored then. Now we are warning about Bihar. We feel that this is just the tip of the iceberg."

Is there anything special about the Ganges? Maybe not. Within weeks of Chakraborti's new findings becoming public, Michael Berg of the Swiss Federal Institute for Environmental Science reported on a study of water from tubewells sunk beneath the Red River delta in Vietnam. They contained arsenic levels up to three hundred times the WHO safe limit. Symptoms of arsenic poisoning could soon emerge, he said. The first tube-wells had been installed seven years before. The delta is home to eleven million people, including most of the inhabitants of the capital, Hanoi.

10

MIRAGES

Over the past twenty years, tens of millions of small farmers across much of the poor world have been pumping underground waters from beneath their fields. As in India, it is a massive revolution born of two factors. First, the failure of government-built irrigation systems tapping rivers to deliver the water the farmers need; and, second, advances in cheap drilling technology that allow them to drill far deeper into the earth for water than the depth reached by their old hand-dug wells, and to buy cheap Japanese pumps to bring the water to the surface.

There are few official statistics, and no way of collecting them. But just three countries—India, China and Pakistan—probably pump out around 400 cubic kilometres of underground water a year from the new tubewells. They account for more than half of the world's total use of underground water for agriculture. And they are living on borrowed time, sucking dry the continent's water reserves.

Every year, perhaps 100 million Chinese eat food grown with underground water that the rains are not replacing. There are, as we have seen, another 200 million or so doing the same in India. In the Pakistani province of Punjab, which produces 90 per cent of that country's wheat, farmers compensate for diminishing deliveries of water from the River Indus by pumping from beneath their own fields. Their pumping is 30 per cent more than recharge, and water tables are plunging by between one and two metres a year.

Overall total pumping in India, China and Pakistan probably exceeds recharge by 150–200 cubic kilometres a year. The boom has so far lasted twenty years; the bust could be less than twenty years away. The consequences of the eventual, inevitable failure of underground water in these countries could be catastrophic. But it is a crisis that has not yet registered on the radar screens of governments or aid agencies. When a river runs dry, it is very visible. But underground water is invisible. Only the farmers know they have to drill ever deeper to find it. And few in the corridors of power talk to farmers about a slow-burning disaster that will one day affect hundreds of millions of people.

It won't happen everywhere at the same time, of course. Each aquifer has its own countdown to extinction. But even so, as Tushaar Shah puts it: "The overuse of water in Asia's underground aquifers will spell disaster for millions of the region's poor people who depend on it." And as each bubble bursts, it will undermine the world's ability to feed itself.

Farmers in other heavily populated countries are beginning to sink tubewells and buy pumps with equal vigour. In the past decade, Vietnamese farmers have quadrupled the number of tubewells to more than a million. Sri Lanka, Indonesia, Iran and Bangladesh are not far behind. These countries are at the heart of what agronomist and environmentalist Lester Brown calls "Asia's food bubble." Record farm outputs in recent years, he says, have been made possible only by an unsustainable assault on this fast-diminishing resource. It is a one-off bonanza, a bubble that is bound to burst. "The question is not if, but when."

Asia leads the way in this unsustainable groundwater revolution. But countries such as Mexico, Argentina, Brazil, Saudi Arabia and Morocco are also increasingly significant players. Sub-Saharan Africa is not far behind. As rivers fail, underground sources provide a third of the world's water. By some calculations, as much as a tenth of the world's food is being grown using underground water that is not being replaced by the rains. Major cities—among them Beijing and Tianjin, Mexico City and Bangkok—are also growing increasingly reliant on pumping out underground reserves.

As water tables sink, there is an urgent need to find new underground water reserves—preferably ones that are recharged by the rain. New water is still being found in the bowels of the Earth. As I compiled this chapter, Chinese scientists reported the discovery of unsuspected water beneath a vast system of sand dunes in the Gobi Desert in Inner Mongolia, which they claim is being replenished from mountains to the south.

And hydrologists reported new research into the likely size of the Guarani aquifer, which stretches beneath more than a million square kilometres of Brazil, Argentina, Uruguay and Paraguay. It may contain 50,000 cubic kilometres of water—as much as flows down the River Amazon in seven years. And it is still being replenished by the rain. The aquifer is already supplying 15 million people with water without any general decline in water tables. Hydrologists now believe it could one day supply as many as 200 million people. They want to build an aqueduct to take the water to the world's third largest city, São Paulo.

But as fast as one door opens, another closes. The High Plains of the Midwest are part of American history. The first white settlers coming west transformed the plains from buffalo hunting grounds into rough pasture for cattle. It was the land of the cowboy. Then came the plough, and pasture became dry prairie—until the drought of the 1930s blew the soil away. Since those dust-bowl days, when millions of *Grapes of Wrath* sharecroppers abandoned the land and trekked west to California, the arid plains have been transformed once again through the pumping of water from a giant underground water reserve discovered beneath the plains.

Known as the Ogallala aquifer after an old Sioux nation that once hunted buffalo here, the aquifer stretches beneath most of Nebraska, southern South Dakota, western Kansas, Oklahoma and Texas and parts of eastern New Mexico, Colorado and

Wyoming. In the 1930s, as the dust-bowl refugees poured west to California, just 600 wells tapped this aquifer. But by the late 1970s, there were 200,000 wells, supplying 27 cubic kilometres a year to more than a third of the US's irrigated fields.

It was a massive US resource, but also a global one. In a good year, the High Plains produced three-quarters of the wheat traded on the world market—restocking empty Russian grain stores, feeding starving Ethiopians and keeping Egyptians fed as the Nile ran dry. The US became the world's biggest exporter of virtual water—but at the expense of draining the Ogallala.

The problem is that much of the aquifer is to all intents and purposes a fossil resource laid down in wetter times. Little water is added to it from the region's meagre rains. And, starting in a few isolated southern pockets, wells have been drying out now for more than thirty years. The first to hear the news, records US water researcher Sandra Postel, were the farmers of Deaf Smith County in the Texas panhandle. During the summer of 1970, a well that had been pumping water since 1936 suddenly went dry. And many others have followed.

Today, more than a quarter of the aquifer is gone in parts of Texas, Oklahoma and Kansas, and over wide areas the water table has fallen by more than thirty metres. All well-sinking is banned in some places, and fewer than twelve cubic kilometres are now pumped annually, less than half the output in the 1970s. Fly over the land and you see can see the circular marks where rotating sprinklers once kept the soil wet and the fields green— but where the soil is now dry and the fields brown. The sagebrush and buffalo grass are returning. The buffalo may follow.

Nationally, the US is not heavily dependent on underground water. Aquifers provide less than one per cent of water supplied in New England, for instance. But a third of all its irrigation water does come from underground, and some states in the south and west would be more or less literally lost without it. The US's three major aquifers—the Ogallala, the Central Valley aquifer in California and the Southwest aquifer—are all in the arid west. The Southwest aquifer in particular is vital. In Arizona, it is virtually the only water source from within the state. No wonder that, across the west, cities are buying up farms to access their rights to pump these aquifers.

But overpumping is as widespread as on the High Plains. For many years, Arizona has been removing underground water at twice the rate that rains can replace it. In California, they pump out 15 per cent more than the rains replenish—an overdraft of 1.6 cubic kilometres a year. The combined annual overpumping of the Ogallala, Central Valley and Southwest aquifers in recent years has been 36 cubic kilometres—a cumulative total of around a thousand cubic kilometres. And, as the aquifers empty, the honeycomb rocks that once held the water in their pores are gradually being crushed by the rocks above. One estimate is that this crushing has permanently reduced the water-storage capacity of the Central Valley aquifer by half—the equivalent of blowing up a dam the size of Grand Coulee.

Some of the most serious, indeed scandalous, groundwater disasters are being played out in the Middle East. Saudi Arabia has virtually no rain and no rivers or surface lakes of any kind. It has spent $10 billion on desalination works to fill its taps. But during the 1980s, the government spent another $40 billion of its oil revenues sinking pumps into the vast aquifer beneath the desert, and marking out a million hectares of desert for wheat farms to use the water. All of the water was provided to farmers free of charge. Sprinkler arms 300 metres long swept over the sands, distributing water pumped up from as much as a kilometre below. Nobody cared how much water was wasted and most of the time most of it evaporated in the sun. For every tonne of wheat grown, the government supplied 3,000 cubic metres of water—three times the global norm. It was an operation that, as the *Economist* suggested at the time, "made about as much economic sense as planting bananas under glass in Alaska."

What to do for an encore? Since the mid-1990s, many Arabian farmers have converted their wheat fields to growing alfalfa—which uses even more water—to fill the feedlots for a new national obsession with dairy cattle. This time, hi-tech cow-sheds sprouted across the desert. Inside them, fine mists of water controlled temperatures in the baking desert sun. Just as wheat once grew in the desert, now Frisian cattle were milked in the land of the camel.

There is undoubtedly a lot of water beneath the Arabian peninsula, but much of it is very deep and very old. Virtually none of it will ever be replaced. At the start of the 1980s, the country was calculated to have proven underground reserves of around 500 cubic kilometres. But since the mid-1990s, that water has been removed at a rate of more than twenty cubic kilometres a year. Saudi experiments in farming the desert have so far wasted 300 cubic kilometres of water, says Elie Elhadj of the School of Oriental and African Studies in London. Some 60 per cent of the water is gone.

Saudi Arabia is slowly waking up to its profligacy. In 2004 it launched a water conservation drive aimed at halving domestic consumption of its desalinated sea water. Crown Prince Abdullah publicly replaced his toilet cistern with a more efficient model. More significantly, water vice-minister Abdullah al-Hussayen promised a root-and-branch review of agricultural water use. "We need to examine whether we need to produce the whole domestic consumption of wheat, or perhaps make do with half," he said. Indeed.

Meanwhile, Saudi pumping is raising tensions with its neigh-bours. Jordanian hydrologists fear that the Saudis are draining the Disi aquifer, which lies beneath their joint border. Jordan is one of the driest states on Earth, and lacks cash for desalination. Disi represents its "last substantial unexploited water resource," according to a UN study, which said it should be kept "for emer-gency use only." There's no chance of that. While the Saudis pump as hard as they can from one side of the border, Jordan is rushing ahead with plans to pipe Disi water 300 kilometres north to the capital, Amman. Whoever gets the water, the aquifer seems doomed.

But whatever Jordan may face in the future, Gaza faces now. The densely packed Palestinian enclave, a narrow coastal strip between Israel and Egypt, is running out of drinkable water today. Aside from Kuwait, which lives on desalinated sea water, Gaza's million-plus inhabitants have the lowest per-capita availability of natural fresh water in the world.

Palestinians pump at least 125 million cubic metres a year from their aquifer beneath the sands. The recharge rate is about 90 million cubic metres. Unsurprisingly, the water table is plunging. Meanwhile, the porous rocks are being invaded by sewage from Gaza's towns and refugee camps and by salty sea water from the coast. The aquifer's bacteria count and salinity level rises inexorably, making the water nasty to drink and increasingly poisonous for crops.

The crisis is partly of the Palestinians' own making. Two-thirds of the water is brought to the surface by Palestinian pumps for irrigation—much of it from wells never licensed by the Palestinian Water Authority. But they are not the only people with pumps. Israelis farm the Negev desert right up to the Gaza border. Seen from Gaza, their greenhouses glint in the sun, guzzling up water that could be growing Palestinian crops.

Some clean water does enter the Gaza aquifer. Some arrives as rain and some comes down the Wadi Gaza. This is the coastal end of a desert drainage basin that begins in Palestinian territory on the West Bank south of Jerusalem, then passes through the Negev desert in Israel and flows to the sea through Gaza, where it replenishes the aquifer through a small coastal wetland. Or it did. For the Israelis have built dams on the wadi (which in the Bible and on Israeli maps is called Besor). These days, little water ever reaches Gaza. Most of it is grabbed to irrigate Israeli fields. And the wetland has turned into a sewage sump.

The international community has plans to improve Gaza's water supplies by building infrastructure to recycle irrigation drainage water and catch more of the sparse rains. The US government also wants to build a desalination plant. "It may take twenty to thirty years, but we'd hope to get the situation into equilibrium, with abstraction from the aquifer no greater than recharge," Alvin Newman, the US point man, told me in his high-security offices in Tel Aviv.

But there may not be enough time, says Clemens Messerschmid, a German hydrologist working for the Palestinian Water Authority and the British government's aid agency. UN studies suggest the aquifer could be effectively dry within fifteen years. The situation "is a catastrophe. It is an emergency case." To save the aquifer, he says, the Palestinians have to close their wells and the Israelis have to supply water. "It is as simple as that. Israel has plenty of capacity in the south of the country. The Gazans will have to pay, of course, but Israel should supply."

During the intifada, the continuing disputes and armed conflicts in Gaza got in the way of action to halt the catastrophe. Everything was "on hold," I was told. But whatever the politics, the hydrology will not wait.

PART THREE

WHEN THE RIVERS RUN DRY ...
THE WET PLACES DIE

1 1

THE COMMON WEALTH

From the peat bogs of Scotland to the backwaters of the Mississippi delta, from the lagoons of Venice to the flooded forests of Cambodia, and from the frozen tundra of Siberia to the salt lakes of the Australian outback, wetlands are an in-between world. Sometimes wet and sometimes dry; sometimes land and sometimes water; sometimes saline and sometimes fresh. They change their character with the seasons. Their wealth is tied up in hard-to-measure intangibles such as flood pulses and the fertile silts suspended in their waters. They may stay virtually dry for several years before being replenished in violent floods. Their wildlife is similarly transitory, with migrating birds, fish and even mammals coming and going. And like rainforests, they are generally not owned by anyone. Their rippling waters, shifting land and migrating wildlife are a common resource available to anyone willing to brave the elements to get them.

These are all unhelpful attributes in the modern world, where certainty in nature is valued more than fluidity, where floods are a "bad thing," where private property is the universal currency and where resources constantly on the move are hard to own. In every sense, the wealth of wetlands can slip through your fingers. The modern world wants to enclose and privatize and tame them—rather as the water in flowing rivers is captured by damming it. The owners of wetlands, despairing of exploiting

105

the moving feast, often prefer to drain the lot, fence in the land and start again. And for generations, engineers have regarded any water draining into wetlands as somehow wasted, and ripe for diversion to other human uses.

So, the world's wet places are being emptied. By some estimates, half of them have gone already. Next to rainforests, they are the most productive ecosystems—for humans as well as for nature. Yet they are disappearing with far less fuss: drained, dyked, canalized, concreted over, turned into shrimp farms and rice paddies, dammed, dredged and filled with solid waste.

As one recent international research project on wetlands economics published by the journal *Nature* observed, "the social benefits of retaining wetlands, arising from sustainable hunting, angling and trapping greatly exceeded the agricultural gains" if they are drained. And yet they are still drained because the social gains often accrue to people beyond the wetland, while the agricultural gains can be captured entirely by the owner of the land. The study concluded that "our relentless conversion and degradation of remaining natural habitats—including wetlands—is eroding overall human welfare for short-term private gain." As scarce natural resources become rarer, the social benefit from protecting them grows rather than diminishes. Preserving what remains "makes overwhelming economic as well as moral sense."

This is a truth that the inhabitants of wetlands—the people willing to get their feet wet to harvest the waters—have known for a long time. Take the case of the English Fens, a wide expanse of low farmland stretching from the great cathedral city of Ely to the North Sea. Today, it is an entirely man-made landscape. Well, almost. Fly over it and sometimes, in among the straight lines of drains and roads and field margins, you can see meandering across the black peat the ghost-like, silty remains of long-vanished riverbeds.

Until the late Middle Ages, the Fens were a world of bog and marsh, wandering streams and great natural wealth. Locals set out from patches of higher land, such as the Isle of Ely, to harvest that wealth from flat-bottomed boats, casting nets in the muddy waters. Chroniclers in the twelfth century wrote of salmon and sturgeon in the waters in quantities "as to cause astonishment in strangers, while the natives laugh at their surprise." Fast coaches took live fish and fowl and eels to London markets. Eels, after which Ely was named, were the most abundant commodity and acted as a local currency. Fenlanders paid their rent in eels and the Domesday Book records that in 1086 the town of Wisbech paid tax amounting to 33,260 eels.

Wealthy landowners like the Duke of Bedford eyed this common wealth with envy. But it was too mobile: hard to catch and difficult to fence in. So they determined that they could make more money more easily by draining the fens and replacing the eels and fish and wild duck, with cattle and sheep. Dutch engineers were the drainage masters of the age. They had built an entire country with drains. In the late sixteenth century, Dutch engineers began to arrive in England, making their pitches in the drawing rooms of the gentry and the corridors of the Treasury to be allowed to remake the Fens. Soon, lavishly remunerated, they were setting up their windmills across the marshes.

The most celebrated and industrious of the new Dutchmen was Cornelius Vermyuden. He dug six great artificial rivers across the marshes for the Duke of Bedford. But the Fenlanders saw no advantage for themselves in this draining and fencing in of their marshes. They protested with stones, shovels, axes and a chant: "For they do mean all fens to drain/And water over-master,/All will be dry and we must die,/'Cause Essex calves want pasture."

One of the champions of the Fenlanders in the 1620s was Oliver Cromwell, who had inherited a fenland estate from his radical uncle. He first tasted armed rebellion here. The Fenlanders helped to build his reputation. But the shifting waters of wetlands seem to breed traitors. Two decades later, having led the English revolution and beheaded King Charles, he joined forces with the Earl of Bedford in a project to drain the Fens, and sent his army onto the marshes to suppress the protesting commoners.

For a long time, the drainage engineers' reach exceeded their grasp. In their efforts to drain the Fens, they caused drought and flood. Bankruptcies were frequent. Their great public works were constantly bailed out with public funds. And all the time the winners in the enterprise seemed less numerous than the losers. Even today, while the drains have finally succeeded in their task and Fenland farmers make good profits, the public expenditure to keep the pumps running far outweighs the private gain.

The story of the Fens is worth telling because it is so similar in so many ways to modern efforts round the world to tame the wetlands. Most such efforts result in huge public expenditure that wrecks natural ecosystems of staggering fecundity in order to generate private profits that are puny by comparison with the former common wealth.

Let us settle for three examples here, from three of the world's largest wetlands—the Sudd swamp on the River Nile in Sudan, the Pantanal in the heart of South America and the Okavango delta in southern Africa. Two of these involve plans for canals that would rush waters past the wetland: in one case to reduce evaporation, in the other to aid navigation. The third is an apparently modest attempt to tinker with a virgin ecosystem for laudable development goals. But it could have huge unintended consequences. In all three cases, the potential beneficiaries have little to lose by the demise of the wetland. In each case too, a common resource of global importance is at risk of being destroyed for narrow self-interest.

The Sudd is the world's second largest swamp. It occupies a swathe of southern Sudan on the White Nile, one of two great tributaries of the River Nile. Places do not come much more remote than this, and the Sudd is a formidable natural obstacle on the Nile. It prevented navigation upstream by generations of European explorers seeking one of the great Holy Grails of geography, the source of the Nile.

It is a natural wonder of the world. Its numberless channels contain an ever-shifting maze of papyrus islands. They are the *sudds* (Arabic for blockages) that give it its name. *Sudds* can be up to a kilometre long and many metres thick—thick enough to carry large herds of hippos and elephants. Sometimes they block the whole channel until, like a dam, they burst. This must be an extraordinary sight. One British colonial officer on a rare nineteenth-century foray into the swamp described how, after such a burst, "crocodiles were whirled round and round, and the river was covered with dead and dying hippos." Others were not so enthused by the Sudd. The Victorian water engineer Sir William Garstin said of it: "No-one who has not seen it can have any real idea of its supreme dreariness and its utter desolation. To my mind the most barren desert is a bright and cheerful locality compared with the White Nile marshland."

The Sudd is a 500-kilometre lay-by on the long journey of the White Nile's waters from Central Africa to the Mediterranean. The river's water takes upwards of a year to pass through the swamps, during which time half its volume, some five cubic kilometres, is lost to evaporation. Those are cubic kilometres that people downstream have long wanted to get their hands on. It was the unenthused Garstin who first proposed either dredging the Sudd or diverting the White Nile away from its suffocating embrace in order to preserve its water from the sun. He never got his way, but modern engineers have not lost the urge. Egypt, which is already using every drop of the Nile that flows through its land, wants to turn dreams into action. And that is why, sitting in the middle of the bush of southern Sudan, for the past thirty years there has sat a vast Heath Robinson machine called a "bucketwheel."

The bucketwheel is the canal diggers' answer to the combine harvester. It is a giant laser-guided digging wheel, weighing 2,300 tonnes and as tall as a five-storey building, a fearsome parody of an ancient Persian water wheel with twelve buckets attached to the wheel to grab earth rather than water. It was in fact constructed in the 1960s to dig a canal across the Punjab in Pakistan. Job done, it was dismantled and carried by truck, train, steamer and finally camel to the edge of the Sudd. Its new task was to dig a channel 260 kilometres long and 50 metres wide to allow the Nile to skirt the eastern side of the marshes.

In June 1978, it began excavating what was called the Jonglei Canal. The giant wheel rotated once every minute, night and day. At each revolution its buckets ate up and threw aside enough Nile sand to fill an Olympic swimming pool. The machine consumed 40,000 litres of fuel a day—more than all the buildings in Juba, the regional capital.

This, however, was not a good moment to dig a canal through the backwoods of southern Sudan. The route passed through the land of Dinka cattle herders. They were seriously inconvenienced by the canal, which cut their lands off from dry-season pastures on the fringes of the Sudd. Moreover, the Dinka and other groups in the non-Muslim south of the country were about to embark on a war of liberation from their Muslim masters far to the north in Khartoum.

By February 1984, the bucketwheel had carved out a third of the route, at a cost of $100 million. Then the Sudanese People's Liberation Army struck the contractors' camp. They destroyed everything except the great machine itself, and ran off with foreign hostages. This was no ignorant piece of terrorism. Its perpetrator, the leader of the SPLA, was John Garang, a young Dinka tribesman who had received a US university education in the 1970s. While at Iowa State University, he had written a Ph.D. thesis on the iniquities of the Jonglei plan. In it, he argued that the canal would suck southern Sudan dry of its greatest resource— the waters of the Sudd.

Though the hostages were released unharmed a year after their capture, the contractors never returned to their project. Civil war raged round the Sudd for twenty years, and the bucketwheel has sat, more or less intact, beside the wetland ever since. At the end of 2004, Garang and the authorities in Khartoum concluded peace talks that provided a fair degree of autonomy for southern Sudan. Insiders said that, twenty years on, Garang was better disposed towards the Jonglei project and might finally consent to the construction of the canal, with proper safeguards for his

Dinka people. After Garang's death in an air accident in 2005, it was far from clear what the consequences might be for the Jonglei. But Egypt was certainly keen to put up the cash to recommission the bucketwheel. The new millennium saw it engaged in a giant new Saudi-funded irrigation project in the Western desert, known as the Toshka Lakes scheme, which will eventually require five cubic kilometres of water—coincidentally precisely the anticipated yield of the Jonglei Canal.

The scheme may now finally get built. However, in their concern to end evaporation of Nile water from the Sudd, the Egyptians seem to have lost sight of an even bigger evaporation loss far closer to home. For, though it is rarely mentioned, roughly three times more water evaporates every year from the surface of Lake Nasser, the vast reservoir behind their own High Aswan dam, than from the Sudd. This Russian-built symbol of Egyptian independence, the crowning glory of the rule of Colonel Abdul Nasser in the 1960s, loses roughly fifteen cubic kilometres a year from its huge surface every year. In a dry year that is more than a third of the river's entire flow. But nobody is suggesting the reservoir should be emptied. Curious, that.

The engineers' second great target is the Pantanal. The largest freshwater ecosystem in the world, it is bigger even than the Sudd. Sprawling across the huge floodplain of the River Paraguay, it spreads from Brazil into Bolivia and Paraguay in the heart of South America. Its swamps cover an area five times the size of the Netherlands, and are home to huge populations of jaguars and armadillos, caiman and anteaters, giant otters and anacondas, the world's largest snake. Above them all stands the giant "too-yoo-yoo" bird, the Jabiru stork, one of more than six hundred bird species that live here.

A fifth of the wetland, the biologically richest part, has been made a World Heritage site. And a recent economic assessment of its "ecological services" put its value at $16 billion a year, primarily for its regulation of water. It is like a vast natural sponge, maintaining a regular water flow downstream through

Paraguay's two major cities, Asuncion and Concepción, all the way to the Argentinean capital Buenos Aires.

It is, like all such areas, being encroached on by farmers and hunters. But their effect is small in comparison with the likely impact of a plan to turn 3,400 kilometres of the meandering and often impassable River Paraguay into a giant shipping canal to the sea. The $3-billion Hidrovia project would pass right through the Pantanal, allowing ocean-going ships to jostle with the wildlife as they head upstream to the Brazilian inland port of Caceres at the northern end of the wetland. There, they would load up with gas brought by pipeline from Bolivia and timber and soybeans harvested in remote Brazilian bush. The canal would, its proposers hope, act like the navigation on the Rhine in the nineteenth century, as a conduit and magnet for industrialization in all three countries. And its influence could be greater still. It might link up with other waterways proposed for the Amazon and Orinoco basins, ultimately creating a water highway across South America from Argentina to Venezuela and Bolivia to the Atlantic.

The Hidrovia project, like the Jonglei Canal, has been on the stocks for a while. The region may be peaceful, but the opposition to the scheme is still intense. Locally they call it "hell's highway." The proposal was last abandoned by Brazil in 2001. But it keeps coming back. Government scientists insist that "the work in the Pantanal will be like a needle to an elephant—it will not feel a thing." But independent hydrologists say that the waterway would drain seventeen cubic kilometres of water out of the Pantanal and dry up half of the wet areas in the dry season when the few areas that remain flooded serve as important refuges for aquatic animals.

In truth, the Pantanal is not some unchanging wilderness. More than 90 per cent of the land is privately owned for cattle ranching. The protected natural wetland is just a 1,000-square-kilometre core. But it is remote. The Chamacoco Indians in the southern tip of the wetland can be reached only by boat or plane.

In recent years, river flows into the wetland have been heavy. Many of the ranches have flooded. And as wildlife flees economic development in the adjoining forests and grasslands, the Pantanal has become an increasingly important refuge for South America's remaining wildlife. Its loss would be an ecological tragedy to set beside the razing of the Amazon jungle. And its hydrological impact, in increased droughts and floods, could be of huge importance to millions of people downstream all the way to Buenos Aires.

Finally, there is the Okavango delta in southern Africa. This is an inland basin—the swampy endpoint for the River Okavango in the Kalahari desert in Botswana. Its waters come from the forests of Angola, pass briefly through Namibia in an area known as the Caprivi Strip and end up in a wide, flat, fan-shaped delta in the desert. The delta is a land of papyrus and hippo grass, lily-covered lagoons and peat islands that occasionally dry out and burn. It is home to tens of thousands of elephants, hippos, zebra, buffalo and antelope, and has for centuries been an oasis for the tribes of northern Botswana.

Unlike many desert wetlands, where water evaporates in the blinding sun, its water stays fresh. This is because the half million tonnes of salt that the river brings to the delta each year become concentrated in underground water that flows into small islands, where the salt is bound to sand that is also brought down in the rivers. It is a remarkable process and ecologists are fearful that almost any meddling with the delta's hydrology could destroy it.

Now, Namibia has plans to dam the Okavango River for hydroelectricity on the Caprivi Strip, just fifty kilometres upstream of the delta. And Angola, now freed from a generation of civil war, also wants to build dams in the headwaters of the river. Fears for the future of the Okavango are growing. Engineers say the ecologists are panicking unnecessarily. The Namibian dam would be only about six metres high and would hold back only a small amount of the river's flow, they say. But Terence McCarthy of Witwatersrand University in South Africa warns that even this dam, which is really little more than a weir, would block the river in the dry season, preventing around 100,000 cubic metres of sand from being washed into the delta annually. That sand, he says, is critical to the process of quarantining the salt. Without the sand, the salt will spread through the delta, destroying its complex ecosystems one by one. Not only would that be a wildlife tragedy, it would also destroy one of the linchpins of the Botswana economy—wildlife tourism, which is concentrated round the delta.

Will the bucketwheel finally carve its way across the savannah lands of southern Sudan, draining one of the continent's most fecund environments to fill the irrigation channels of Egypt? Will the hidden wealth of the Pantanal slip through South American fingers like so much silt? Could dams doom the Okavango? We can make the moral and the environmental cases for saving these oases. But much may in the end depend on the abstractions of economists, and whether they can come to recognize that commonly owned wealth has as much value and importance to society as privately owned wealth.

12

LAKE CHAD: TRAGEDY OF THE FLOOD PLAINS

The death of a wetland is a terrible thing, particularly a wetland in a desert. When it happens, lakes shrivel, crops go brown in the baking sun, fishing nets empty, trees die and herders slaughter their animals for what pitiful cash they can raise. The land curls up and dies. The people depart. Usually this happens when the rains fail. How much more terrible when the drought is man-made; when the wetland dies because humans have decided to divert the rivers that should replenish it; when the water is taken for little purpose, more as a statement of the power of one community over another; and when even hard-nosed economists say what is going on is madness.

Welcome, then, to the death of the Hadejia-Nguru wetland in northern Nigeria. This dramatic kite-shaped expanse of green and blue stretching for more than a hundred kilometres along the edge of the Sahara desert was once a bulwark against the advancing sands. Its lakes were full of fish and their fertile waters washed annually across the land, creating lush pastures that sustained tens of thousands of cattle, and watering almost a quarter of a million hectares of fields that farmers planted with crops as the floodwaters receded. The wetland supported a million or more people, and provided exports of fish and vegetables to cities across the largest country in Africa.

Some of this remains. But much has been destroyed as dams divert water upstream for irrigation projects, the lakes shrink and the summer flood dies. In a region of Africa better known for drought and famine, the Nigerian government promised that the dams and irrigation works would green the landscape and bring bounty. But they have been doing the opposite. They have been destroying a natural bounty of far greater value.

Westerners are used to having rivers kept within narrow channels. For us, floods are generally a bad thing. When African engineers train in Western colleges they learn the same thing, and go home to banish floods. But in Africa and much of the developing world, poor farmers and fishers and cattle-herders need floods. They bring free irrigation water and silt to fertilize fields and sustain pastures and fisheries. When engineers capture the flood flows, the millions who depend on the flood suffer.

The Hadejia-Nguru wetland is a complex network of natural channels and lakes that mingle the waters of the Hadejia River, coming in from the west, and the Jama'are, coming from the south. But two dams have been built on tributaries of the Hadejia. Between them, they capture 80 per cent of that river's flow. The area of wetland regularly inundated has fallen by two-thirds. Lakes like the Punjama and Nguru have shrunk, and the water table has declined by as much as twenty-five metres, unleashing a further round of desiccation. Meanwhile, on the Jama'are River sits the half-completed Kafin Zaki dam. The money for this ran out long ago, but the government still wants to finish it. If that happens, Kafin Zaki will be the largest dam on the system and will dry out the remainder of the wetland for good.

A journey across the wetland shows the hydrological devastation and the tensions the dams are creating. On the east side, Gorgoram was once a sizeable town in the heart of the wetland. It had a famous fishing festival to which teams of youths came from hundreds of miles around to net the biggest catches in the last pools as the flood retreated. Dignitaries from across northern Nigeria came too, awarding prizes and lobbying for votes. But now Gorgoram is an emptying village. The festival is failing because the floods are poor and there are no fish. And all around, the landscape is littered with fallen trees, victims of the falling water table.

Many villages have lost their wells and lakes and woodlands. At Adiani, on the south shore of Lake Nguru, villagers told me how they once lived by keeping bees in the village's tiny forest reserve. But the forest is dying, and with it the bees. On the road to Nguru town, I drove through an empty wasteland that went on for miles. It seemed deserted, until suddenly a man appeared from behind one of the last trees left standing. He was like an apparition, and probably sensed it. He advanced on our car with rage in his eyes. "This is how men are suffering in the bush," he roared, and would say no more.

On Lake Punjama, the waters were still high and hundreds of birds were swooping low. Locals took me fishing in a flat-bottomed boat. We landed some catfish. And in the soft early evening light, we rowed for home past boys paddling on large pumpkin shells. They had knives to cut the tall lake grasses to use as floats for their fishing nets. And nearer the shore, two brothers were wading waist deep in the water, driving their cattle to the same grasses to feed. The first group of boys shouted to the second to keep the animals clear of their fishing lines, which we saw paid out across the water.

It appeared an idyllic scene. But an hour later I met a family of Fulani cattle-herders, setting up camp for the night on an island in the lake, who had a different story. They, like other Fulani, came to the wetland during the dry season to find water and graze their animals on the lake edges and on stubble in fields after the harvest. The woman rounded up the cattle, shooed them into a stockade and lit a fire of dung and straw to keep away the mosquitoes. But her husband was morose. "Once there were many Fulani coming here," he said. "There was more water then, and more grazing land. Now there is little grazing. We still come because there is nowhere else to go, but there are always disputes with the farmers." The previous year there had been pitched battles between the Fulanis and gangs of settled farmers, he said. By the time the fighting died down, there were bodies in the water and ten people were dead. "Every year, people get killed."

The first dam was built on the Hadejia in 1974. The Tiga dam stored water to supply a state irrigation project south of Kano, the biggest city in northern Nigeria. Each wet season, the rain must replenish the reservoir and supply the irrigation project before any surplus can flow down into the wetlands. In the early 1990s, the government completed the Challawa Gorge dam on another Hadejia tributary. It was built to supply water to the 12,000-hectare Hadejia Valley irrigation project on the edge of the wetland.

This later project has turned to farce. For more than a decade, French engineers formed a garrison in the wetland, surrounded by earth-removing equipment waiting to build the $100-million scheme. But the money kept running out. When I visited, huge areas of forest had been cleared to make way for the irrigation channels. I spoke to the emir of a nearby village who hoped his people could move onto the land within a year or so. But after years of promises, the only crops growing here were in the French project director's vegetable garden. I had some of them for lunch. Today, less than half the project has been completed. Soils that had nourished a forest before the trees were chopped down have baked hard. Some believe the whole project is doomed. Some just hope so.

Since the completion of the dams, what water has come down the rivers and onto the wetland has often caused mayhem. It has come at the wrong time, fed the wrong channels and caused damaging floods rather than nurturing the ecosystem. Take the sixty-kilometre-long Burum Gana channel. Once it was just one among many that distributed the Hadejia's waters. It was wet for just a few months a year. But it is now the only channel that gets any water, and it is wet all year. The perennial flow has attracted bulrushes that now choke the channel, often blocking it entirely so that the water overflows and destroys crops in surrounding fields. Some communities have been forced by the floods to abandon their villages. Birniwa, once among the more parched parts of the wetland, is now flooded almost every year. Meanwhile, the bulrushes are invading fields where rice once grew. And the fields have attracted a huge invasion of quelea birds that roost among the bulrushes and forage for crops all across the wetland. According to local press reports, in some villages children are kept home from school to frighten the birds away.

Occasionally there are bigger floods when, after very heavy rains, dam managers hurriedly release water downstream to protect their structures. In August 2001, 140 people died and thousands more lost their homes as a wall of water rushed across the parched wetland.

Is this hydrological mayhem the price that has to be paid for economic progress? Well, no. Economists have concluded that the big dams and irrigation canals here have been a huge waste of money. The British government's aid agency calculates that the income from each hectare of land has fallen since the dams were built from $167 to $20. The value of the crops grown on the irrigation projects, it says, is tiny compared with the lost benefits on the wetland from farming, fishing, timber, livestock, honey, straw for construction and bricks.

Ed Barbier, an environmental economist from the University of Wyoming, agrees: "Gains in irrigation values account for at most around 17 per cent of the resulting losses on the flood plain." There is, Barbier says, "a clear choice between using the water for irrigation upstream or allowing it to enter the wetlands to support agriculture, fishing and other economic activities there." And in economic terms, he says, there is no contest. The wetland wins every time. The half-completed Hadejia Valley project should be abandoned along with the mothballed Kafin Zaki dam on the Jama'are. The only sensible use for the existing dams, he says, is to re-create the natural flood. But the bigwigs in Nigeria have yet to take such advice.

I moved on to Gashua, the easternmost town on the Hadejia-Nguru wetland. It is where the various channels coalesce again to form a new river, the Yobe, which heads for Lake Chad, an inland sea in the heart of the Sahel. These days only a quarter as much water emerges from the wetland as before the dams were built. In Gashua, fish were in short supply in the town market, owing to the declining productivity of the wetland and the river. What the town's traders did have, I discovered, were bags of potash—the salty crust of desert soils, scraped by villagers from shrivelling oases to the north. It was the one local commodity in plentiful supply.

I took a detour to one of these oases, Garin Momadu. Even here there was desolation. The wells at the oasis were running dry, dead palm trees lay across the ground, and sand dunes were taking over the houses on the edge of the village. Heading back to Gashua, we passed a camel train—a dozen animals all bearing yet more potash to the market. The animals had just crossed one of the beds of the Yobe, which hydrologists say feeds the oases. But it had been dry, locals said, ever since the Tiga dam was finished. That probably explained the crisis at Garin Momadu. The bed was just a sand-filled depression, and the air was full of dust whipped up by desert winds. Camels walked where fishermen once threw their nets. Ahead of the camel train a man walked alone in white robes, carrying a sword. The desert was on the march.

On again, to Maiduguri, a town with another ominous warning of what awaits the wetland. It is the largest town in the area, had already exhausted two aquifers and was pumping from a third. Officials from an EU anti-desertification project in the town told me that, without river flooding, this final aquifer would never recharge. The town had built a reservoir to take water direct from the river. But the river was nearly dry and the reservoir lost more than two metres of water a year from its surface due to evaporation. The town would die unless another source of water could be found.

Does it have to be like this? Well, no. Witness events on another river that drains into Lake Chad, the River Logone in the neighbouring state of Cameroon. The Logone is rather bigger than the Hadejia ever was because it flows out of the rain-soaked fringes of the great Congo rainforest of Central Africa. Its waters have for centuries been the lifeblood of a thriving flood plain rich in wildlife and with rich pickings for fishers and hunters. Farmers planted traditional varieties of rice on the wet soils left by the retreating floods each year. The flood plain also attracted Fulani nomads and their cattle herds from neighbouring countries. It is said to have been one of the great centres of the Fulani, the largest nomadic pastoral group in the world.

But in 1979 a state-owned rice company built the Maga dam to capture water entering the Logone from the Mandara Mountains to the west. The idea was to divert that water to irrigate new fields of modern rice varieties on the flood plain. Modern "green revolution" rice is more susceptible to excess water than traditional varieties, so, to prevent possible flooding from the river, the company raised a hundred kilometres of embankments to separate the river from the paddy on its old flood plain. The result was to deprive the river of water and wreck the flood plain ecosystem. A hundred thousand people who had depended on the floods for their livelihoods were left destitute.

Paul Loth of the World Conservation Union conducted a comprehensive assessment of this project and its aftermath. He concluded that it was spectacularly inefficient even in its own terms. Little rice was grown most years, and by some measures only around a tenth of the water collected by the dam has ever been productively used. Like the irrigation projects in northern Nigeria, it "diminished rather than improved the living standards and economy of the region as a whole. A once fertile flood plain was turned into a dustbowl."

The litany of disasters assembled by Loth is terrifying. Rich pastures of perennial grasses died and some 20,000 head of cattle had to move away. Fish yields declined by 90 per cent. Water tables fell for more than 1,500 square kilometres, emptying wells and water holes. Yields of the local varieties of sorghum and rice fell by 75 per cent. Meanwhile, elephants and lions in the Waza National Park, one of their last refuges in Central and West Africa, fled as their water holes dried up. Those that stayed were

mostly killed by desperate farmers who moved in to poach them.
With the entire flood plain in crisis, the human inhabitants
fought pitched battles over water and pastures. Many left for
distant cities.

But, unlike in Nigeria, that was not the end of the matter.
Local leaders joined foreign scientists to implore the rice company to allow water back onto the flood plain. They argued that
it could be done without destroying the irrigation project. And
the dam managers briefly relented. In 1994 and again in 1997,
they let water downstream from the dam, flooding about a third
of the former flood plain. Zanankay Yap, a traditional leader in
Tekele town on the flood plain, remembered when the embankment was broken. "We all waited to see the water arrive with our
own eyes," he said. "And then when it came, there was instant
joy. We farmed well and we fished well that year."

The pilot releases had a lasting effect. The perennial grasses
returned. Cattle numbers increased threefold. Fish bred again in
the pools. Wildlife began to return to the park. Wells filled and
the greater availability of clean drinking water improved local
health. Economists from the World Conservation Union measured the short-term economic benefit and used the results to
calculate what had been lost by the dam drying up the flood
plain. The dam and embankments, they said, had cost 8,000 of
the poorest and most vulnerable households in this part of Africa,
a total of $2 million every year for over twenty years. That is
almost a dollar a head per day and far greater than the gains from
the expensively watered rice fields. "Often nature is a triple-A
company, and its dividends go to its shareholders—the rural
poor," said the economists.

The lesson is obvious. The water should be given back to
those who most need it, and who evidently use it most effectively—the residents of the flood plain. And yet, extraordinarily,
those pilot releases—at the time of writing, almost a decade old—
have never been repeated. The embankments that cut the river off
from its flood plain have been put back. In March 2004, after
several years pushing for a permanent resumption of the flooding,

the scientists from the World Conservation Union packed their bags and left.

It is too easy to see communities that depend on natural wild resources and the vagaries of untamed rivers as somehow left behind by progress. The truth, quite often, is the opposite. It is they who have unlocked the truth about how to make the maximum use of natural resources. It is the urban sophisticates with their engineering diplomas who haven't got a clue. The pilot studies on the Logone, and the similar research done on the Hadejia-Nguru wetland, cement the case for a completely different way of managing flood plains and the rivers that sustain them, not just on the fringes of the Sahara but right across Africa, where millions still depend on their free water services.

What does all this mean for Lake Chad, the great inland sea on the edge of the Sahara into which the Yobe and Logone, along with other rivers like the Chari, drain? The lake drains an area as big as France, Spain, Germany and the UK put together, and atlases show it as having a shoreline in four countries: Nigeria, Niger, Chad and Cameroon. But it is naturally temperamental, given to huge changes in size. This is partly because the rivers themselves are temperamental, even without human influence. And it is partly because the lake is so shallow, currently averaging only 1.5 metres in depth. So it is hugely prone to water loss from irrigation, and very dependent on the rivers for renewal. Ten thousand years ago, the lake filled its basin and overflowed through Nigeria into the Atlantic Ocean. And yet it entirely dried up four times between 1400 and 1910, when it divided into two small pools.

After 1910, it grew again, reaching a peak in 1962, when it covered 25,000 square kilometres. Since then it has been in retreat once more. By the late 1990s, it had lost 95 per cent of its surface area. The open water had again been divided in two, with a large swamp in the middle. By 2004 it had shrunk again and was reportedly down to 523 square kilometres. All this happened because, for forty years, the amount of water coming down the rivers has halved. Hydrologists reckon that between a half and two-thirds of this decline has been due to diminishing rainfall and the rest to diversions for the irrigation projects in Nigeria and Cameroon.

The retreat has caused massive disruption. Niger and Nigeria no longer have a lake shoreline. Nigeria and Cameroon have long disputed where exactly in the lake the border between them runs. But it only mattered after the lake retreated and farmers moved onto the disputed bed. The International Court of Justice finally ruled that Darak and thirty-two other villages were part of Cameroon.

Worse, government infrastructure and Western aid projects have everywhere proved quite unable to cope with the lake's decline. Three decades ago, British engineers began to build what should have been one of Africa's greatest irrigation schemes, the South Chad Irrigation Project. The scheme was intended to irri-gate rice and wheat on a vast 67,000-hectare stretch of the lake's southwest shore. There was a 30-kilometre intake canal from the lake. But even that wasn't enough to keep up with the retreating waterline. Most of the project area has spent most of the time since then high and dry. Its grain mills are rapidly becoming of interest only to industrial archaeologists.

But the local farmers and fishing communities, who generally have little to do with central government and rely on their tradi-tional systems of rule, have taken hydrological events much more in their stride. British social economist Terri Sarch has sent sev-eral years visiting the lake. She says that while the South Chad Irrigation Project sat abandoned, the farmers who were supposed to benefit from it simply moved with the lakeshore to cultivate the lake bed. There were no roads, no government wells and no police—but there was wet, fertile land. Roughly half a million hectares of it. And that was far more important.

Interestingly, the constant moving and establishment of new farms on new land has been a remarkably peaceful process. Sarch says the farmers fell back on their traditional systems of authority for allocating land. A typical community, from the Nigerian village of Tumbun Naira, moved east in 1985 to farm on the lake floor close to an abandoned fishing camp. They stayed a few years farming, before upping sticks again in 1994 after rising lake levels flooded their settlement. But they returned and rebuilt the following year, as the lake retreated once more. It sounds like a recipe for conflict, failed crops and famine. Yet, "They did better than merely cope," she says. "Many are producing a food surplus." The evidence included an influx of pickup trucks driving across the lake bed.

The lesson of all this? When the rivers run dry, it need not be disaster, provided societies can adapt to cope with it. And the traditional attributes of flexibility associated with communities living on wetlands serve remarkably well. One of the ironies of today is that we have grown disturbingly good at disrupting river flows, while at the same time losing our capacity for coping with, let alone prospering from, the consequences.

13

SEAS OF DEATH

For thousands of years, under a dozen different empires, the Hamoun wetlands have been a refuge and a source of food and water in the fierce deserts of Central Asia on the silk road to China. Overlooked by the mysterious Parthian citadel of Kuh-e Khwaja, the Sistani people of the wetlands on the remote border between Afghanistan and Iran were always left to their own devices. Or so it was until a lethal combination of drought, US engineering and Taliban fanaticism turned their oasis to dust at the start of the new millennium.

The Hamoun wetlands covered 4,000 square kilometres. Even in bad years, half that area was wet. Leopards lurked in the marshes; and carp and otters swam the three lakes at their heart. It was a mecca for flamingos, ducks and pelicans migrating from Siberia to the Indian Ocean. And, of course, for the Sistani, who lived apart, fishing, hunting, farming and punting the lakes in traditional flat-bottomed reed boats called *tutans*. They herded their animals across the rich pastures round the lakes, and tapped the waters to irrigate wheat and barley, grapes and melons, even a little cotton and sugar cane. As recently as the mid-1990s, they pulled tens of thousands of tonnes of fish from the lakes each year.

The water came from the snowfields of the Hindu Kush in the east of Afghanistan. The River Helmand flowed for 1,300 kilometres across Afghanistan, through the Margo desert and into the

Hamoun wetlands of Sistan depression, which straddles the border with Iran. There, its water slowly evaporated in three lakes, each usually not much more than half a metre deep. The upper lake, which got water first, was in Afghanistan; the two lower lakes were in Iran. Unusually in such an environment, they each contained fresh water because the occasional years of floods overflowed the lakes and flushed the salt into salt flats to the south.

But all that disappeared in 1998, when all three lakes dried out. The reed beds vanished; the wet marshes were replaced with salt flats; and the wildlife largely disappeared. It was a major environmental catastrophe: more complete and devastating even than the destruction of the Aral Sea a thousand kilometres to the north. And for the wetland's quarter-million inhabitants, it was a human catastrophe. But you might not have read about it. For the wetland was on a remote border between a pariah state then run by warlords and another run by a member of George Bush's "axis of evil." Only satellite images of a new desert and a few voices from refugee camps have revealed what happened.

The origins of the tragedy go back to the repeated efforts by Afghans and their Western friends over more than a century to modernize agriculture by irrigating fields along the Helmand. From the start, the risks to the Hamoun wetlands were understood. As early as 1926, under a British-brokered deal, Afghanistan promised to leave half the river's water for the Iranians and the lakes. But the deal has rarely been honoured. Upstream Afghanistan has regularly taken more—especially in dry years when the downstream need is greatest.

After the Second World War, US engineers arrived in Kabul intent on transforming the Helmand valley. They began digging dams and irrigation channels and installing hydroelectric turbines. The centrepiece was the hundred-metre-high Kajaki dam, which captured most of the river's flow behind a fifty-kilometre reservoir. Half a century on, it remains the largest and most ambitious civil engineering project ever undertaken in modern Afghanistan. It is also a model of how things should not be done.

While the hydroelectric dam at Kajaki lit the lights of Kandahar city, the irrigation works proved a disaster. Less than a third of the canals intended to irrigate 200,000 hectares of the Helmand valley were ever built. Many of the nomads brought down from the hills to farm the desert soon returned. But the canals that were dug consumed huge amounts of water, most of it eventually seeping into the ground or evaporating in the sun. The new canals took six times more water to irrigate a hectare of land than had traditional systems, which the new canals often replaced.

Under a deal struck in 1973, the Afghans agreed to leave at least half a million cubic kilometres in the river each year. Various estimates put this at between a fifth and a third of the long-term average flow. The Hamoun lakes diminished but survived. But the Taliban seized control of Afghanistan in the early 1990s and all the treaties were off. In 1998, the Taliban closed the sluice gates on the Kajaki dam. Henceforth, no water was allowed to flow down the river into Iran until the reservoir was full. It was an act of extreme hydrological provocation. Iran protested to the UN. But nobody was listening.

Matters were made worse because 1998 also proved to be the start of a drought that, at the time of writing in early 2005, continues. The combination of drought, the US–built dam and the Taliban proved terminal for the lakes and the wetland. With rainfall at only a quarter of the norm, and no flow in the Helmand, all three lakes dried out for the first time in recorded history. The marshes turned to dust bowls. Hundreds of villages on either side of the border were overwhelmed by shifting sand dunes and ravaged by summer dust storms known locally as the "wind of 120 days." The old irrigation channels round the lake disappeared beneath the sand. "Many who had lived around the Hamoun for generations moved away or lost everything," says Hassan Partow, a researcher for the UN Environment Programme who made a rare visit.

The Sistan depression became a humanitarian disaster zone. An estimated 300,000 refugees crowded into camps there in 2002. Some had been made destitute by the environmental catastrophe; others were fleeing from the war in Afghanistan to an area where, in past crises, their ancestors had always found refuge. With unpleasant irony, some of the trucks ferrying water to the camps had filled up at the same distant reservoirs that emptied the rivers in the first place.

The removal of the Taliban in Afghanistan changed little. In late 2002, the new Afghan government announced that "to show goodwill" it would open the Kajaki sluices. Some muddy water from rains in the Afghan mountains flowed across the border. Iranian peasants rushed to divert the water into their wells for storage. But after two weeks the river dried up again. "It is still dry and there is still no agreement between Afghanistan and Iran on sharing the waters of the Helmand," Partow told me in late 2004.

Kabul claimed in its defence that it no longer had control of the river. Many Afghan farmers had built their own dams to divert any water that passed through the Kajaki dam. Ministers added darkly that Iranian farmers were using any water they got to plant opium poppies. If so, then they were not alone. In Afghanistan, the Helmand valley, still an outpost of Taliban insurgency, had become a major centre of poppy cultivation. In retaliation, the Iranians took to blaming US "provocation" for the failure of the river to flow. It wasn't clear what they meant. But the anger can only have been exacerbated when the US announced plans to raise the height of the Kajaki dam as part of its aid work to "rebuild Afghanistan," and when the World Food Programme began feeding farmers in the Helmand valley in return for their labour cleaning out abandoned irrigation channels.

In the spring of 2005, nature intervened. Heavy rains far away in eastern Afghanistan broke dams and drowned an estimated 200 people, but finally brought water roaring down the Helmand into the parched Hamoun. Two of the lakes reflooded. But as engineers rushed to rebuild the Afghan dams, and Afghan farmers grabbed as much water as they could, it was not clear how long the reprieve would last. There was still no breakthrough in the UN efforts to broker a deal over the river.

14

MEKONG: FEEL THE PULSE

The diminutive king and queen of Cambodia appeared on the
balcony of the Royal Palace overlooking the Tonle Sap River.
Like toy-town monarchs, Norodom Sihanouk and his queen
Monineath serenaded their subjects—upwards of a million of
them—gathered on the riverside promenade of the beautiful old
colonial capital of Phnom Penh. It was the high spot of the
Cambodian year, and the audience between monarch and subjects
was part of one of the world's oldest boat-racing festivals, the
Bon Om Touk.

This year, 2003, around four hundred boats, each decorated
with paintings of water serpents, rushed two-by-two down the
river to a finish line right by the Royal Palace, where the Tonle
Sap flows into the mighty Mekong. In some boats there were seventy frenetic oarsmen, all standing in a line, pounding the water
from the narrow vessel. Altogether, thousands took part in the
races, while, from across one of the poorest and least urbanized
nations on Earth, thousands more Cambodians flooded into the
city for a weekend of eating and camping on the riverside.

This festival has taken place since the twelfth century, always
at full moon in late October or early November. It is a celebration
of one extraordinary fact about the river on which it takes place.
The Tonle Sap is one of the few rivers in the world that reverses
its flow. It does it every year, right in front of the Royal Palace.

It happens because every year, at the start of the monsoon rains, the often quiet Mekong becomes a raging torrent that overwhelms its tributary, forcing it to surge back upstream for some 200 kilo-metres. At the height of the monsoon, this reverse flow swallows a fifth of the Mekong's prodigious waters, and the tiny Tonle Sap is for a few months one of the world's great rivers—albeit flowing backwards. The river backs up into a great lake that itself spills over its banks, flooding a wide area of rainforest, which turns into a vast fish nursery for the Mekong in the heart of Cambodia.

For five months, fish grow in profusion in the silty forest waters, before being washed back into the main river as the mon-soon abates and the Tonle Sap resumes its proper flow. The annual boating festival marks this unique spectacle and celebrates the great flush of fish that leaves the forest with the water. It is a flush that, in the months to come, will feed tens of millions of people up and down the Mekong river system.

Or that is how it should be. For in 2003 there was consterna-tion on the river. The Mekong floods had been the poorest on record; the reversal of the Tonle Sap's flow had been short and tentative; and the fishing had been terrible. Some in the crowd said that mysterious changes far upstream on the Mekong had neutralized the flood. Fears grew that the reverse of the Tonle Sap, the beating heart of the Mekong river system, might be about to come to an end. Something else was afoot, too. In the Royal Palace. This turned out to be the eighty-year-old king's last serenade of his people. In failing health, he abdicated a few months later. Was this, his subjects asked, the end of an era? The end even of the great flood?

Once, the world's rivers teemed with fish. Then, during the twenti-eth century, most of the rivers were barricaded by dams and their wild flows tamed. Almost everywhere this has caused a drastic decline in wild fisheries. Natural fish nurseries have been wrecked and fish migrations disrupted by the unnatural flow rhythms cre-ated by the dams. But on the Mekong, the great artery of southeast Asia, half a century of warfare has kept the dam-builders away.

The natural seasons of the river have continued uninterrupted. The river has remained free to trespass over its banks and flood forests in summer, then retreat to small pools and rapids in winter. The fish have prospered. And not just the fish. For the fishing communities have enjoyed a bonanza now extremely rare round the world. In Cambodia, where the river flood is most intense, the people live off wild freshwater fish to an extent unknown anywhere else. Even the poorest can dine like kings.

The Mekong remains true to its popular image as the "sweet serpent" of Southeast Asia. It winds for 4,500 kilometres out of the ice fields of eastern Tibet and through a long series of deep gorges in the mountains of southern China, before tumbling down rapids to flood the rainforests of Laos and Cambodia, and sliding into the sea through its delta in Vietnam. The Mekong is far from being the world's largest river. Its average annual discharge of 470 cubic kilometres makes it fourteenth in the riverine pecking order. But its flow is today the most variable of any major world river. During the summer monsoon, it contains up to fifty times more water than in the long dry season. Then, it has the third biggest flow of any river in the world, exceeded only by the Amazon and Brahmaputra.

"The Mekong is not just another river," says Chris Barlow, fisheries researcher at the Mekong River Commission, an inter-government science agency. "It is the least modified of all the major rivers in the world. Animals have evolved to exploit its flood pulse, and local societies have developed that way too." Four-fifths of the population of Cambodia is involved in fishing and processing the harvest. Some sixty million people in the Mekong's lower basin—in Laos, Cambodia and Vietnam—draw their food and income from the river and its wetlands, catching some two million tonnes of fish a year. That is over 2 per cent of the entire world catch of wild fish from both rivers and the sea. Among rivers, only the Amazon produces more.

The Mekong is a salutary lesson in what the world has lost since it began erecting concrete barriers across nature's finest. There are more than a thousand species of fish living in the

Mekong, again more than anywhere bar the Amazon. Hundreds of species are regularly caught and eaten, but the most important is the humble *trey riel*, a small sardine-like relative of the carp that turns up in almost every fishing net on the river. It is, says Joern Kristensen, head of the river commission, "both meat and milk," because it provides both protein and calcium. Oxfam says that the river fisheries of Cambodia "make a bigger contribution to economic well-being and food security than in any other country." Cambodians are more dependent on wild protein than almost any nation on Earth. But as a result, one of the world's poorest countries is one of its best fed.

The biological heart of this extraordinary fecund river lies in the upper reaches of its reversing tributary, the Tonle Sap. In particular it lies where the river opens out into the Great Lake, the largest body of fresh water in Southeast Asia. Every monsoon season, as the Tonle Sap backs up, the lake floods rainforest for up to forty kilometres around it.

After the boat festival, I took to the water: up the Tonle Sap, through the Great Lake and into the flooded forest. It is a topsy-turvy world. Giant trees poke from the water. Tens of thousands of people live in floating villages that loose their moorings and cruise slowly across the lake. Where there are no trees, paddy fields lie beneath the waters, waiting to emerge in the dry season. One French author described Cambodia as the land where fish grow on trees. And that, more or less literally, is what most of them do. Except for the striped snakehead, which lives among tree roots in swamps and can slither overland when the swamps dry up.

This flooded forest is one of the most productive natural ecosystems in the world. Each summer, billions of fish fry are swept here on the monsoon surge to feed on the floating vegetation. Then, as the forest drains each autumn, the fattened fish exit. And the local fishers are ready. Much of the flooded forest is in private hands—divided into five hundred fishing lots that are auctioned by the government. Many are managed by Vietnamese, who are regarded as the master fishers. The biggest lots can cover hundreds of square kilometres and make their owners $2 million a year. From October to March, virtually the entire lake is ringed by bamboo "fences" erected by the lot managers to trap fish as they swim out of the forest.

The forest is also a magnet for tens of thousands of Cambodia's poorest, who take their nets into the "open access" areas outside the private lots. The flooded forest currently has one of the fastest-growing rural populations anywhere in the world. In the mid-1990s, there were only 350,000 people round the lake; today there are a million. Many are landless refugees of the great expulsions by the Pol Pot regime in the 1970s. They depend for survival on the free resources of the lake.

Some say all this activity is destroying the fishery. I clambered aboard a wooden floating platform-cum-office and met Sreng Sokhak, a fishing-lot owner with twenty employees. "I've been fishing on this river for twenty years. We used to catch a hundred tonnes a year. We get nothing like that now," he said. He complained about his neighbours, and unlicensed fishers who come in with batteries and electrodes, sending an electric charge through the water to electrocute the fish. But others argue that a much greater danger would be the loss of the forests and waters that make the system so productive. They say that ultimately the fishers are the true friends of the fish because they prevent the flooded forests from being felled by farmers and converted to rice paddy.

Whatever the truth in this debate, the fecundity of the ecosystem is extraordinary. During their time in the flooded forest, the fish are the main food for a cornucopia of wildlife that in turn also becomes a target for human hunters. Gangs of villagers collect the eggs and chicks of cormorants, pelicans, storks and ibises. Others hunt squirrels and rats, pythons and cobras, turtles and lizards. Up to a million water snakes are netted each year.

Conservationists are here too, policing the various protected areas. Sleeping in a tree house above the water in the Prek Toal nature reserve, I met a pair of local villagers employed by the Wildlife Conservation Society in New York. Their job was to stay out in the flooded forest for a week at a time to protect migrating birds from hunters. Their charges that week included a magnificent fish eagle, hundreds of Indian cormorants and forty pairs of greater adjutants, which are reckoned to be among the world's rarest storks and breed only here and in the Indian state of Assam.

Traders come to the lake from Thailand, Vietnam and even China to buy crocodiles, fish, snakes and monkeys. A Vietnamese monkey farm was in the market for macaques to breed for Western laboratories. Crocodiles have been hunted to extinction in the lake and forest, but the floating villages now farm them. Stepping unawares out of my boat onto a jetty in Kaoh Chiveang village, northwest of the lake, I was surprised by a rush of water beneath my feet. Looking down, I saw between the wooden slats a score or so young crocodiles, each about a metre long, in a cage suspended in the water.

The village was an upmarket suburb on the lake. The floating homes were immaculate, with flower and vegetable gardens at their doors, electricity generators hooked up to long lines of car batteries and TV aerials on every palm-frond roof. The water-ways were lined with stores, karaoke bars, filling stations and elaborate cranes for lifting boats out of the water for repairs. I soon found out the source of the wealth. The village of some three thousand people had at least as many crocodiles. Most fed on water snakes harvested from the flooded forest all around. A fully grown reptile fetched about a thousand dollars. Every household with the capital to spare had set up crocodile cages. The open water might now be empty of the beasts, but the cages probably contain more than ever lived in the lake.

While people working the lake today live a life afloat, their ancestors had a much more sedentary existence. On the lake's northern shore sit a series of truly spectacular temples, headed by Angkor Wat. They are the remains of the capital of the great Khmer empire that lorded it over the flooded forest, the Great Lake, the Tonle Sap, the lower Mekong basin and much of Southeast Asia a thousand years ago. Beside the lake, they created what historians believe was probably the largest urban area on the planet, growing rich on the fish of the lake and the rice grown on its shores. The thousands of carvings depicting fish and fishing that festoon the walls of the temples are testimony to the huge importance of the lake to the wealth of the empire, and to the enduring productivity of the ecosystem here.

Just as Angkor once ruled across much of Southeast Asia, so the flooded forest is an ecological dynamo of importance far beyond its immediate surroundings. It feeds the whole ecosystem of the Mekong basin. Two-thirds of all the Mekong's fish are nurtured in and around the Great Lake. The waxing and waning of the lake is, say ecologists, the "beating heart" of the river and its fishery—sucking in silt, larvae and water, and expelling grown fish a few months later. "If the heart stops, the system dies," says Anders Poulsen, a fisheries biologist at the river commission.

And the artery to the heart is the Tonle Sap River. During the five months when the lake drains, the length of the river is usually a hive of activity. Organized bands of fishers suspend wooden scaffolds over the river and suspend from them wicker bag-shaped nets, each about 25 metres wide and 120 metres long. These "bagnets" are like a fixed trawl, in which the water does the moving rather than the boat. They can fill with a quarter tonne of fish in fifteen minutes. At the height of the season, more than thirty tonnes of fish can be caught every hour in the Tonle Sap, day and night.

Just occasionally, the bagnets bulge with a giant catfish. This is the largest freshwater fish in the world. It grows up to three metres long and can weigh as much as a cow. It migrates more than a thousand kilometres up and down the river from the Great Lake into Laos, where kings once sacrificed a man and a woman before daring to go hunting for the beast. These days, the giant fish is a protected species. In Phnom Penh, the bagnet fishers reach for their cell phones when they catch one and call Zeb Hogan. He is a biologist from the University of California at Davis, but spends part of each year in Phnom Penh on catfish alert—ready to measure, tag and release them whenever they get caught in the bagnets. The day we met, he had been up at 2 A.M. recording a 2.4-metre monster. They are still revered, he said. Even at that hour, women came out to sprinkle perfume onto the fish in an act of homage before their husbands released it into the water.

But the end of 2003 and early 2004 was a desperate time on the Tonle Sap. The summer flood had been poor. The reversal of the Tonle Sap into the Great Lake started late and finished early. A five-month reversal had become a three-month reversal. Less forest was flooded and the fish had less time to mature. The bag-nets caught a mere 6,000 tonnes—less than half the usual haul and the worst on record. Nguyn Van Xia, a riverside buyer for a wholesale market in Phnom Penh, stopped to talk on a landing point just a hundred metres from one of the main bagnet fishing spots. It ought to have been the height of the season, but he had plenty of time. There should be twenty truckloads of fish leaving this spot every day, he said. But the current average was five. Several of his friends were so short of work they were playing volleyball on the beach.

Why? He shrugged. "The flood was bad this year, so we have a bad catch." Out on the river, most of the fishers said their catches had never been so poor. Most blamed low flows. One, heading back to his floating village across the lake with empty nets, told me simply: "When the water is shallow in front of the Royal Palace, there are no fish in the river."

The Mekong is weird. For one thing, the pulse of life on the river seems to be mediated by the moon. The *trey riel*, the most common fish in the river, times its long migrations with phases of the moon. And then there are the hundreds of Naga fireballs, which rise from the river during the October full moon. Even sophisticated townies are spooked by these small orbs of red, pink and orange light, each about the size of a tennis ball. They are named after a giant mythical serpent, Naga, who is said to release them from her lair in caves beneath the river.

The balls are a genuine natural phenomenon. One explanation is that they are pockets of methane drawn from rotting vegetation on the riverbed by the moon's gravitational pull. But, though there may be no Naga serpent, there are in fact mysterious wildlife lairs on the bed of the Mekong. They are giant pools scoured by the enormous whirlpools that form between rapids. There are fifty-eight known pools and they are immense. Some of them extend for a hundred metres below the regular riverbed—making them deeper than the English Channel. They are essential dry-season habitat for huge numbers of fish, including real monsters of the river such as catfish and the equally rare Mekong population of Irrawaddy dolphins.

But these pools and rapids are threatened by the dynamiting that can now be heard on long stretches of the river in Laos, Burma and Thailand. China—the river's secretive and overbearing big brother—has embarked on a plan to make the river navigable for ships. That means removing the rapids. Blasting began in 2001 in an area on the border between Thailand and Laos once known for its catfish. Since then, not a single catfish has been seen in that region. And Isabelle Beasley, an Australian researcher studying the Irrawaddy dolphins in the pools, found fifteen dolphins dead in 2003. Ten more bodies were discovered in early 2004. Most of the dead, she says, are caught accidentally in fishing nets. But Beasley's big fear now is the destruction of the pools as the Chinese blasting moves south. "If we lose the pools, we will lose everything."

And with the dynamiters come the dam engineers. The Mekong and its tributaries have been a mouth-watering prospect for hydroelectric engineers for half a century. For almost a thousand kilometres in China and the mountains of Southeast Asia, the main stem of the river carves a path down narrow gorges, falling almost a kilometre in the process. The gorges make the river easy and cheap to dam; the drop means the power that can be generated is stupendous. In the 1960s, the US government's dam-builders at the Bureau of Reclamation sought to cement Uncle Sam's tenuous hold on the region by offering to build hydroelectric dams in the canyons. But leaders like North Vietnam's Ho Chi Minh turned the Bureau down, before war engulfed the region.

But forty years on, Southeast Asia is finally at peace, and demand for water and electricity is soaring. For engineers, the river is the obvious source for both. Thailand, Vietnam and Laos have already built dams on tributaries of the Mekong, and hydroelectricity is now the biggest legal export from Laos. Most of these dams have proved problematic in one way or another. Vietnam's blocking of the Se San at Yali Falls is causing chaos as unannounced releases of water flood villages over the border in Cambodia. Thailand's Pak Mun dam on the Mun River wrecked local fisheries. The Nam Theun II, for which Laos wants international funding, has become a cause célèbre before a stone has been laid because locals fear it too will kill their fish.

China, meanwhile, is building a cascade of eight huge dams on the main stem of the Mekong, which it calls the Lancang. The first two are already operating and generating concern downstream all the way to the sea. As the turbines are switched on and off to meet changes in demand for power, and their reservoirs empty and fill, water levels in the river fluctuate by up to a metre a day for hundreds of kilometres downstream. Peter-John Meynell of the World Conservation Union, who regularly sails on the river, says, "I feel the wash myself going down the river. Even big boats find it difficult because of the surges from the dams. Local fishers are losing their livelihoods as a result."

Meanwhile, the initial filling of the first two dams—the Manwan in 1993 and the Dachaoshan in 2003—both coincided with unusually low flows on the Mekong all the way down to the Tonle Sap, and with poor fish catches. And in other years, hydrologists have measured a reduction in the Mekong monsoon flow that they suspect is due in part to the dams holding back the floodwaters for release through the dry season. The Mekong's pulse is being weakened.

But this is just the start. Construction began in 2002 on a far bigger dam. The Xiaowan dam will tower 292 metres over the river, as high as the Eiffel Tower. Its reservoir, at 170 kilometres long, will be twenty times the size of the two existing reservoirs combined and second in China only to the Three Gorges on the Yangtze. After that will come a 250-metre-high dam, the Nuozhadu, which will have an even bigger reservoir. By early next

decade, the cascade of dams will be able to store forty cubic kilometres of water—more than half the river's flow as it leaves China.

According to Chinese operational plans, the river's dry-season
flow out of China will triple after the cascade is finished, and the
huge wet-season flow will fall by a quarter. The effect will diminish as you go downstream but, with 40 per cent of the river's flow
coming from China in the dry season, it will still be enough to
halve the strength of the flood pulse in Cambodia as it passes the
Royal Palace. The effect of that on the reversal of the Tonle Sap is
harder to predict. In a worst-case scenario, though, the reversal
could give out altogether.

Some old-school river scientists argue that these changes could
be a good thing, moderating floods and enhancing water supply
downstream in the dry season. Ted Chapman of the Australian
National University's Mekong Research Network told me: "My
own view is that the Mekong cascade could be very beneficial to
the Mekong region." Not so, says Eric Baran, a French biologist
investigating the Mekong. "Western engineers think of flood
extremes as bad news, and engineers in Cambodia have absorbed
this Western philosophy. But in Asia, floods are generally a good
thing because they drive the natural ecosystem on which millions
depend for their food." Hans Guttman, senior hydrologist at the
river commission, agrees: "There is a strong relationship between
flood flows and fish migration. Flattening the flood peaks would
have a severe effect on the river's ecosystem."

And that effect would be felt nowhere more than in and
around the Great Lake. Matti Kummu of the Helsinki University
of Technology, who is modelling the river's hydrology, reckons
that the cascade of dams would not end the Tonle Sap's reversal,
but would delay it by about a month. That would be enough to
reduce the area of flooded forest by more than a million hectares,
he says. But the greatest danger might be the curtailing of the pro-
nounced dry season. Without that, much of the forest would die.

Perhaps just as important as the changing water flow would be
the loss of the river's load of silt. And here the Chinese dams are of
even greater significance. Around one half of the 160 million

tonnes of silt coming down the river each year begins its journey in China. Much of it ends up in the flooded forest round the Great Lake, fertilizing the vegetation and feeding the growth of fish. According to Kummu, the first two Chinese dams are already capturing half the silt flow from China. They may be as much to blame for declining fisheries as the faltering water flows. "If the whole cascade of dams is built, it would trap some 94 to 98 per cent of the sediment load coming from China," says Kummu. That would be a catastrophe for the fertility of the Mekong flood, the flooded forest and the entire ecological infrastructure on which much of Southeast Asian rural life is built.

The Mekong matters to the people who live round it perhaps more than any other river on Earth. Some communities in Cambodia live as much as fifty kilometres from the nearest road. For them, the river is the road and the annual flood is the basis of their lives. "Fish are landed virtually every kilometre along the river by tens of millions of people from tens of thousands of communities," says Barlow. Yet the Mekong fishery's place in Cambodian society and its economy is largely hidden from urban elites and government. Most of the fish caught on the river never reach commercial markets and never appear in government data.

As societies in Southeast Asia urbanize, the lines are being drawn for a final battle for the Mekong. Engineers see the river as a potential powerhouse for industrialization and urbanization. And politicians are taking the lure. Ministers are seduced by "hard figures, megawatts of power," says Barlow. "They are far less impressed with what we tell them about the livelihoods that depend on the fish. They really don't appreciate what is at stake. It's not just about money; it's the food, the protein and the jobs. The fisheries are a source of natural wealth for the poor. It belongs to them. But if the fisheries are destroyed, their only alternative would be a job in a factory in Phnom Penh making textiles for the West." Full nets or full factories: maybe that's the choice.

PART FOUR

WHEN THE RIVERS RUN DRY ... FLOODS MAY NOT BE FAR BEHIND

15

CHINA: THE HANGING RIVER

In early June 1938, at the height of the Sino-Japanese War, Chinese generals perpetrated what remains the single most devastating act of war ever. On their own side. Fighting to hold back Japanese invaders, they sent 800 troops to the great dyke that holds in check the Yellow River as it falls onto the wide North China plain. They told the troops to dig pits beneath the 400-year-old dyke and fill them with explosives. And on the morning of June 9, the generals ordered the detonation of the explosives and the firing of artillery shells to widen the breaches. The aim was to destroy the dyke and create a great wall of water to hold back the Japanese army.

At first, the water flowed only slowly through the kilometre-wide gap in the Huayuankou dyke. It seemed as if the plan had failed. But gradually, as the summer monsoon floods came downstream, more and more of the river escaped the confines of its channel and spread across the plain. By the end of June, villages, towns and farmland across three provinces had flooded and millions of Chinese had fled their homes.

More than half a century later, I discovered hanging in a small museum near Huayuankou a small, dog-eared photograph taken in July 1938 from the remains of the dyke. It shows a scene of utter and total devastation. I have only ever seen one picture like it—taken shortly after an atomic bomb was dropped on

Hiroshima in 1945. The flooding delayed the advancing Japanese for about a month. But thousands upon thousands of Chinese drowned as the Yellow River marauded across the wide plains. And as the flood swelled, famine and disease spread. Chinese historians put the final death toll at a staggering 890,000 people, virtually all of them Chinese.

Stop a while and take that number in. It is three times greater than the number killed by the Indian Ocean tsunami of Christmas 2004. It is greater even than the combined death tolls of the atomic bombs dropped on Hiroshima and Nagasaki and the fire-bombing of Dresden and Berlin and Tokyo during the Second World War.

During the floods, the river abandoned its old course altogether and chose a new path, finally reaching the ocean almost seven hundred kilometres farther south than before, near the mouth of the Yangtze River. There the river stayed for almost a decade, till 1947, when engineers managed to divert it back within its old dykes. All that remains on the rebuilt Huayuankou dyke today, to remind visitors of the destruction once wrought there, is a small stone memorial. On the day I visited, most of the people milling round it were uncomprehending young Chinese taking the last autumn sun. But occasionally older citizens stopped for a while, consumed in thought. As well they might.

The Chinese have always called the Yellow River their "joy and sorrow." Joy, because control of its waters to irrigate crops has sustained more people for longer than anywhere in history. But sorrow because of what happens when the river fails or the control gives way. Unlike the Mekong, where floods are still good news, flooding along the Yellow River is usually disastrous. The river has probably killed more people than any other natural feature on the Earth's surface. Controlling those floods has always been the single most important activity of Chinese governments. Many historians argue that it is the single most important reason for the creation and survival over the millennia of the vast Chinese state with its draconian powers. The Chinese sum up the relationship in a word: *zhi*, which means both "to regulate water" and "to rule."

But fast forward sixty years from the great disaster of 1938 and the news is all about the river running dry. The Yellow River first failed to reach the sea in 1972. Between then and 1998 the river stopped short of its delta for part of almost every year. In 1997 it did not reach the sea for more than seven months. For most of that time, it trickled into the sand on its bed at Kaifeng, 780 kilometres inland, and just downstream of the site of the 1938 breach.

I set out to discover why the river seems to have so changed its character—why the killer floods are giving way to drought. But on my journey I began to conclude that the river has changed less than it appears. I found that the two phenomena of flood and drought on the river are inseparable. Like yin and yang. And while Chinese commentators rail against the river running dry, many experts at the Chinese government's Yellow River Conservancy Commission, whose job is to manage the river and prevent disasters, believe that the next great disaster could be another major flood. "The flood threat of the Yellow River is still the hidden danger in China," says the commission's director, Li Guoying.

Flood remains, as the late Harold Dregne of Texas Tech University put it in 2001, "the most fearsome threat on the river. A minor breach of an embankment could cause one of the worst catastrophes in human history—the threat is very real." The truth, I discovered, is that floods and droughts have always gone together on the river. Every year of low flows increases the chances of a future lethal flood. And modern engineering has only upped the stakes.

The Yellow River begins high in the mountains of eastern Tibet. It loops first north through the Gobi desert and then south and east, through the heart of the world's most populous nation, to the Yellow Sea. It is a journey of more than 5,000 kilometres. The river is the fifth longest in the world. Almost half a billion people depend on it for water to drink and to grow their food. Irrigation water from the river has made China the world's largest producer of wheat and second largest producer of maize. But this Chinese success story is threatened today by growing water shortages.

The river is running low all the way from its source to the sea. Up on the eastern edge of the Tibetan plateau, the area where it rises used to be known as "the county of thousands of lakes." But over half the lakes have disappeared in the past twenty years and a third of the pastures have turned to desert. In the river's middle reaches, irrigation canals are running dry, fields are being abandoned and desertification is generating huge dust storms that spread east, choking lungs in Beijing and closing schools in Korea, dusting cars in Japan and raining onto mountains across the Pacific in western Canada. Near the river's mouth on the fertile expanses of the North China plain, springs no longer gush, the meadows are gone and few of the old lakes that once dotted the plain survive.

The desiccation of the Yellow River and its basin is an economic, as well as an environmental, disaster. As its waters have faltered, millions of hectares of farmland in the river's lower reaches have been abandoned. The wheat harvest fell by a third in six years from the late 1990s. A new dust bowl looms in the breadbasket of China, reminiscent of the disaster on the High Plains in the US in the 1930s. The World Bank warns that the desiccation will bring "catastrophic consequences" for China's ability to feed itself. This matters to the world. As China's grain imports soared, the world's granaries emptied and global grain prices rose by a third.

What has gone wrong? For one thing, there has been drought. Historically, the river has an average annual flow of 57 cubic kilometres. But in the 1990s, the average was just 43 cubic kilometres. The drought may prove to be a cyclical change, or something more permanent. It could be an early sign of global warming. But an equal cause of the river's fitful flow is a dramatic rise in abstractions to feed irrigation and China's fast-growing cities. State irrigation projects dotted down the river cover 75,000 square kilometres and soak up the majority of the river's water—so much so that, in dry years, the total official allocations are greater than the actual flow.

China has put a giant bureaucracy, the Yellow River Conservancy Commission, in charge of the river. I travelled the river with its staff, constantly struck by how their comments jumped from civil service reticence to open candour. One of the problems, they said, is that "the most inefficient irrigation schemes are always in the driest places." On the fringes of the Gobi desert—in the provinces of Gansu, Ninxia and Inner Mongolia—it typically takes four times as much water to grow a field of wheat than it does in the lower river basin. Yet in many years, all the water is taken in these dry upstream provinces and little or nothing is left for Shandong and Henan on the North China plain, where the soils are better, evaporation less and the water would be much more productive.

At the start of my journey, in an office way upstream at Langzhou, capital of Gansu province, one commission official pointed to a map of local irrigation projects. One pumped water 600 metres up from the Yellow River onto sandy hilltops. Another sent the precious liquid through ninety kilometres of tunnels to reservoirs where much of it evaporated. Was this a good use of the water? The local state officials who built the projects say yes. The water grows crops: end of story. The commission's river managers said no. The irrigation projects are hopelessly uneconomic, built more for prestige than profit, and are vastly wasteful of water.

Meanwhile, China's fast-growing cities want the same water. Altogether, about ten cubic kilometres of the river's water—getting on for a quarter of the flow today—is piped out of the river basin, much of it to distant cities. And that is putting ever greater stress on the river. Taiyuan and Hohhot, capitals of the Shanxi and Inner Mongolia provinces, are both digging canals a hundred kilometres long to connect to the spluttering lifeline. Taiyuan, ironically, only needs the water because the city's old source, the

River Fenhe, itself a tributary of the Yellow River, has dried up because of huge abstractions for the state's vast coal mines.

To see some of the downstream consequences of this upstream mismanagement, I went to the People's Victory Irrigation Project. It is just over the river from the Huayuankou dyke, where the river flows out onto the North China plain. The project is a fifty-year-old Communist totem—one of Chairman Mao's first public works to feed his people. The project's canals irrigate an area about the size of Greater London, where a million people live and work. But things are in a bad way. The main distribution canal is badly polluted with foam from a local paper works. Much of the equipment has not been replaced since the fifties. The original iron sluice gate that the "great helmsman" Mao opened more than half a century ago is still in place. And worse, the water is giving out.

In the old days, the project was literally awash with water. It sucked almost a cubic kilometre from the river each year. The entire project was shut down for a while because it became waterlogged. No such luck today. "We are always short of water now," sighed director Wang Lizheng, in between nervous puffs on his People's Victory cigarette. "We are allowed to take only half as much water from the river as we used to." Shortages are made worse because more than half the water he does get his hands on disappears into the ground through the bottom of leaky canals. Wang's main task today is finding cash to line the canals. So far he has lined only a fifth of the main canal. "We do about two kilometres more a year." At that rate, it will take another twenty years to finish the job. Farmers are drilling wells to catch the water that seeps from the canals. But even so, only about a quarter of the original area is still farmed.

In Tianzhuang village I met Shang Sumei, who was carrying a small child on her hip. "Most people now work in factories and only farm in their spare time," she said. She is a teacher and her husband works in a paper factory. "My children won't be farmers. They will go to college and work in the city," she said. Her neighbour Jiao Zhilong said there were often water shortages, so he spent most of the time selling electrical goods in the local market. Another, Pu Yujun, dismissed his agricultural activities in a sentence and took me instead on his motorbike to see his workshop, where eight staff mill wheat to make noodles. In the yard outside, I met a man who has his own workshop making plastic sheeting for electric cables. "There are five hundred households in this village and fifty factories," he told me. Anything but farming.

Mao's greatest investment to feed his people, his symbol of what he saw as the "people's victory" over nature, is now quietly capitulating. Mao is still revered here, but later leaders who have starved his favourite project of both funds and water are not. Wang took me to the tiny project museum where—roped off beside old black-and-white pictures of happy peasants digging dykes with spades and bullock carts carrying bumper harvests—he showed me a chair on which Mao sat after he opened the project's sluice gate in 1952. It has pride of place still (even though, as one of the party gleefully pointed out, when one of Mao's successors later sat on the chair, "he broke it with his fat arse").

Symbolism counts for a lot in China. As we drove on, my guide drew the lesson: "The government is becoming weak. It cannot maintain these projects any more." An old dictum holds that governments in China live or die by their control of the waters of the Yellow River. If so, then here, at least, the current regime is in big trouble.

Downstream from the People's Victory project, on the North China plain, water shortages are even greater. In a good year, the coastal province of Shandong can produce a fifth of China's maize. But in the 1997 growing season, the river failed to reach the province, which is China's largest with a population of ninety million. Crops died in the fields. There was panic in the government. An edict was issued from Beijing. The Yellow River shall not dry up. Ever. The government for the first time began to enforce limits on how much water each province could take from the river, and it told the Conservancy Commission to manage the river so that a minimum flow of fifty cubic metres a second always reached the sea.

In the headquarters of the commission in Zhengzhou, I watched the giant control system in action. One wall is covered with a huge electronic map of the river with real-time readings of key hydrological data. A klaxon sounds if any of the dozens of automatic monitors on the lower river detect that the flow is getting down to the limit. The operators know who is taking what water from the river at any moment and can press a button to shut off sluice gates and reverse pumps to stop all abstractions. To make the point, the engineers reset the emergency shutdown limit to just above the flow on the day of my visit, so I could hear the alarm sound. The sense of power over a mighty river was palpable.

The government can now truthfully say that the river never runs dry. Since 1999, the river has always flowed. But despite the macho politics and state-of-the-art engineering, not much has changed. The river's managers say they still don't have effective control of what happens far upstream where most of the water is wasted. Their political writ often does not run up there. And the tiny trickle that always gets through to the delta is "largely symbolic," they admit. Certainly it hasn't stopped the sense of crisis.

As the river empties, farmers and cities alike try to keep going by pumping water from beneath the ground. In Shandong, more than half the irrigation water now comes from underground. But they are now pumping up water twice as fast as it is being replenished by rains and the river. The underground reserves on the North China plain are being emptied thirty cubic kilometres a year faster than the rains replenish them. In the 1960s, the water table was almost at the surface; now it is thirty metres down. In places round Beijing, 90 per cent of the replenishable water is gone and in places the city is tapping water a thousand metres down in "fossil aquifers" that will never refill. Fearing the worst, the city has banned new water-guzzling industries and even emptied the lakes in front of the Summer Palace.

In the summer of 2000, the year after the minimum flow was established, water wars broke out in Shandong as thousands of farmers made illegal connections to a reservoir that had been earmarked to supply cities. When police intervened, there were riots. One police officer died and more than a hundred protesters were injured. Meanwhile, the problems are spreading upstream, where low flows are becoming ever more frequent. In both 2002 and 2004, the river nearly dried up in Inner Mongolia—1,500 kilometres from the sea. China, superficially the most ordered of nations, seems to be subsiding into hydrological chaos.

They don't call the river Yellow for nothing. Its waters are thick and silty. Standing at the Hukou Falls in the river's middle reaches, a popular spot for Chinese tourists, I watched what looked like chocolate mousse churning over the giant boulders into a narrow gorge. Every year roughly a million tonnes of silt flows over these falls and on down the Yellow River. It is by some way the world's muddiest river. Every tonne of water contains about forty kilograms of silt, twice the load of its nearest rival, the Colorado in the US, and seventy times that of the Mississippi. The silt, like the water, brings joy and sorrow. Joy because it makes the lower valley supremely fertile. But sorrow because of what the silt can do to the river when it is not properly managed. As the river's successful rulers have always known, managing the silt is as important as managing the water.

My first destination on a journey that uncovered the truth of this was a region in the river's middle reaches, where it cuts through steep terrain known as the Loess Plateau. The plateau is the source of 90 per cent of the silt in the world's siltiest river. Nowhere on Earth loses as much soil to erosion. This is because the Loess Plateau is not a proper mountain range at all. There is no underlying geology. It is just a huge pile of loose sand, several hundred metres thick and covering an area five times the size of England.

The sand blew here from a distant desert thousands of years ago and has been left out in the rain ever since. Four-fifths of it is bare, without any kind of vegetation. Every drop of rain falling on the bare slopes eats away at the sand pile. During the monsoon season, the water washes in torrents down the plateau's quarter of a million gullies (that's the total so far; but only those more than half a kilometre long have yet been counted). These muddy torrents can carry almost as much silt as water.

Erosion on this scale changes the landscape fast. Five thousand years ago, this pile of sand was a true plateau, dotted with fortresses that have since earned it the title "the cradle of Chinese civilization." But today, the "plateau" has become a maze of steep-sided hills and valleys with occasional surviving flat hilltops, some still occupied by villages and fields. For China, the erosion of the Loess Plateau is an environmental disaster—both for the plateau itself and for the river downstream, where the silt clogs reservoirs and the riverbed itself.

The silt in the Yellow River has been a constant source of embarrassment to China's leaders, ever since they ordered the building of dams on the river be started. The faces were reddest after the completion of the Sanmenxia dam. The first dam on the main stem of the river, it was intended as another engineering triumph for Chairman Mao—simultaneously a means of regulating water for the People's Victory irrigation district downstream, for preventing floods and for generating hydroelectricity. Mao expelled 400,000 people to make way for the reservoir, and was so proud of it that he had its image printed on the country's banknotes. It was part of his 1950s campaign for "the mountains to bend their tops and the rivers to give way."

But this particular river did not give way. Within two years, it had filled the Sanmenxia reservoir to the brim with mud that eventually backed up for a hundred kilometres, causing flooding on the River Wei, a tributary of the Yellow River. Chinese engineers have since learned how to avoid catching the worst of the river's silt flows in reservoirs, but even so the twenty large reservoirs on the river currently hold more than ten billion tonnes of the stuff. And ever since the Sanmenxia disaster, China's leaders have dreamed of stabilizing the Loess Plateau to eliminate erosion and make the Yellow River "run clear."

To this end, they have spent half a century remaking the steep eroding hillsides into staircases of terraces, planting swathes of trees and bushes, and plugging the gullies with small dams known as checkdams. This work began back in the 1960s with another of Mao's slogans: "Let bald hills become green fields." In most of the world—from Peru and India to the Philippines and the Holy Land—ancient agricultural terraces are being abandoned. But here in the Loess Plateau they are still being built, probably in record numbers.

It is a huge and continuing enterprise of the kind that only a Communist society could attempt. Upwards of 30,000 workers are involved at any one time, often digging terraces and forming chain gangs to plant trees on the steep slopes. So far, a third of the fields have been terraced. And the plan is to have 60,000 check-dams to trap soil flowing down gullies by 2010.

The World Bank has funded much of the recent work. James Wolfensohn, the bank's president, lauded progress during a visit to China in 2004. A decade before, he said, "The hills in an area the size of Switzerland had looked arid, terrible, stark with no trees. Now they've got grass and trees and animals. It's an area where you'd like to have a holiday...it looks like Switzerland." I went to see.

I began on a hilltop in Dingxi county in Gansu with the county's head of soil and water, Cheng Hangjun. In the valley below, dozens of old terraces had been renovated over the previous year and planted with cypress trees. "Until last year people grew crops right up here. Now that's banned," Cheng said. The aim was to trap 80 per cent of the soil and water that used to flow off the hills in the heavy rains. "You can see an effect already. Only clear water flows into the valley now."

The official word is that peasant farmers are happy to have their hillside plots planted with trees. And certainly in areas where I was taken in Gansu and neighbouring Shaanxi, that seemed to be true. They were being compensated with deliveries of as much grain as they would have grown on the plots they had given up. And they got help in growing high-value produce that they could sell in nearby towns.

Farmers said that terraces had made them richer, too. Liu Kequang in Kongge Lao village in northern Shaanxi told me that "the terraces trap water, so we get better yields on the fields where we still grow crops. I used to get two hundred kilos of maize for every *mu* [a fifteenth of a hectare], but now I get more than four hundred kilos." He also grew potatoes and apples, sold to a private trader who takes them to southern China. Liu's diminutive, eighty-five-year-old grandmother wandered round the homestead tending pot plants, a reminder of the days before Mao and the Party. But his brother had just bought the family's first-ever car.

A few valleys away, in the village of Ermaoqu, I met Wang Shiping. His village had recently replanted grain fields with cash crops such as green beans, peanuts and watermelons, and turned many of the old hillside terraces over to apple orchards. Three times a week, Wang went to the nearby town of Qinghuabian to sell his watermelons. "Five years ago we had only ragged clothes, but now we buy good clothes in the town market. We can all afford TVs and motorcycles. My income has increased four times," he said while wielding a massive chopper to cut melons in half and distribute them to our party. The village showed the sign of wealth that holds across most of rural China: it had more motorcycles than donkeys.

For several days, local officials took me to the top of hills to show off their terrace-digging and tree-planting prowess and to introduce me to happy farmers. The work is genuinely remarkable and the gains for some farmers at least seem unquestionable. But the declared purpose of all this work is to make the Yellow River run clear all the way to the sea. So does it? Can it? And why should we care? To find out I had to return to the river's lower reaches—and to backtrack to some history; the history of why silt matters so much.

The story of China's love–hate relationship with the Yellow River and its silt goes back eight thousand years to the dawn of farming on the river's flood plain. The first farmers set up here to take advantage of the smear of silt brought down from the eroding Loess Plateau and dropped onto the flood plain as the river meandered back and forth. But while the farmers grew good crops in the fertile silt, they were at the mercy of a river that flooded huge areas during the annual monsoon, and regularly changed course. So, the farmers started to build dykes to keep the river on a single path.

But from that point on, the river stopped spreading its silt. It left it instead on the bottom of its new permanent channel. The layers built up. Every year, the riverbed was a little higher. It soon began to rise above the level of the surrounding flood plain. The "hanging river" was created. It was a point of no return. From that time on, the dykes had to be raised higher to keep the river in. The task of holding back the river could never be shirked.

The consequences of failing to contain the river became ever greater as time passed and the river rose higher. There were repeated disasters. Between 600 BC and 1949, the river changed its course across the North China plain twenty-six times—or roughly once a century. The regular cataclysms often brought down dynasties. In ancient times, if the river shifted ground the emperor was thought to have lost the mandate of heaven and could no longer rule. And sometimes there were global consequences. The Black Death that killed up to half of Europe's population in the fourteenth century may have begun when rats that carried plague fled China after the Yellow River changed course.

As recently as 1855, the river broke its dykes so decisively that it abandoned one route to the sea almost overnight and took over another river channel that entered the sea a thousand kilometres farther north. Since then the river has resumed its ascent above its flood plain, held back only by dykes that have to be constantly raised and maintained by press-ganged peasant labour. In places, the river is now some twenty metres above the land outside the dykes. The river has never been as high as it is today; nor has it ever risen so fast as it has in the past couple of decades. Never have the human and political consequences of a breach been so great.

Why the apparent rush to disaster? The problem is the rate at which the modern Yellow River is accumulating silt in its lower reaches. Till the mid-twentieth century, at least half of the silt flowing down the river made it to the sea. But today only about

10 per cent gets there. Most of the rest accumulates either behind dams or in the "hanging river." This accelerated build-up of silt is happening, say scientists at the Conservancy Commission, because less water is coming down the river, and because when it comes it is travelling more slowly. In the 1950s it took floods seven days to make it to the sea; now it takes eighteen days. A slower river has less force to bear the silt to the sea.

So with 90 per cent of the sediment now ending up on the riverbed, the hanging river is rising ever higher. By early this decade it was rising by ten centimetres a year, or a metre every decade. Dykes can no longer be raised to keep up, so the capacity of the river channel is getting smaller. Its ability to contain summer floodwaters is falling alarmingly. In 1950, the Yellow River flow could reach 8,000 cubic metres a second before it spilled over the inner dykes. By 1990, that was down to 4,000 cubic metres, and by the end of the 1990s to a measly 2,000 cubic metres.

In recent years, drought has kept river flows low enough to avoid disaster. And river engineers have helped by emptying their reservoirs before each monsoon season, so they are ready to catch whatever floods come down. But this only exacerbates the problem in the long term because the slow flow adds to the silt accumulation.

A crisis is approaching. A breakdown of the dykes and a breakout of the river seem imminent. It was something I pondered as I stood on the Huayuankou dyke. On one side the water was surging past. On the other, there were 87 million people living in a flood zone as large as England. I looked at the marks on the dyke showing high-water levels during past floods in 1958 and 1996. The 1996 flood contained only a third as much water as the 1958 flood, but it rose a metre higher up the dyke wall. In September 2003, just a year before my visit, a flood of just 2,600 cubic metres a second broke an illegal dyke erected by villagers and inundated 100,000 people near Caiji village in nearby Henan. Ten thousand soldiers fought the breach and prevented disaster.

What should be done to prevent disaster? Some believe it is time for another change of channel—preferably a managed change rather than one borne of catastrophe. Richard Cowen at the University of California Davis argues that China should abandon the existing hanging river and start digging an entirely new route for the river to the sea. But, he says, "It seems far more likely to me that there will have to be a catastrophe before China summons the resources for a major renewal of the river."

In China, they have adopted two approaches. One is to cut the amount of silt coming down the river and clogging the channel. That is the national purpose of the great works on the Loess Plateau. But is it working? A lot of inflated claims are being made for public consumption, and the official line from the Conservancy Commission is that the works on the Loess Plateau have cut silt flows downstream by a fifth, to 1.2 billion tonnes a year. But when I asked about this within the commission, its scientists were decidedly cautious.

Xiong Weixin, deputy director of its bureau of soil and water conservation, told me that average figures mean nothing. Annual silt discharges range from three billion tonnes in a wet year to less than half a billion tonnes in a dry year. The low figures were mostly from recent years. That could reflect the conservation work, but it was at least as likely to be the result of poor rains. Most of the silt comes downstream after a few intense storms and, as many farmers told me during my travels, they hadn't had a big storm for five years. Nobody could yet disentangle the two effects.

Even optimists at the commission doubt that it will be possible to cut silt flows much further. Massive erosion, they point out, is a natural feature of the Loess Plateau. And to try and halt it would be decidedly unnatural. The dream of making the river run clear, they say, is just that: a dream. The Chinese, brought up on the wisdom of managing the Yellow River, sensibly have an idiom: "when the river runs clear." Meaning never.

The second approach to preventing disaster is to increase the amount of water coming down the river. This sounds crazy. But the thinking is that more water discharged at the right time will flush the silt to the sea without causing floods. "It's like an inoculation," one engineer said. "We have to have regular small floods in the river in order to prevent major flood disasters." The problem here is that there is not enough water in the river these days for proper flushing. The current estimate is that efficient flushing requires at least nineteen cubic kilometres of water to reach the sea each year. That's more than a third of all the water that enters the river in a typical year, and almost half of the river's flow in some recent years. As the Conservancy Commission puts it, "This challenge will be vitally serious and difficult to meet." For that, read: politically impossible.

So the river's engineers are trying to use the dams on the river to send an artificial flood pulse to flush the river of silt. It's a genuinely innovative idea, never tried on this scale anywhere in the world. They store up water behind the dams and then release it all at once—like a giant water cistern on a toilet—to flush away the sediment on the riverbed downstream. At the start of the monsoon seasons of 2002, 2003 and 2004, they successfully flushed away some 200 million tonnes of silt, lowered the bed by 30 centimetres in places and increased the capacity of the channel to some 3,000 cubic metres a second.

The Conservancy Commission engineers are divided about how much further the flushing can go. But they hope that annual flushing from the reservoirs can stabilize the channel's capacity at its current level. This would be a help, but the capacity of the river channel to handle floods is still not much more than a third what it was half a century ago. While the droughts continue, and the upstream reservoirs can handle what floods do come downstream, that may not matter much. However, it means that the river is primed for disaster if ever a big flood comes.

So could a massive human disaster happen again? The answer has to be yes. And it is the years of low flows, which have clogged the riverbed with silt, that have made it possible.

I asked the engineers what floods they feared most. What might trigger a disaster? The river, they say, has two Achilles' heels. The first vulnerability is to ice. On its long journey to the sea, the river twice makes giant excursions to the north, first into Inner Mongolia in its middle reaches and, second, as it crosses the North China plain to the sea. Sometimes the water in these northern reaches freezes and blocks the river. With water continuing to flow on downstream, the result is floods. Historically, about a third of the big floods on the Yellow River have been a result of ice blockages. They are notoriously difficult to prevent—so much so that there was a saying in the Qing dynasty that a river official, who would normally lose his life for not anticipating a flood, could not be executed for an ice flood. In modern times, there have been big ice floods in 1951 and 1955. As recently as December 2002, a build-up of ice along a hundred kilometres of the river in Shandong threatened to cause flooding. Half a million people were mobilized on Christmas Day to fight threatened floods by strengthening dykes and dynamiting ice. It worked. It needed to.

The second Achilles' heel is intense local flooding that no dam can contain. Li Guoying, the director of the Conservancy Commission, said in a recent paper on the long-term security of the river that the river's flood defences have a weak point between the lowest dam, the Xiaolangdi, and the Huayuankou dyke—the one that the generals chose to break back in 1938. "Although this area is not too big, it is a district with extreme rainstorms," he said. One rainstorm not far away in June 2000 produced half a metre of rainfall in twenty-four hours, and dumped in the order of six cubic kilometres of water into local rivers, luckily without disaster. But, said Li, "If that storm had moved a hundred kilometres west, to the area between Xiaolangdi and Huayuankou, [the consequences] would have been unimaginable."

Chinese society along the Yellow River is the supreme example of what historians call a "hydraulic civilization," a centralized autocratic society built around the paramount need to control its water resources, to harness them for food and tame them to prevent the destruction by floods. The struggle is encapsulated by the legend of Yu the Great, a leader credited with taming the floods on the Yellow River four thousand years ago by dredging channels and allowing the water to flow to the sea. On a ridge near Zhengzhou, not far from the headquarters of the modern Conservancy Commission, his statue towers above the flood plain of the river. One hand is outstretched, bestowing prosperity on his people. But the other hand carries the tools with which he cleared the river. His face looks defiantly towards the river. Taming it had been a grim, remorseless task. And, once undertaken, it is a task without end.

Standing on the dykes outside Zhengzhou, I considered Yu's legacy and imagined the huge endeavour by hundreds of millions of people over thousands of years to keep the Yellow River in check. The dykes constructed in the last fifty years alone have a volume equivalent to thirteen Great Walls of China. But the risks that China runs with this river seem to be ever greater. I have no doubt that the engineers do their best. But the country seems to be sleepwalking to the next disaster, believing against all the evidence that history will not repeat itself. Dyke- and dam-building cannot save China forever from the wrath of the Yellow River. And it is hard to escape the conclusion that the next disaster may not be so far away.

16

CHANGING CLIMATE

Nobody can say for sure how much of the declining rainfall across the basin of the Yellow River is due to man-made climate change, and how much to natural fluctuations. In the short term, it is probably unknowable. What can be said is that a good number of rivers have experienced serious declines in the amount of moisture reaching them in recent years; and that much of this is in line with the predictions of climate researchers.

Equally clearly, rivers in these desiccated regions are also being emptied by direct human activity, often to irrigate fields parched by the lack of rain. Earlier chapters have looked at how the combined effects have reduced flows on the Rio Grande in the American West, the rivers feeding Lake Chad in the African Sahel, and the rivers of Central Asia, such as the Helmand in Afghanistan. In later chapters we will come across more, from southern Europe to the heart of Australia.

But, as climate change gathers pace in the coming decades, the desiccation won't be universal. Modellers in organizations such as Britain's Met Office predict that in some cases, there will be increased river flows. The one certainty is that change is taking place quite rapidly on many rivers, and the hydrological statistics on which dam-builders, river managers and irrigation districts rely to build their structures and make their plans often have little meaning anymore.

First the global picture. Higher air temperatures will increase evaporation from the world's oceans and so intensify the water cycle. By later this century, there could well be 8 to 10 per cent more water vapour in the atmosphere on an average day. That is a thousand cubic kilometres or so extra, enough to fill twenty Niles. This will almost certainly increase global rainfall. Also, shifting trajectories of rain-giving climate systems, like Atlantic cyclones, will mean that the total rainfall will be redistributed. Many middle latitudes will become drier. Meanwhile, the higher temperatures will also mean faster evaporation of water on land. So soils will dry out more quickly. That means less of the rainfall will reach rivers.

Future flows on individual rivers will depend in large part on the balance between the competing effects of changing precipitation patterns and greater evaporation. The rule of thumb seems to be that dry areas will become drier, while wet areas will become wetter. Globally, climate will become more extreme, and rivers will respond in kind.

As a result, many of the rivers that provide water in the world's most densely populated areas, and where water is already in the shortest supply, will be in still deeper trouble soon. In northeast China, the savannah grasslands of Africa, the Mediterranean, the southern and western coasts of Australia and even the chalk hills of England, the rains will probably diminish, evaporation will certainly be greater—and the rivers will run dry.

The US government's Scripps Institution of Oceanography estimates that reservoir levels on the Colorado River will fall by a third as declining rainfall and raised evaporation combine to reduce moisture by up to 40 per cent across the southern and western states of the US. The River Niger, which waters five poor and arid countries in West Africa, is expected to lose a third of its water; and the Nile, lifeblood of Egypt and Sudan, could lose a fifth. Inland seas will be at special risk, as many rivers in continental interiors lose flow. Lake Chad has almost succumbed and may suffer further in future. Also under threat are the Caspian Sea and Lake Balkhash in Central Asia, Lakes Tanganyika and

Malawi in East Africa, and Europe's largest, Lake Balaton in Hungary.

But giant tropical rivers like the Amazon and the Orinoco in South America and the Congo in Africa may become even more bloated than today, the models predict. Similarly, the great Arctic rivers of northern Canada and Siberia will probably gain water as warmer air holds more moisture and more rain falls on their catchments. So the Mackenzie and Yukon in Canada and the Ob, the Yenisei and Lena in Siberia will rage even more fiercely—40 per cent more, according to one big study.

There is some evidence that these trends are already well under way. In early 2005, US climatologist Kevin Trenberth showed that, after a century of little change, there has been a surge in instances of severe drought round the world since 1970. The proportion of the Earth's land surface suffering very dry conditions rose from 15 per cent then to 30 per cent at the start of the twenty-first century, he said. Meanwhile, scientists from the Met Office reported that "far northern rivers are discharging increasing amounts of fresh water into the Arctic Ocean due to intensified precipitation caused by global warming." There had been an annual increase in river flow into the Arctic of nine cubic kilometres since the 1960s, they found.

But there will certainly be anomalies. In some places, neighbouring rivers could have very different futures. The Indus and the Ganges both rise in the Himalayas and flow south. But while models say the Indus could be flowing at half present levels by the end of the century, the Ganges could have gained half. In Britain, the rivers of the north and west, like the Clyde and the Mersey, will probably run fuller as more intense Atlantic cyclones increase winter rains, while those in the south and east, like the Thames, the Stour and the Kennet, will waste away as summer evaporation goes into overdrive.

And some rivers will live a switchback life in a greenhouse world. They will become increasingly unpredictable and dangerous, with flood and drought alternating even more than today. That will sometimes be good for wildlife. It could even help revive flood pulses lost to dam-building. But the danger is that the pulse will prove too irregular and unpredictable for either nature or man to benefit.

Some rivers will change dramatically with the decades, first running full to overflowing, and then shrivelling. This is most likely on those that drain the great glaciers of the Himalayas, Tibet, Alps and Andes. As their glaciers melt in the early decades of this century, the flow of some are predicted to increase, especially in summer. Already the Alps in Europe have lost a quarter of their ice. Alpine melting in 2002, during the warmest-ever summer in the northern hemisphere, contributed to unprecedented floods in central Europe. But, as the glaciers disappear, the meltwaters will disappear too.

A British study in the Himalayas found that the Indus could increase its flow by between 15 and 90 per cent in the first half of the twenty-first century as glaciers melt, and then decrease to between 30 and 90 per cent of current flows later in the century. Likewise, American researchers believe that the spring meltwaters from the Sierra Nevada snowpack, which today sustain summer irrigation of crops and lawns across the desert lowlands of California, could diminish by 70 to 80 per cent over the next fifty years. As the rushing meltwaters become a trickle, some of the most productive agricultural lands in the world could dry up.

One important effect of existing glaciers is to stabilize river flow between years. They absorb highly variable monsoon rains and provide a strong, regular flood pulse in the summer melting season. This is vital to people living downstream. The glaciers of the Himalayas and Tibet feed seven of the greatest rivers in Asia—the Ganges, Indus, Brahmaputra, Salween, Irrawaddy, Mekong and Yangtze—ensuring reliable water supplies for two billion people. But in half a century or so, the glacier flows in many of these rivers will dwindle and be replaced by much more fickle flows from rain in the mountains. That is a serious threat to Asia's future.

"Once the glaciers go, you're down to whatever happens to fall out of the sky," says British glaciologist Martin Price. And not just Asia. Down the Andes, cities like La Paz, Lima and Quito—

capitals of Bolivia, Peru and Ecuador, respectively—depend on the Andean glaciers for secure water and hydroelectric power. But the glaciers are disappearing fast.

Uncertainty, then, is the greatest difficulty. Some of the above predictions assuredly will not come true. Equally certainly, there will be real-life horror stories unconsidered in the climate models. This creates huge dilemmas for water engineers. How can they design dams and irrigation schemes, with expected lifetimes of fifty or a hundred years, to cope with such uncertainty? In all probability, they can't.

Already the white elephants, the victims of recent climate change, litter the landscape. In Ghana in West Africa, the Akosombo dam has been left high and dry by declining flows down the River Volta. The dam was designed by British colonial administrators who wanted to kick-start industrialization in Ghana as it became independent in the 1960s. Instead, it virtually bankrupted the nation. The dam was built at a time when rainfall was at a historic high. But these days, the reservoir rarely gets above 50 per cent full. Its electricity output is a fraction of that anticipated. Industrialization never happened.

Likewise the Victoria dam, which was built by the British in Sri Lanka in the 1970s. It too was a bid to industrialize a newly independent nation. It too languishes half-used most of the time, because the River Mahaweli has only 40 per cent of the flow anticipated by British hydrologists. And near Lake Chad, as we saw in chapter 12, the British-designed South Chad Irrigation Project sits high and dry because the lake has long since receded beyond the reach of its intake pipe. These boondoggles warn of a growing crisis of confidence about cherished notions of how much water rivers can be expected to deliver.

Most of the world's population currently lives where there is a history of ensured water. That is not by chance. Humans require reliable and predictable water in order to flourish. Modern, highly engineered methods of exploiting water often test reliability to the limit. Now climate change is undermining the predictability, too.

PART FIVE

WHEN THE RIVERS RUN DRY ...
ENGINEERS POUR CONCRETE

17

WONDERS OF THE WORLD

He cut a startling figure. Daniel Beard, the recently retired commissioner of the Bureau of Reclamation, the US government agency that has built more large dams on more rivers than any other body anywhere in the world, had taken off his suit, donned a T-shirt, and was striding through the streets of Nagaragawa in southern Japan at the head of a thousand protesters. He was yelling: "*No more dams!*"

The demonstration was headed for a newly completed concrete barrage on the estuary of the River Nagara. It was a project with an unusual history. Costing $1.7 billion, the barrage began as a scheme to supply water to the city. When it transpired that the water was not needed, it turned into a flood-protection project. The saga reeked of Japan's seemingly insatiable desire to keep the construction industry hammering away, almost regardless of whether its structures were needed.

Beard was in no doubt that the barrage should never have been built. "This is one of the most awful dam projects I have ever seen—and I've seen some," he told the demonstrators that afternoon through a crackling megaphone. "It will supply water that nobody needs, will probably destroy a salmon fishery on a beautiful river and may actually increase the risk of flooding."

Beard's public conversion to the anti-dam cause had begun a few years before, in 1995. He was at the time still in charge at

BuRec, and was attending a meeting in South Africa of the International Commission on Large Dams, a professional association of the global high priests of dam engineering. One quiet morning he declared to an astonished workshop audience that "the dam-building era in the United States is over." Such heresy. The agency that raised the Hoover dam across the Colorado River, built the Grand Coulee on the mighty Columbia River, that was the US's largest water wholesaler and fifth-largest electricity generator, and that had poured concrete and rock and earth across thousands of other rivers in the US and around the world had, he said, stopped building forever. No more dams.

Now in Japan, a country with dams on virtually every river, Beard went further, condemning a huge global industry in which his organization had played a central role. He linked arms with Japanese opponents of the Nagara barrage; with Phil Williams, then president of the International Rivers Network, and an arch foe of the old BuRec who believes every dam is a bad dam; and with Dai Qing, a former missile engineer from Communist China who became the country's best-known and most courageous opponent of dams. He was, he said, proud to stand that day beside the anti-dam protesters of the world.

Treachery? Enlightenment? Dams have always excited intense passions. You are, to coin a phrase, either for them or against them.

Modern water engineering began in earnest with BuRec's Hoover dam—the first superdam. The 220-metre plug across the Boulder Canyon on the Colorado River was completed in 1935. It was taller than a sixty-storey building, bigger than the Great Pyramid of Egypt and contained enough concrete to pave a highway from San Francisco to New York. Behind it grew Lake Mead, which could hold more than twice the river's annual flow. As Francis Crowe, the BuRec surveyor on the project, later put it: "I was wild to build this dam—the biggest dam built by anyone, anywhere." This was not the language of technical reports, but it was perhaps the truest reflection of the motivation behind much large dam construction on the Colorado and round the world.

The white concrete of the Hoover dam became a symbol of Franklin Roosevelt's New Deal of public works projects, and of a wider lust to remake the landscape. It was soon joined by the equally talismanic Grand Coulee dam on the Columbia River. The folksinger Woody Guthrie wrote a collection of songs celebrating the re-engineering of the Columbia River with the Grand Coulee dam. In it he called the dam the newest wonder of the world.

These dams ushered in a post-war world in which dams became symbols of modernism, of economic development and of mankind's control over nature. Russia wanted its own Hoover dam; so did Egypt and Japan and China and India; they sprouted across Latin America; Britain built replicas for their colonies as parting gifts before independence. No nation-state, it seemed, was complete without one.

"Except for global warming, there has been no more drastic human alteration of the landscape in the last fifty years than the damming, regulation and diversion of the world's rivers," Beard told the Japanese demonstrators. But he was not boasting now; he was apologizing. "Those who promoted dam projects were not honest about costs and benefits. The truth is that dam proponents would say just about anything to get a dam project approved."

The decisions to build were "political, benefiting particular politicians or their benefactors rather than solving a problem. In our experience at BuRec, the actual total costs of completing projects exceeded the original estimates typically by 50 per cent. And the actual contribution made to the national economy by these dam projects was small in comparison to the alternative uses that could have been made with the public funds they swallowed up. We are now spending billions of dollars to correct the unanticipated impacts such as lost fisheries, salinized soils and desiccated wetlands." Ouch.

Rivers today are worth more in America as amenities for fishing and tourism than as water for filling reservoirs, he said. "We've started tearing down dams." Is the US a special case? Far from it. "In my view, we are starting down a similar path throughout the world," Beard said. "The time when large dam projects are a realistic answer to solving water problems is behind us."

Like Beard, modern environmentalists have come to see large dams as engines of environmental destruction. But it was not always so. For many years, greens in both North America and Europe supported the dam-builders. Rather like wind power today, hydroelectricity was seen as a new, clean, cheap source of electricity. In Europe, concern that dams might interfere with the natural flow of rivers such as the Danube, Rhine and Rhone was tempered by the fear that the alternative was pollution from fossil-fuel power stations. As late as 1996, the head of World Wildlife Fund in Austria told me, "Even though we love the mountains, most environmentalists in Austria still support the construction of dams in their valleys."

And hydroelectric dams do generate a huge amount of electricity—around a fifth of the global total. More than sixty countries depend on them for more than half their power. One dam, at Itaipu on the River Parana between Brazil and Paraguay, has a generating capacity of 12,600 megawatts—equivalent to a dozen conventional power stations. It supplies São Paulo and Rio de Janeiro, two of the world's largest megacities. China's Three Gorges on the Yangtze will be even bigger. Most modern dams serve dual or triple functions, also supplying water for irrigation projects and city taps and sometimes claiming flood-prevention capabilities as well.

The world's large dams now hold approaching 7,000 cubic kilometres of water. Most big river systems, including the twenty largest and the eight with the most biological diversity—the Amazon, Orinoco, Ganges, Brahmaputra, Zambezi, Amur, Yenisi and Indus—all now have dams on them. Most of the surviving untamed rivers of the world are in the empty Arctic tundra and northern boreal forests. The largest is the Yukon in northern Canada. The handful in tropical lands are rapidly becoming extinct. The Salween, which runs for some 2,600 kilometers from China through Burma and Thailand, is about to be tamed for the first time.

On rivers like the Colorado, the Volta in West Africa and the Nile the dams can hold two or three times the actual annual flow. And yet, they remain an essentially experimental technology. Their hydrological, ecological and social effects have been huge. But for many years their status as symbols of modernism insulated them from serious appraisal. Even in the 1990s, fewer than half of all proposed dams had an environmental impact appraisal before construction began. And even fewer had the consent of the people they displaced. Only since the late 1990s have serious steps been taken internationally to establish if their benefits outweigh the environmental, social and economic downsides.

The focal point for this re-evaluation has been the World Bank. In the second half of the twentieth century, the Bank spent an estimated $75 billion on building large dams in ninety-two countries. But by the late 1980s, its own cost-benefit analyses questioned the value for money represented by this investment bonanza. They catalogued huge cost overruns, billion-dollar corruption scandals, poor design and bogus hydrology that left reservoirs empty, turbines that were never connected to national grids and promised downstream irrigation works that never got built at all. Bank-financed dams, it also discovered, had caused the forced resettlement of ten million people.

Amid a rising chorus of opposition round the world, the Bank pulled out of contributing to the funding of a high-profile dam on the River Narmada in India. And in a quandary over how to proceed, it appointed a World Commission on Dams to assess the successes and failures of large dams, and to come up with some ground rules for what a successful dam project might look like.

The final report from the commission was launched in a blaze of publicity in London in late 2000 under the benign gaze of Nelson Mandela and the rather sterner visage of World Bank president James Wolfensohn. It was even more scathing about large dams that the Bank could have feared at the outset. It endorsed many of the environmentalists' most trenchant criticisms. Most dams just don't deliver as advertised, the commission said. Average cost overruns were 56 per cent. Half of hydroelectric dams produced significantly less power than promised; two-thirds of dams built to supply water to cities delivered less water than promised; a quarter of them delivered less than half what their brochures claimed. Dams built to irrigate fields were no better. A quarter of them irrigated less than 35 per cent of the land intended. Even dams that promised to protect against floods "have increased the vulnerability of river communities to floods," often because their reservoirs have been kept full to maximize hydroelectric production.

And dams have taken huge amounts of land—land on which people once lived. All told, at least 80 million rural people worldwide had lost their homes, land and livelihoods, the commission found. The Akosombo on the Volta in Ghana expelled 80,000 people, the High Aswan in Egypt 120,000, the Damadur in India 90,000, the Kariba in southern Africa almost 60,000, the Tarbela in Pakistan more than 90,000. And for what? My own estimates show that the High Aswan dam generates just 5 kilowatts of electricity for every hectare of land flooded; Kariba generates just 3 kilowatts, Akosombo 0.9 kilowatts. Others are even worse: the Kompeinga dam in Burkina Faso generates just 0.7 kilowatts per hectare and Brokopondo in Suriname is worst of all at 0.2 kilowatts.

Dams' destruction of ecology has been extensive. The commission found that, far from "greening the desert" as promised, many dams may have encouraged its advance by desiccating wetlands and delivering salt to fields. A quarter of the world's irrigated land, much of it watered by dams, was damaged by salt and waterlogging. Meanwhile, accumulations of silt had more than halved the storage capacity behind a tenth of older dams. And by stopping the flow of silt downstream, dams had universally reduced the fertility of flood plains and "invariably" caused erosion of riverbanks, coastal deltas and even distant coastlines. Coastal lagoons are being washed away all along the West African coast, owing to dams.

Most of the remaining untamed rivers are in the empty Arctic tundra and northern boreal forests. The largest surviving wild river system is the Yukon in remote northern Canada, the world's twenty-second-largest river by volume. Europe's last three undammed river systems are all in northern Russia. But Christer Nilsson, a landscape ecologist at the University of Umea in Sweden, who led the research, said that many dry parts of the world have become "totally devoid of unaffected river systems." And surviving rainforest rivers are under increasing attack. Rivers about to be dammed for the first time include the Salween— which runs for 2,400 kilometres from China through the jungles of Burma and Thailand—the Rajang in Malaysian Borneo, the Joquitinhona in Brazil, the Ca in Vietnam, and the Agusan on the Philippine island of Mindanao.

By interrupting natural river flows, dams have wrecked fisheries from the Columbia to the Ganges. Fish stocks established in the reservoirs behind dams rarely come close to compensating. The Grand Coulee and its fellow dams on the Columbia River in the US have destroyed one of the world's largest and most lucrative salmon fisheries. The fish, according to one study submitted to the commission, would have been worth more than the electricity generated by the dams.

The commission report trashed some of the most treasured icons of the industry. Typical was the billion-dollar Kariba dam, built by the British on the River Zambezi in 1959. It created the largest man-made lake in the world on a rich flood plain where 57,000 Batongan people had lived. It was intended to generate hydroelectricity to boost the future independence and economic development of the peoples of Zambia. But far from benefiting from the project, the Batongans found themselves expelled and left destitute in refugee camps, while the electricity and water from the dam went to multinational corporations running copper mines. Was this development? The commission rather doubted it.

It also catalogued how the Manantali dam on the River Senegal in West Africa eliminated floods that provided free irrigation for half a million farmers, and how the Akosombo dam in Ghana flooded an area of fertile farmland the size of Lebanon, while providing a paltry amount of power sold at knockdown price to an American aluminium-smelting company. The loss of silt downstream of the dam has caused massive erosion at the River Volta's mouth and along the West African coastline. Some 10,000 people who lived along the coast of neighbouring Togo have seen their homes disappear beneath the waves.

Commission chairman Kader Asmal did not in the end condemn dams as a technology. "Shortcomings are not automatic and can be avoided," he said. Future dams could be justified if they showed that they overcame the drawbacks and had the consent of the people affected. But even so, his report revealed that there are just too many horror stories for each to be dismissed as arising from problematic local circumstances, whether hydrological, social or political. It was an extraordinary condemnation of what, for much of the past fifty years, has been one of the world's largest construction industries, and a cornerstone of world strategies for economic development, soaking up an estimated $2 trillion.

I admit to a sneaking love of large dams. The sheer grandeur of them takes the breath away. I can empathize with Franklin Roosevelt, who said on opening the Hoover dam in 1935: "I came, I saw and I was conquered." With Woody Guthrie, who felt similarly about the Grand Coulee. And with Jawaharlal Nehru, who called his dams "the new temples of India, where I worship." But clearly dams do both good and harm. A balance, as the World Commission insisted, can be drawn. But it is not an easy balance.

Usually the benefits are short-term, while the costs are long-term. Usually urban elites gain most, especially from hydroelectricity, while the poor in the countryside lose most, as their fields are flooded or the rivers and wetlands on which they depend are wrecked. Water, as they say in the American West, flows uphill to money. That is why, everywhere around the world, farmers and fishers are being forced to give up their water resources to cities and industry.

It is perhaps no surprise that, notwithstanding the New Deal idealism of the early days, it is autocratic, corrupt and militaristic governments that have come to like dams best. Marshall

Goldman, the analyst of Soviet Russia, identified "an almost Freudian fixation... nothing seems to satisfy the Soviets as much as building a dam." Communist China, with 22,000 large dams, has almost 50 per cent of the world total. Spain, under the fascist leadership of General Franco, built more dams than any nation of comparable size on Earth. Dams, if nothing else, have proved an exceptionally effective technology for turning the unruly flow of rivers into private or state property.

Can we ever draw the balance? At the World Water Forum in Kyoto in 2003, I heard hundreds of scientists deliver a string of serious indictments of the failings of many water-engineering technologies, especially dams. They also made numerous proposals for less ecologically damaging and socially divisive solutions to water problems, which we will explore later in the book. And yet water ministers attending the same meeting, but apparently hearing a different message, almost unanimously supported calls for a doubling in the planet's stock of large dams during the twenty-first century. The simple image of the giant dam delivering water and power and control over rivers seduces them still. It begins to look as if Baird's fond hope that the era of dam-building is over may be rather wide of the mark.

The most persuasive mantra is that poor nations must have dams if they are to grow rich. The latest rhetorical version of this claim has been doing the rounds of ministers and international-aid officials ever since being road-tested by the dam-building industry in Kyoto. A typical version came from Kristalina Georgieva, director of the Environment Department at the World Bank. "Look," she told me during a visit to London, "countries need infrastructure, and that includes dams. Ethiopians have fifty cubic metres of water storage each; Australians, with a similar climate, have more than three thousand." And Americans, she might have added, have double that.

But this is sloppy thinking. Some developing countries might be best advised to build dams. But it is far from self-evident. Anti-dam campaigner Paddy McCully, head of the International Rivers Network in California, says such an analysis "does not explain why Ethiopia is poor, or prove that building lots of dams will end its poverty. Zambia and Zimbabwe have around twice the water-storage capacity per person that Australia has, but they remain desperately poor. Paraguay generates nearly ten times more hydroelectric power per capita than Australia, but has a per-capita GDP just a tenth as big."

A list of the twenty-five countries most hooked up to hydro-electricity includes such economic under-performers as Burundi, Rwanda, both Congos, Malawi, Afghanistan and Laos. The only wealthy nation among the twenty-five is Norway. I was struck too by the situation of the tiny landlocked southern African state of Lesotho. It is one of the most water-rich nations in Africa, with the tallest dam on the continent. That dam has enough reservoir capacity to give each of the country's two million citizens about 1,500 cubic metres of water each a year. But in early 2004, Lesotho faced famine as parched crops withered in the fields. The government appealed for food aid. Why? Because almost all the water stored in the mountain kingdom's two giant reservoirs was earmarked for sale to its neighbour, South Africa. The problem for Lesotho was not the absence of water or even of a dam; it was an absence of money.

18

SUN, SILT AND STAGNANT PONDS

You could fill every tap in England with the amount of water that evaporates each year from the surface of Egypt's Lake Nasser. This is one of the more staggering statistics I uncovered while researching this book. According to Egyptian hydrologists, between ten and sixteen cubic kilometres of water disappear annually from the surface of the great reservoir behind the High Aswan dam—that is, a quarter of the average flow of the river into the reservoir, and approaching 40 per cent in a dry year.

This huge waste of water in a country dependent for its survival on the Nile should come as no great surprise in Cairo. In the early twentieth century, British colonial engineers forcefully advised against building a dam in the Nubian desert precisely for this reason. Far better, they said, to capture water farther upstream in Ethiopia, where most of the river's water rises. There, a cooler, cloudier climate would reduce evaporation rates and the steep valleys would reduce the surface area of the reservoir. But in the 1950s, when Egypt gained the independence to do what it liked, its leader, Gamal Abdul Nasser, decided on a dam on Egyptian territory, whatever the water losses. He created the second-largest man-made lake in the world, with water spreading for five hundred kilometres along the flat Nubian desert deep into Sudan.

Lake Nasser is not alone in such losses, of course. Right across the tropics and beyond, evaporation is a major drain on reservoirs. In the American West, as in Egypt, more than two metres of water evaporate annually from reservoirs like Elephant Butte on the Rio Grande and Lakes Mead and Powell on the Colorado. A tenth of the flow of the Colorado River, lifeblood of the American West, evaporates from Lake Powell alone. A typical reservoir in India loses 1.5 metres. In the parched Australian outback, the losses can exceed three metres a year.

What proportion of the reservoir's water supplies this represents depends on the ratio between surface area and capacity, and the amount of time the water spends in the reservoir. Like the High Aswan, the Kariba dam on the River Zambezi loses around a quarter of its annual inflow, which is more water than is consumed annually in Zimbabwe. In Namibia they estimate that the amount of water evaporating from the Epupa reservoir annually could supply the capital, Windhoek, for forty-two years.

Among the worst offenders must be the Akosombo dam in Ghana, which holds back a larger surface area of water than any other—approaching 10,000 square kilometres. An evaporation rate of 1.5 metres would lose 15 cubic kilometres a year, which is roughly half the reservoir's input from the River Volta in an average year. Rainfall into the lake may compensate for some of that, but the rain would have fallen anyway, whereas the evaporation would not have happened without human intervention.

Could this evaporation be prevented? Technologists have come up with an ultra-thin layer of organic molecules that can reduce evaporation on small reservoirs by up to a third. But for larger reservoirs, wind breaks the thin surface. And the ecological effects of cutting off the exchange of gases like oxygen and carbon dioxide between air and water remain largely unknown. So, for now we are stuck with the problem.

Igor Shiklomanov, a Russian hydrologist, reckons one litre in every twenty drawn from rivers for human use disappears in reservoir evaporation. That works out at 350 cubic kilometres a year, of which 40 per cent is lost in Asia, a quarter in Africa and a sixth in North America. In Australia, twenty million people lose something like 4 cubic kilometres of water a year—or 200 cubic metres a head. Peter Gleick, author of a biennial report on the world's water, estimates that an average US hydroelectric dam loses 400 cubic metres of water per year for every person supplied with electricity. Of course, reservoir evaporation will cause rainfall somewhere else. But, even so, it is a lot of water to mislay.

Fetid, choked with weeds and swarming with mosquitoes, the Balbina reservoir in the Amazon rainforest 150 kilometres north of Manaus is a billion-dollar boondoggle. The dam rises fifty metres above the forest floor on the River Uatuma, a tributary of the River Amazon. The reservoir floods an area the size of an English county. But much of it is less than five metres deep. Philip Fearnside, from Brazil's National Institute for Research in Manaus, has counted 1,500 islands and "so many bays and inlets it looks rather like a cross-section of a human lung."

Even the introduction of a herd of grazing manatees has failed to staunch the spread of weeds across the surface. Stagnant water slips through the reservoir's flooded forest for years before reaching the dam's hydroelectric turbines, which have a piffling generating capacity of 112 megawatts—not enough to power a tenth of an English county. The reservoir needs to flood the equivalent of a soccer pitch to deliver enough power to run a small air-conditioning unit back in Manaus.

Even in the Amazon rainforest, that sounds like a waste of land. But the true insanity of this hydroelectric dam has only recently emerged. The rotting vegetation in the flooded forest is producing huge amounts of methane, one of the greenhouse gases thought responsible for global warming. The reservoir was created in the 1980s to provide pollution-free electricity for the capital of the Amazon. But by Fearnside's calculations, it produces methane with eight times the greenhouse effect of a coal-fired power station with a similar generating capacity. This is not green electricity.

Balbina is not alone. Brazil is largely powered with hydroelectricity, and Marco Aurelio of the Cidade University in Rio de

Janeiro says up to half of Brazil's hydroelectric reservoirs warm the planet more than an equivalent fossil-fuel power plant. The World Commission on Dams warned that greenhouse gases bubble up from every one of the reservoirs round the world where measurements have been made. While probably only a handful are emitting more than fossil-fuel power stations, almost all make a significant contribution to atmospheric concentrations. "There is no justification for claiming that hydroelectricity does not contribute significantly to global warming," the commission said.

Vincent St. Louis of the University of Alberta has tried to calculate the global effect of all this methane. He says reservoirs produce a fifth of all the man-made methane in the atmosphere, and make up 7 per cent of the man-made greenhouse effect. That is a bigger impact than, for instance, aircraft emissions. His calculation is controversial but persuasive. Until recently, scientists investigating the phenomenon believed that the gases came mostly from vegetation trapped underwater when the reservoir filled. They reasoned that the rotting vegetation would soon be gone and emissions would cease. Not so, it turns out. As reservoirs round the world age, most continue to produce substantial quantities of methane.

Why so? For one thing, rotting can be very slow. It takes up to five hundred years for a tree to rot in a stagnant Amazon reservoir. For another, a lot of the rotting vegetation does not come from the reservoir but floats down the rivers that drain into the reservoir. As long as the reservoir continues to flood, the vegetation will continue to arrive and the reservoir will continue to give off greenhouse gases. Of course, most of this vegetation would have rotted anyway. But without reservoirs, says St. Louis, the decomposition would most likely occur in a well-oxygenated river, producing carbon dioxide—whereas tropical reservoirs usually contain little oxygen, and as a result they generate methane instead. Methane is twenty times more potent as a greenhouse gas than carbon dioxide. Reservoirs thus change the way significant amount of the Earth's vegetation rots, and with it dramatically raise the "greenhouse effect" of the rotting.

This could be political dynamite when the Kyoto Protocol on climate change is discussed. The inclusion of reservoir gases would transform the estimated emissions of greenhouse gases for some nations. If St. Louis's average figure for emissions from tropical reservoirs holds for the Akosombo dam in Ghana, the reservoir must be emitting five times as much greenhouse gas each year as all the country's fossil-fuel burning. The tiny South American nation of French Guiana is in a similar position. Once thought of as one of the world's most greenhouse-friendly nations, French Guiana has a small population and its industrial emissions are minuscule. But a new dam built in the jungle to power the launch site for Europe's Ariane space rocket is a greenhouse boondoggle on the scale of Balbina. It produces three times as much greenhouse gas as an equivalent coal-burning power station. As a result, French Guiana's real per-capita emissions of greenhouse gases are three times those of France and greater even than those of the US.

Reservoirs are not permanent structures. Or not permanently useful, anyway. However well they are managed, they accumulate silt brought down from the headwaters of the rivers they trap. The extreme case is the Yellow River, the world's siltiest river, which succeeded in filling the Sanmenxia reservoir in just two years. China's dam engineers are more sophisticated about how they manage silt flows these days, allowing the siltiest surges to pass through the reservoir. But the reservoirs on the river currently still have a half-life of less than two decades.

No other river beats this, but most rivers flowing out of the Himalayan heartland of Asia carry substantial silt flows. Many dams on these rivers are likely to be as good as useless in forty or fifty years. The reservoir behind the Tarbela dam, the largest and most upstream on the Indus, is now more than a quarter full of silt. An island of silt has already broken the surface and is moving ever closer to the dam itself. By 2025 it will be three-quarters filled and effectively useless. Pakistan is looking for a site for a replacement.

Overall, the world's reservoirs are thought to be losing their storage capacity at a rate of at least 1 per cent a year. In China, which has more reservoirs than any other country, the figure is 2 per cent. That is a loss of tens of cubic kilometres of reservoir capacity a year. "This loss should be of the highest concern for governments across the globe," says Rodney White of HR Wallingford, a British consultancy. "The world requires between three hundred and four hundred new dams every year just to maintain current total storage."

In theory, clogged reservoirs could in future be replaced with new ones. But the trouble is that most of the world's best potential sites for dams are already taken. Any replacement for the Tarbela will be only a fraction as effective. Future dams will get second and third and fourth best, with less water storage and less hydroelectric potential. And their ecological impacts are likely to be much greater. However good or bad the current crop of dams have been for the world, their successors will flood much more land for far less benefit—and be very substantially more expensive.

19

DAMS THAT CAUSE FLOODS

Sofia Pedro gave birth to her daughter Rositha in a tree. She couldn't go home or to hospital because everywhere for miles around her tree was flooded. It was her only refuge. In February 2000, Mozambique had suffered the worst floods in living memory. TV images taken from a helicopter of Sofia's plight in the midst of the flood transfixed the world. As water engulfed the lowlands of Mozambique, torrential rains got the blame for the inundation. But matters were made worse by the operators of dams upstream in South Africa, Botswana and Zimbabwe, who had kept their reservoirs almost full at the start of the rainy season.

When the floodwaters came down the rivers, dams that promised to provide flood protection became a lethal liability. Dozens of dams were washed away. The resulting floodwaters came as a surprise to people downstream, who thought the dam protected them against floods.

Most dams are built with the promise that they will capture floodwaters from the rivers that they barricade. But one of the hidden secrets of dams is how often they make floods. This happens because of the contradictory hydrological requirements of the different uses to which dams are put. In order to catch floods, reservoirs need to be kept empty; whereas for most day-to-day operations, like feeding irrigation systems and city taps or generating hydroelectricity, they need to be kept as full as possible. Sensitive dam managers try to reconcile these aims. But, says Bryan Davies, a river ecologist from the University of Cape Town who watched the buildup to the Mozambique floods in 2000, put it: "The tendency everywhere is to store like hell when you can."

In times of very high rainfall, a dam's very capacity to capture water becomes a menace. As the reservoir fills to the brim, its operators are faced with the choice of risking the catastrophic failure of their dam if it overfills, or of making emergency releases of water down spillways. Often they leave it too late to make the fateful decision. The result is releases that are far greater and more sudden than would have happened during natural river flooding.

Nobody keeps proper records, but it is increasingly clear that inept dam management is contributing to a growing toll of flood catastrophes around the world. And many fear "the big one"—a major disaster in which thousands die after a dam bursts or panicking operators release a huge volume of water to save their pride and joy. The risks are greatest when natural sponges on river catchments like forests and wetlands are being destroyed; when dams are designed with poor knowledge about the history of floods on the rivers they block; and when climate change is making all hydrological statistics useless anyway. All three applied in Mozambique.

Because nobody knows what the "worst flood" might be, dams are often built without adequate spillways for emergency releases. A World Bank survey in India in 1995 found two that could cope with only one-seventh of what its experts estimated to be the possible peak flows. For these, said the report's author, William Price, "the consequences of dam failure during a major flood would have to be described with some adjective beyond disastrous." Perhaps he had in mind India's worst dam failure, in 1979, when the Machu II dam in Gujarat drowned two thousand people.

One of the Indian dams the Bank labelled a disaster waiting to happen was the Hirakud dam on the River Mahanadi in Orissa.

When Sir Hawthorne Lewis, the British colonial governor, laid the foundation stone back in 1946, he promised that it would provide a "permanent solution" to floods on the Mahanadi. Wrong. The dam's managers regularly kept the reservoir too full. And ever since, far from disappearing, the frequency of serious floods in the river's delta has more than doubled. In July 2001, when engineers made emergency releases from the dam, eighty people drowned and two hundred villages were inundated. Two years later, more than sixty died.

The failings of Indian dams are not unusual. In 1998, the *China Daily* reported engineers' fears that thousands of that country's dams were at risk of catastrophic failure. Quoting unnamed experts, it said that "most of the old dams built in the fifties and sixties are seriously deformed [and] are all threatened by the hidden danger of dam collapse." It suggested that politicians were more keen on building "new star dams dazzling people's eyes" than on repairing old ones, which "have been forgotten."

In half a century, 322 Chinese dams had failed, the agency said. Failures included the world's worst dam disaster. It happened one hot August night back in 1975. The operators of the 120-metre-high Banqiao dam in Henan province in central China believed they had nothing to fear when a typhoon hit the hills behind their dam and the River Ru swelled. Their manuals said the dam could survive a once-in-a-thousand-years flood on the river. But, unknown to them, another dam upstream was getting into difficulties. And shortly after midnight, the upstream dam burst, emptying 120 million cubic metres of water down the river. When the water reached the Banquiao dam, it gave way under the onslaught, unleashing half a billion cubic metres of water, mud and masonry downstream.

One woman, so the Chinese later reported, leapt clear with the cry, "The river dragon has come." The water formed a wall of water twelve kilometres wide and six metres high, travelling downstream at upwards of fifty kilometres an hour and crashing into the town of Huaibin with the force of a tsunami. Estimates of the death toll that night vary from 80,000 to 200,000 people.

But such was Chinese secrecy back in the 1970s that it was years before the outside world learned of this man-made holocaust.

Hurricane Mitch hit Central America in October 1998. It was the most destructive storm in the western hemisphere in two hundred years and dumped record amounts of rain onto steep hillsides saturated by a month of heavy rain. Landslides and flash floods turned small mountain streams into torrents that killed at least ten thousand people. But many died because of the extra force and suddenness of torrents unleashed as dams collapsed.

Records of the night Mitch struck Tegucigalpa, the capital of Honduras, are less than complete. But when I visited the country six weeks later, I met many people who described how a "wall of water" had struck poor, low-lying shanty areas in the south of the city shortly before midnight. Several hundred died there. Scientists from the US Geological Survey discovered that minutes before the wall of water struck, the Los Laureles reservoir had burst, unleashing floods along the River Guacerique as far as the city's southern suburbs. Then, on another stream south of the city, the Concepcion dam overflowed, causing what the operators' log called a "high-flow release" through the heart of the capital that lasted for seven hours.

Similar explanations may lie behind other mysterious "walls of water" that hit other Honduran towns that night. I visited Pespire, a town of 30,000 people in the south of the country. It suffered forty-one dead and lost more than three hundred houses after the level of the river that runs beneath the town rose by some fifteen metres within a matter of minutes. Nobody could remember anything remotely like it from the normally placid river. But I noticed that the town was immediately downstream of a dam that would normally have impounded floodwaters. The dam was physically intact. But had operators made emergency releases? Did the dam trigger the disaster in Pespire that night?

In the chaos of heavy rains and already swollen rivers, it is often far from clear where nature's influence ends and mankind's begins. Even so, it seems odd that nobody has tried to assess the scale of disasters caused by flood releases from dams. So, alerted by what I heard in Honduras, I carried out a survey of media reports of dam-related flood incidents round the world over the three years after Mitch. What I found was, I think, at least a cause for concern.

A year after Mitch, the annual rains were unusually heavy in West Africa. Dams were in trouble. Engineers in the landlocked state of Burkina Faso opened spillways to relieve water pressure on the Bagre dam on the River Nakambe. Downstream, across the border in northern Ghana, forty-eight people died during the resulting sudden river surge.

Later in the month, large areas of central Nigeria were submerged after operators opened the spillways of Nigeria's giant Kainji dam, unleashing part of the contents of its 130-kilometre reservoir down West Africa's biggest river, the Niger. It later emerged that the operators had been jittery about the thirty-year-old dam after it got too full and almost collapsed during floods the previous year. If that had happened, it would have washed away the town of Kainji. So when the floods returned in 1999, they took no chances. They opened the spillways. Sixty died and 80,000 refugees needed food and shelter as their homes and fields were under water.

The following month, on the other side of the Atlantic, media reports held that releases of water from La Esparanza dam in the Mexican state of Hidalgo were implicated in floods that left a hundred dead. No follow-up study seems to have established the truth of these claims.

Then came the Mozambique floods, when rivers such as the Limpopo and Zambezi broke their banks, flooding farmland over a wide area of southern Africa. Nobody would claim that dams were responsible for all, or even most, of the flooding. The rainfall was truly exceptional. For three months the Limpopo valley, which drains out of the African interior, received five times its usual rainfall. At the height of the floods enough water flowed down the Limpopo in just eight days to fill all twenty-four dams in the river's catchment five times over. But, said local hydrologists, if the reservoirs had been left empty before the rains, the capture of two days of floodwaters could have made all the difference in some places.

And events were equally confused farther north, on the Zambezi, the largest river in southern Africa. The lake behind the Kariba dam is more than 250 kilometres long. Through the wet weeks of early 2000 it filled rapidly, until engineers relieved the pressure on the dam by opening three of its five spillways. Initially there was much local excitement. People had never seen anything like it and rushed from miles around to watch. But some 12,000 people living along the riverbank below the dam saw the water surge through their fields, grain stores, schools and villages. The Mozambique town of Zumbo, 250 kilometres away over the border, was flooded.

The Zambezi River Authority argued that "if the Kariba dam had not been there, the areas downstream would have been subjected to worse floods." That may be true. But Kariba's builders had promised that the dam would protect communities against floods. Taking them at their word, tens of thousands of people had moved onto its flood plain below the dam. The authorities obviously took a similar view of the protection offered by the dam. As the BBC reported at the time, "There seems to be no contingency plan in place to help people or businesses....A year's supply of food for thousands of people who farm along the banks of the Zambezi was wiped out in just nine hours."

In August 2000, monsoon floods in the Indian state of Andhra Pradesh cracked the Roxsagar dam. Thousands of labourers rushed in to mend the breach but retreated as ever more water gushed through and surged towards the state capital, Hyderabad. Nearly 40,000 people fled as water filled their homes.

A month later and 1,500 kilometres north, in West Bengal, engineers made emergency releases from several dams during a flood that left more than a thousand dead. The worst flooding happened around the town of Murshidabad, through which dam releases on the River Mayurakshi flowed, and on the lower reaches of the River Damodar, where, at the height of the floods, 40 per cent of the water came from emergency dam releases. The floods soon spread into Bangladesh. Wide areas of low-lying land along the border disappeared under three metres of water. In Bangladesh, water officials said only those rivers coming from India were in flood. "We consider this flood unnatural and unprecedented," said the director of the country's Water Development Board.

Every year, there are more such incidents. In August 2001 over a hundred people died in northern Nigeria after water was released without warning from two dams, sweeping away two hundred villages. The following year, twenty people died in Syria when a dam on the River Orontes burst, burying more than a hundred square kilometres of farmland in river mud. And in 2003, it was Nigeria's turn again. At least thirty-nine died after the state power company again sought to save a dam by opening spillways. The incident, on the Shiroro dam, was a virtual repeat of a similar incident at the same dam in 1999.

In February 2005, more than a hundred people drowned after a 300-metre-wide dam burst in heavy rains on the Shadikor River in western Pakistan—just two years after a previous dam on the same site had been washed away. The following month dozens more died when a dam burst in southeast Pakistan. And in April, on the River Narmada in western India, more than sixty pilgrims camping on the river's banks were washed to their deaths when managers of the Indira Sagar dam upstream released water downstream without warning.

Considered individually, each case might be put down to bad luck or poor management. Cumulatively, however, they tell a different story. It is that when they are needed most, dams designed and promoted as preventing floods often end up creating floods.

20

SAVING THE GORGES

Sometimes opposing the constructing of dams is just a matter of aesthetics: about the protection of scenery. Anti-dam campaigning in the US began with lovers of wilderness denouncing the New Deal dam enthusiasts and fighting to protect their most treasured vistas. David Brower, a veteran US environmentalist who founded Friends of the Earth at the end of the 1960s, began the movement and helped secure its most celebrated victory, preventing the drowning of the Grand Canyon on the Colorado River. It is almost unbelievable today, but the flooding of this national monument in order to generate hydropower nearly happened.

The anti-dam flame soon crossed the Atlantic in the hands of people like Brice Lalonde, who was one of Brower's first lieutenants in Europe, establishing Friends of the Earth in France. One of that organization's greatest European achievements was to save one of the continent's last wild rivers, and France's longest—the Loire. By chance I was there in the mountains of the Massif Central in the January snow, when the victory was won.

It was a wonderfully French occasion. Clutching a basket loaded with bread, wine and cheese, Jacqueline Arnould erupted from a victory press conference in a bar in the Auvergne hill town of Le Puy to declare, "*C'est une grande victoire!*" And, for my benefit: "We are the poorest region of France and they thought they could walk over us. But we have won. There will be no dam

in the Loire gorge." And with that, she set off to begin the celebrations on a snow-covered campsite at the end of a beautiful
gorge, where the dam was to have been built.

There, in the days before cell phones, she was able to break
the good news in person to three burly French youths who had
stuck to their post, keeping the camp permanently occupied
through some of the coldest weather in the Massif Central for
years. As the winter sun disappeared behind the gorge, they were
settling in for another night under siege. They could scarcely
believe it was over.

Le Puy has for centuries been best known for its twin volcanic
peaks, one capped by a statue of the Virgin Mary. Now it had
won a famous victory for Les Verts, the new green movement carrying all before it in France in the mid-1990s. The argument was
won on a legal technicality. A tribunal had concluded that the
local prefect had exceeded his powers when he granted permission for a seventy-metre hydroelectric dam that would have
flooded the famous gorge at Serre de la Fare outside Le Puy. For
such an important project, only central governments could grant
approval. But with Lalonde in the environment ministry and the
Green Party that month at 22 per cent in the national polls, central government was in no mood for giving the go-ahead.
Everyone knew the battle had been won.

During its two years, the campsite had attracted international media coverage for the preservation of the "Loire
Sauvage." Twice, camp residents had physically stood in the
paths of bulldozers sent to begin work on the site. But for that
heroism, the legal decision would have come too late to halt
construction, said the cheese-bearing Jacqueline. And this, for
her, was a family affair. Her husband, Jean-François, was president of the SOS Loire Vivante committee, and her son, Martin,
ran the campaign office above a hair salon in the town. Sales of
T-shirts and badges had been so brisk they opened a shop. But
much of the funding had come from WWF in Paris. Campaigners
believed a turning point came when the fund's international
president, the Duke of Edinburgh, had visited mud flats at

nearby Bec d'Allier and declared that the dam would destroy this magnet for wintering birds.

The campsite celebrations on victory night were all goats' cheese and Gallic emotion. A girl who had kept vigil with the boys through the cold winter danced with an elderly, Gauloise-smoking peasant farmer. Somebody wondered what would happen to the camp dog, bought for a thousand francs from an angry pro-dam farmer who had chained it up for daring to visit the camp. The campaign lawyer quaffed wine, shrugged and smiled his most enigmatic smile at the suggestion that politicians from Paris, even the sainted Brice Lalonde himself, might have engineered the surprise comeuppance for the city bosses of Le Puy. But this was France. We all reckoned we knew the score.

I had stumbled on the victory celebration when I made a brief visit for the *Guardian* newspaper in London, intending to report on the second anniversary of the protest camp. Before we heard the news a penurious local musician, Henri-Claude Portal, had spent the day showing me the threatened sights of the gorge. We had visited the haunts of kingfishers, seen breathtaking views of the gorge and dropped in on the tiny stone village of Colempce, which would have been drowned by the dam.

There, housewife Andrée Lyotard sat at her kitchen table and denounced neighbours who had taken offers of compensation and left. She almost spat the name of the village mayor, who wanted the dam built because it would attract cash from Paris. Afterwards we clambered down the hillside to a remote stone hut by the river, from where Portal solemnly collected water from a spring and talked about his music. "The river provides me with inspiration," he said. His new CD, *Serre de la Fare*, carried a picture of the gorge on the cover. I still have it. And the people of the Loire still have their gorge.

In China, they have been trying to save not one gorge but three. The Three Gorges that form a long corridor along the middle reaches of the River Yangtze have been among China's most treasured scenes, pictured by its artists for more than a thousand years. And yet, in pursuit of modernization and industrialization in today's China, such sentiment has counted for little. Since the 1940s, China's engineers and politicians have dreamed of inserting a plug in the last of the gorges and flooding all three to create a reservoir more than 300 kilometres long. As a totem of modernism, it bears a resemblance to the US's scheme to dam the Grand Canyon. But unlike the US, China went ahead.

The project, now under construction, will create the world's largest hydroelectric power station on the world's fourth-largest river. And, its engineers claim, it will simultaneously protect the lower reaches of the Yangtze flood plain from the catastrophic floods that have plagued it over the centuries. But opponents see it in a very different light. And their motives have as much to do with high politics as protecting scenery. They are fighting Communist totalitarian rule as much as a dam.

The world of Dai Qing, China's foremost opponent of China's foremost dam, could not be more different from that of Jacqueline Arnould and her wine-and-cheese party on the banks of the Loire. "For me, the campaign against the Three Gorges is a matter of the integrity of science," she told me when we met in Beijing in the winter of 2001. "I became involved when many of the big names in Chinese science opposed the dam."

Dai Qing was born into the Communist military elite. Her father was an early Chinese Communist, a card-carrier before the party took over in Beijing. He worked for Lenin in Moscow in the 1920s, and was a high-level military intelligence officer until he was killed in prison at the end of the Second World War. Then, his daughter came under the wing of another top man, Marshall Ye, who sent her to study military engineering. She was groomed for the top. On graduation, she became a rocket scientist working on gyroscopes for guided missiles. That stopped during the Cultural Revolution in the 1960s, when scientists were sent to work in the fields. But afterwards she returned, this time developing spy cameras and importing Western computers to take them apart and see how they worked. She was also briefly a spy, but had to leave when her boss was caught in a CIA honey trap.

That was when she became a journalist. Her involvement with the Three Gorges saga began in 1986, when scientists from the Chinese Peoples' Political Consultative Committee, a government advisory board that normally toes the party line, went to the Yangtze to report on the scheme. The scientists came back adamantly opposed to the dam. The reservoir would flood huge areas of fertile farmland and ancient archaeological sites, they said. The resettlement of around 1.5 million people from the valley on the surrounding hilly land would create destitution over a wide area of southern China.

And all for what? The dam would quickly silt up because of all the soil coming down the river from the eroded uplands, they said. And it would not even control flooding downstream, as the politicians claimed, because most of the flood-prone arms of the Yangtze reach the main stem below the dam. The electricity would be too expensive to sell in the country's new privatized power markets. And far from improving navigation on the Yangtze, the dam would cause the harbour in the huge city of Chongqing at the head of the reservoir to silt up.

This defiance was, says Dai Qing, "the first time under Communism that scientists as a group had started to say something different from the official view." The Communist Party leadership responded in the only way it knew. It declared a news blackout on the dissent. But a leader of the group, an old friend of her mother, had invited Dai Qing to go along to the meetings of the scientists as they prepared their explosive evidence against the dam. This was a time of growing political tension in China in the run-up to the demonstrations at Tiananmen Square in 1989. And as that crisis came to its head, Dai Qing decided to publish the scientists' findings in defiance of the ban.

She conducted nine interviews with the dissident scientists, and assembled them into a *samizdat* book called *Yangtze, Yangtze*. Some of the interviewees lost their jobs as a result. But the publication stimulated widespread opposition to the dam both in China and outside. I had first learned about the book and about Dai Qing when a London publisher asked me for advice on whether to publish it in English. Following publication in the West, the campaign to save the Three Gorges became an international cause célèbre. By 1992 the furore reached the National Peoples' Congress, where a third of the delegates defied the leadership to vote against the scheme.

Dai Qing left the Communist Party during the massacres at Tiananmen Square. She tore up her party card on the day the tanks rolled over the student protesters in their tents. This made her finally an outsider. And her writings on Three Gorges gave her a dangerously high profile. She was castigated by political leaders as a "bourgeois liberal," arrested and held without charge for almost a year. Since then, she has had her freedom. She is allowed out of the country, and has become a frequent visitor to the US, lecturing about Three Gorges and China's water policies.

But she is still barred from publishing her work in China.

I first met her on the Japanese march with Dan Beard. There she discovered that even the engineers of BuRec, who had first tutored Chinese engineers on constructing the Three Gorges dam sixty years ago, now opposed the scheme. But China is not the US, and she has not been able to stop the dam. Its reservoir will be full later in the decade. She is convinced, however, that its technical failings mean the dam is destined to be a failure. "I will continue my opposition even when the dam is finished," she insisted to me. "Even then, it will be better if the dam is not used. And a lot will depend on how it is used." The scientists who sparked the debate have petitioned for the completed reservoir to be only partially filled. That way, she says, it need displace only half as many people, but could still get 85 per cent of the planned electricity.

The authorities seem to have decided that Dai Qing is safe enough when abroad. But they keep a close eye on her at home. As we talked in a quiet hotel lobby in Beijing for a magazine interview, she spotted a shadowy listener at the next table. Was he a government spy? Was he a casual sneak looking for a useful tidbit to pass on? It is still dangerous being an anti-dams campaigner in China.

PART SIX

WHEN THE RIVERS RUN DRY ...
MEN GO TO WAR OVER WATER

21

PALESTINE: POISONING THE WELLS OF PEACE

Ahmad Qot is a poor Palestinian farmer. He spends between three and four hours every day walking his donkey to get water for his nine children and five farm animals. I met him by chance at a shaft to an ancient tunnel that channels water from the hills above Madama, his village on the West Bank near Nablus. He repeatedly dropped his bucket down the shaft and hauled it up, gradually filling a long line of plastic containers with water. His donkey stood patiently waiting to be laden with the containers. "I come here three times a day," he said. "I have three cows and two sheep; this is the only water for them."

His life is breathtakingly meagre. He has less than a hectare of land. He grows a little wheat, to make bread, and some vegetables. His sheep provide his family with meat. His cattle produce milk that he sells in the village. And the lifeline for his animals is a shaft in the road—a shaft with a beautifully made stone surround that has been deeply grooved by centuries of ropes hauling buckets. Centuries of people getting by as Ahmad is doing.

The villagers say the shaft and tunnel are "Roman," which means no more than that they are very old. The tunnel concentrates seep from tiny springs in the hills and brings their flow to the village. Similar tunnels are to be found all across the West Bank. Hydrologists call them spring tunnels. They are an ancient water-catching system that even many Palestinians know little about. Many have dried up as water tables have fallen, but the tunnel at Madama runs all year.

Ahmad and a handful of the poorest in Madama still use it to water their animals. But it has lately become polluted. "Sometimes even the donkeys won't drink it," Ahmad said. Certainly his family cannot drink it. So most days Ahmad makes another, much longer journey out of the village, across a road that leads to a nearby Jewish settlement and past a military checkpoint to another spring in the neighbouring village of Iraqburin. The journey takes two or three hours—much longer if the soldiers hold him up.

"Some days the military let me pass with my donkey, and some days they don't," he said. "Sometimes when I am coming back, they just pour the water on the ground. They never say why. Once they just drove a tank over my water containers." He cannot understand such behaviour. "Water is life." He has no choice but to make the journey, though. He cannot afford the two dollars for a cubic metre of water charged by the driver of the village's tanker, who also collects water from Iraqburin and delivers to the wealthier inhabitants of his village.

The reality of daily life for Palestinian villagers on the West Bank is told in such stories of their fight for the most basic of resources. It doesn't explain the continuing poisonous dispute between Jews and Palestinians in these hills, but it does go to the heart of the daily misery the dispute brings.

The two thousand inhabitants of Madama used to have another source of water. There is a spring two-thirds of the way up another hillside—two-thirds of the way towards an Israeli settlement, high on a ridge, called Yitshar. There is a pipe connected to the spring that takes water down to a tank outside the Madama mosque. It was the village's main source of clean and free water, until the spring became polluted. Everybody in the village assumes the pollution comes from the Israeli settlement—and I could see no other likely cause. Nor could Geoff Graves from

Oxfam, my guide in the village. "We have twice repaired the head of the spring after Yitshar settlers damaged it. The last time we fished soiled nappies out."

Ayed Kamal, head of the Madama village council, told me: "Sometime the settlers shoot at us when we go up the hill. Three of us have had bullet wounds. They killed a donkey." Graves said the settlers, who number between 700 and 1,000, have even shot at Oxfam workers repairing the spring. The settlers on the ridge seem to have decided that they are in danger from potential terrorists if they allow the villagers to climb up the hill to their spring. But, seen from below, their actions are plain vindictive.

Ayed also works as a teacher in the village school, whose outside walls are daubed with pictures of Islamic martyrs and a huge mural of a giant lake surrounded by palm trees. In Madama, he says, getting water is a constant problem. Most families have installed cisterns to collect the winter rains from their roofs and store it underground. "But this water doesn't usually last beyond about May. After that, we all have to buy in water delivered by tankers if we can afford it, or brought by donkey if we can't," he says. But sometimes you cannot even pay for water. The Friday before my visit, a curfew imposed by soldiers on the settler road prevented the water tanker coming in.

There is no lack of outside concern at the situation in villages like Madama. Aid flows in. Oxfam has built a water-recycling system at the school. Thanks to its efforts, a series of pipes collect water from the school sinks and pump it into a tank on the roof, from where it flushes a newly repaired toilet block for girls. Before, girls either went home to use the dismal facilities or didn't go to school at all. But, despite such projects, the villagers feel hemmed in here, by the unknown settlers on the hill above, by the soldiers on the road outside the village, and by the many other checkpoints that can make a brief trip to Nablus just five kilometres away into a twelve-hour odyssey.

My host advised against trying to visit Yitshar, so I Googled it. The first two references said it all, I imagine. The first, put out by the Israeli Terror Victims Association, listed two people,

Shlomo Liebman, aged twenty-four, and Harel Bin-Nun, eighteen, who had been "shot and killed in an ambush by terrorists while on patrol at the Yitshar settlement" on August 5, 1998. The second, from the Israeli Information Centre for Human Rights in the Occupied Territories, was a testament by a local Palestinian, who had been forced to abandon his olive groves by settlers from Yitshar.

There is clearly mutual fear and hostility here. But while in Yitshar there is running water in the taps at all times and sprinklers in the gardens, in Madama times are tougher. Had the villagers ever personally met the settlers? I asked. No, they said, laughing. "They just arrived on the hill. They have never come to introduce themselves."

Most Palestinian villages on the West Bank tell similar stories of conflict in which water plays a central role. I visited Deir Sharaf, another village outside Nablus, where they complained that two Israeli settlements overlooking the village had taken their water. Farther east, Beit Fureik and Beit Dajan are two overgrown villages with a combined population of 15,000 but no piped water. They rely on old wells and more than a hundred rooftop cisterns, installed with aid from the UN Development Programme, to store the winter rains. In summer, tankers bring them water through the security checks that dot the roads to floodlit hilltop settlements, many of them built on the olive groves of the villagers. Here too Palestinians get shot at if they try to tend their remaining orchards. And here too the Israelis have reason to fear. A Palestinian who blew himself up at a bus stop in Tel Aviv on Christmas Day 2003 was from Beit Fureik. The next day the Israeli army entered the village and shot holes in many of the cisterns.

The West Bank has few permanent rivers. But the dolomite hills are honeycombed with caves and crevices, where rainwater collects. Hydrologically, there are three aquifers beneath the West Bank. The largest is beneath the western slopes and drains towards Israel proper and the Mediterranean. The second, around Nablus, drains north and supplies much of Galilee. The third drains east to the Jordan Valley. Collectively they are called the mountain aquifers. They are virtually the only source of water for Palestinians, and they are at the heart of the conflict between Israelis and Palestinians over water. Here is how it happened.

In the 1950s, when the Palestinians lived here under Jordanian tutelage, the West Bank seemed to have ample water. Far more rain was falling here and filling the aquifers than the Palestinians needed. The excess water in the western aquifer gushed from springs along the boundary between the West Bank and Israel. Those springs were the sources of two of Israel's largest rivers, the Yarkon and Taninim, which flowed west into the Mediterranean. But as the Israeli population grew, they began to tap the water of the western aquifer by sinking well-fields close to the border. Soon they were taking far more of the water under the West Bank than the Palestinians ever had, without ever actually setting foot on the West Bank.

"By the early 1960s, we were taking about 300 million cubic metres from the aquifer and the Arabs about 20 million. Between us we were fully utilizing the aquifer, plus a little more," says Ze'ev Golani, who later became an Israeli official on the West Bank. The water table in the western aquifer began to fall and the two rivers died. The Yarkon's bed became an open sewer for the fast-growing communities of the Tel Aviv urban area. So, says Golani, "When Israel took control on the West Bank after the Six Day War in 1967, we said there should be no additional pumping by anyone—certainly not for agriculture. And not much has changed since."

In that way, almost by accident, Israel came to take the lion's share of the western aquifer and, in the name of conservation, decreed that it should take the lion's share forevermore.

Israeli hydrological rule on the West Bank since 1967 has been absolute and unyielding. Across most of the West Bank, Palestinians have been largely forbidden to sink new wells, and rarely get permission to replace old ones. Before the Israelis took control, says Clemens Messerschmid, a German geologist working for the UK Department for International Development and the Palestinian Water Authority, the West Bank Palestinians had 774 wells. Thirty-five years later, only 321 are still operating. The rest have either dried up or are off limits in areas requisitioned by the Israeli military. Israel even prevents Palestinians from expanding use of the estimated five hundred springs and spring tunnels. Its only concession is to sell water to villagers with piped distribution networks. But they are in the minority and constantly fear being cut off.

As the existing springs and wells deteriorate and their population grows, Palestinians find they have less water per capita than when the Israelis invaded. The World Health Organization warns that poor water supplies are behind rising rates of water-borne diseases among Palestinians. Typically, today each Palestinian has less than a quarter as much water as his Israeli neighbour. "We used to bathe and wash clothes every day, now it is every two or three days. We'd love to have water for a garden, trees, even a pool like the Jews do in the settlements," said Siham Khabirat, a mother of six in al-Dhahriyeh. This is hydrological apartheid.

And often Palestinians pay more for their limited supply than do Israelis. Tanker water typically costs two dollars for a cubic metre. A study in the villages round Nablus found that families spend between 20 and 40 per cent of their income on buying water. The highest spending was in Salfit district, which has some of the most productive wells in the country. But most, says Messerschmid, have been confiscated by the Israelis to supply their settlements.

Many outsiders believe that Israel only annexed the water of the West Bank when it took over the territory after the Six Day War. In fact Israel did not have to occupy the West Bank to take the water. It was doing so years before the war. But the subsequent occupation did stop Palestinians from developing their water resources and ensured that Israelis could continue to take the lion's share.

The Oslo Accord, signed by both sides in 1995 as part of the peace process, cemented the existing unequal share-out of the mountain aquifers. It allowed Palestinians 57 cubic metres of water per person per year, whereas Israelis get 246 cubic metres each. But the Palestinians pinned their hopes on what they saw as a promise by the Israelis contained in the accord to develop with the Palestinians new sources of water in the region, and particularly to exploit the eastern aquifer. This had the attraction of being the only water resource in the region entirely within Palestinian borders. "It has been the focus and the hope of the Palestinian Water Authority," says a local British water consultant Jennifer Moorehead. Foreign donors came in to help the Palestinians realize their dreams.

But this hydrological peace dividend is proving to be an illusion. There are growing doubts about how much water is in the eastern aquifer—and even more about how much it will be possible to exploit. "The only good places for drilling on the east side are down in the Jordan valley. But it's just not economic," says Messerschmid. "The water table is 600 to 800 metres down and there have been so many dry boreholes that, at a thousand dollars a metre, the aid agencies don't want to drill any more."

The US government's aid agency, USAID, which has been drilling deep wells to supply Hebron and Bethlehem, agrees. Alvin Newman, head of water resources at the agency's Tel Aviv office, says: "We are getting to the end on the eastern aquifer. If you are pumping water 800 metres out of the ground and then another 1,000 metres uphill to taps in Nablus, that involves very big costs. In fact you can't buy water pumps big enough to do it. We buy oil industry pumps."

Most outside experts put the maximum potential of the eastern aquifer for Palestine at 20 to 30 million cubic metres a year, says Moorehead. That is only about a quarter what was envisaged under the Oslo Accord. The Israelis disagree, in public at least. Yossi Gutman, chief hydrologist for the Israeli water utility Mekorot, says: "Yes, there is a problem in some areas, but I believe we could pump water up to Palestinian villagers. Maybe the Palestinians don't want to invest in this project." But if so, they are not alone. And for now, Palestinian water officials deeply regret the concessions that they made in Oslo. They don't see how they can supply their people without getting their hands on a greater share of the western aquifer. Yet all the time their share seems to be diminishing.

The latest problem is Israel's security fence, which has cut off dozens of Palestinian villages from their wells. The fence nominally follows the "green line," the internationally accepted border between Israel and Palestine, sealing off the West Bank from Israel proper. But it does not follow the border precisely. The "fence" is in fact a complex cordon sanitaire of trenches, barbed wire and electrified fences, turrets, infrared sensors and a security road. It is up to a hundred metres wide and constructed entirely on requisitioned land on the Palestinian side. And in places it plunges for tens of kilometres into Palestinian territory in order to keep Jewish settlements on the West Bank on the Israeli side of the barrier. A number of Palestinian villages have found themselves on the "wrong" side of the fence and others find that, while they are on the Palestinian side, their wells have disappeared behind the fence.

Israel says it planned the fence to keep suicide bombers from gaining unfettered access to Israeli towns. But hydrologically it could not be more divisive. The most productive wells on the West Bank, for both Israelis and Palestinians, lie in a strip of land either side of the green line. So, says Messerschmid, "The wall has taken from the Palestinians many of their best wells." Most notably, at Baqa ash Sharqiya, near Tulkarem, wells supplying half a million cubic metres of water a year to fifteen villages are now on the Israeli side of the walls, while the villages are on the Palestinian side.

In mid-2004, Messerschmid calculated that wells and springs that once delivered five million cubic metres of water a year to Palestinians sat on the wrong side of the barrier. If so, that represents getting on for a quarter of the water the Palestinians once took from the prized western aquifer. Some have concluded that the barrier is a conspiracy to appropriate water. In truth, says Messerschmid, the hydrological implications are probably just an accident of Israeli's security agenda. But that doesn't make them any less painful.

The conflict is having longer-term effects on water supplies in the West Bank that could be catastrophic for both communities. In the fractious frontier lands of the West Bank few care these days what happens to the rubbish and sewage. Both the settlers and the Palestinians pour their waste into old quarries or down the banks of wadis. Graves has seen sewage trucks discharge their toxic load into cracks in the rocks that lead straight to the aquifer. "Month by month, since the intifada and the restrictions on movement on the West Bank, you can see the wadis filling up with sewage," says Messerschmid. "In terrain like this, that means the waste water will go right into the aquifer." Drivers say constant checkpoints leave them little choice.

Outside Deir Sharaf, I saw a stream of raw sewage discharged from Nablus into the Wadi Zeimar, which recharges the western aquifer. In Ramallah, the current Palestinian administrative capital of the West Bank, the city sewage works is overloaded and gives effectively no treatment. But aid projects to build sewage-treatment works for these towns have fallen foul of the security crisis.

Though the Israeli settlers make up only a tenth of the total population, Friends of the Earth in Israel estimates that they may be responsible for a quarter of the sixty million cubic metres of untreated sewage that flows into the West Bank aquifers. "The settlements all discharge untreated waste water into the wadis," says Robin Twite, a former head of the British Council in Israel who is now head of the Israel Palestine Centre for Research and Information.

Israeli boreholes are deep and remain unpolluted. But in many places sewage is already polluting Palestinian springs and wells, causing yet more to be abandoned. At Nazlal'Isa, north of Tulkarem, artesian wells that bring water to the surface under pressure are laced with sewage. "They know the water is polluted, but they have no choice but to use it," Monther Hind, a Palestinian waste-water engineer, told me in his office in Ramallah. The sewer pipe that is leaking, he said, was on the other side of the security barrier. So the villagers could not repair it.

How, ask the Palestinians, are we expected to survive under such conditions? Why are we allowed to have only 20 per cent of the water that falls onto the West Bank? The Israelis, even in the depths of the intifada, agreed that these were valid questions. But while the Palestinians insist that the answer lies in giving them greater access to the aquifers, it emerged in 2004 that the Israelis have another plan: let them drink sea water.

Israel, which has been developing desalination for its own use, has drawn up a plan for a giant desalination plant on the Mediterranean coast that would be dedicated to supplying a network of pipes across the West Bank. It wants the US government to pay for the plant and pipes which could, it says, supply a wide area from Jenin in the far north of the territory to Ramallah in the south, including many of the 250 villages that currently rely on local springs and small wells for their water. Israel says its contribution would be to guarantee safe passage of the water across its territory. But it would only do this in return for an agreement that it can continue to take its current share of the waters of the West Bank—especially the western aquifer, the region's largest, cleanest and most reliable water source.

USAID, which would probably fund the scheme, puts the capital cost of the desalination plan at $800 million. But the running costs would also be high. Large amounts of energy would be needed both for desalination and for pumping the water up between 300 and 1,500 metres to the West Bank communities who need it.

Is this a viable solution? Uri Shamir, director of water research at the Israel Institute of Technology in Haifa, told a US House of Representatives Committee in mid-summer 2004 that the desalination project was "the only viable long-term solution" for supplying drinking water to the West Bank. Later, he told me that the project could be complete in five to seven years. "The plant will be funded by the world for the Palestinians. Israel will not be willing to carry this burden, and the Palestinians are not able to." Newman at USAID agreed.

But Palestinian negotiators are deeply uneasy about the plans being drawn up on their behalf. "Desalination cannot be a substitute for our rights of access to the western aquifer," says Nabil Sharif, chairman of the Palestinian Water Authority. Many outsiders share the unease. Tony Allan of the School of Oriental and African Studies in London, a leading authority on Middle East water, says, "Pumping desalinated water to the West Bank is not the best technical or economic option."

Even leading Israeli hydrologists are incredulous at the plan, which they say would cost up to $1 per cubic metre. "It would be foolish to desalinate water on the coast and push it up the mountains when there are underground water resources up there that cost only a third as much," says Arie Issar of Ben-Gurion University of the Negev, a leading Israeli hydrologist for half a century.

The Israeli water commissioner Shimon Tal sees the issue through the prism of domestic Israeli politics. "It is very difficult to take water from some consumers and give it to others," he says. "We can't solve the problem with natural water. We must start talking about production of desalination water for the West Bank. If we can co-operate to produce more water resources, then the negotiations on natural resources will be much easier."

When Israel first announced plans to build desalination works for its own needs, many liberal Israelis thought it could reduce Israel's demands on the West Bank aquifers, and allow their partial return to Palestinians. But the brute truth is that the current generation of Israeli water planners see desalination as a means of retaining control of those aquifers, not of relinquishing it. And with desalination plans also afoot to supply Gaza, they are looking forward to a future in which Israelis take all the natural freshwater and an independent Palestine becomes more dependent on desalination than almost any other nation in the world.

I spoke to many people on both sides about the potential for redistributing western aquifer water to Palestine. Former West

Bank water commissioner Golani believes Israel makes too much fuss about the western aquifer. "Arab pumping today is only a small fraction of total Israeli use," he says. "If they doubled consumption it would take perhaps ten years and still only be marginal. They should have a bigger share." Issar reckons it would not be unreasonable to increase the Palestinians' share of the water from the mountain aquifers to 50 per cent.

But so far the Israeli government has refused to countenance these ideas, even though they come from the heart of its hydrological establishment. It regards the western aquifer as the hydrological crown jewels of Palestine, a more vital resource for Israelis even than the land of the West Bank. Many Israeli leaders believe that they need to maintain an iron grip on the aquifer in order to keep their own taps flowing. And if that means keeping control of the West Bank itself to prevent new drilling by the Palestinians, then so be it.

But unless the Israelis are willing to unlock those jewels, then Ahmad Qot will go on dropping his bucket down into the Madama shaft—and the prospects for hydrological peace on the West Bank will continue to look dim.

22

THE FIRST MODERN
WATER WAR

In 1964, Israel hijacked the waters of the River Jordan. There is no other way of putting it. The Jordan Valley, a green desert strip that had been cultivated for longer than perhaps anywhere on Earth, was overnight deprived of most of its water. One day the River Jordan poured out of the Golan Heights, into the Sea of Galilee and on down the valley to the Dead Sea, as it had for millennia. The next day, a dam constructed by Israeli engineers blocked its outflow from the Sea of Galilee. Instead, a pumping station lifted the water out of the sea and into a three-metre-wide pipeline that delivered it the length of Israel.

Grabbing the Jordan's flow had been no easy task. Engineering heroics were involved. By the time the river reaches the Sea of Galilee it is more than 200 metres below sea level in a great fissure in the Earth's crust known as the Rift Valley. To divert that water to Israelis taps, it had to be lifted a total of 370 metres back up out of the Rift Valley. But it was accomplished. The pipe is known today as the National Water Carrier. It carries half a billion cubic metres a year and has become the major source of water for the whole of Israel.

The Carrier irrigates fields from Haifa in the north almost to the Egyptian border and fills taps from Tel Aviv to Jerusalem and the Israeli settlements on the occupied West Bank. Some is even sold to Palestinians living in the shadows of those settlements. The pumps that run the National Water Carrier take an eighth of the entire output of Israel's power stations. At the time of writing in early 2005, no fresh water had flowed out of the Sea of Galilee into the lower Jordan Valley since 1991. "It is an article of faith among Israeli hydrologists that to let the water into its own valley is a failure," says Gidon Bromberg of Friends of the Earth in Israel.

The emptying of the River Jordan may have been an engineering triumph, but it was also a geopolitical earthquake. It was done without the agreement of either Syria, which back in 1964 held the eastern shore of the Sea of Galilee, or Jordan, through which the river ran to the Dead Sea. It was as if France had one day unilaterally annexed the Rhine as it flowed out of Switzerland and pumped its contents over the hills to irrigate the plains of northern France—leaving a dribble of water to flow down Germany's main artery.

But this was not the end of the matter. Almost three years later, Israel and its Arab neighbours fought the Six Day War. Most histories of the war discuss its importance and motivation in terms of land and security. They often ignore water. Yet the simple fact is this: prior to the war, less than a tenth of the River Jordan's basin was within Israeli borders; by the end, it was almost entirely controlled by Israel. Israel had taken from Jordan all the land between its former eastern border and the River Jordan. And it had taken from Syria the Golan Heights, the mountains northeast of the Sea of Galilee where the headwaters of the River Jordan rise.

Ariel Sharon, who was a commander in that war and much later became prime minister, is unabashed about the hydrological motives of Israel in that war, though he said the other side started it. In the early 1960s, he wrote in his autobiography, Syria committed the first offensive act on the River Jordan by starting to dig a canal in the Golan Heights to divert the Jordan's headwaters away from Israel. "The Six Dar War really started on the day Israel decided to act against the diversion of the Jordan," he wrote. "While the border disputes were of great significance, the matter of water diversion was a stark issue of life and death."

The Six Day War was, by this account, the first modern water war. And Israel's victory in seizing the River Jordan and its catchment remains an essential backdrop to today's continuing conflicts. Israel today uses far more water than falls on its territory. And it has been able to do it because of its occupation of the West Bank and Golan Heights. That is how hard-line hydropoliticians in Israel see things, at any rate. But almost any final peace settlement with Israel's neighbours will require it to hand back some of its control and some of the water.

Israel has three main sources of water today. The first, used from the day the state was founded after the Second World War, is an aquifer that stretches along the coast from Haifa in the north to Gaza in the south. Ze'ev Golani, an Israeli water engineer and administrator for many years, drilled many wells into the coastal aquifer as the new state established plantations of water-guzzling crops such as cotton, tomatoes, avocados and the ubiquitous Jaffa orange. Soon, he says, the water table fell and—as the Palestinians have also discovered in Gaza—the porous rocks began to fill with salty sea water flowing in from the Mediterranean. Pumping was cut back, but even today much of the aquifer, which supplies up to a fifth of Israel's water, is too salty for drinking.

So in the late 1950s, Israel began to sink wells farther inland, near the Yarkon and Taninim springs. Those wells, as we have seen, tapped the edge of the western aquifer beneath the West Bank. By the early 1960s, the Israelis were overpumping here too. And that was when they decided to annex the third, and currently biggest, source of water for Israel—the River Jordan.

The fate of the coastal aquifer is essentially a private matter for Israelis. The fate of the West Bank aquifers is a matter of intense dispute between Israelis and Palestinians. But the fate of the Jordan involves many more players, including Syria, Jordan, the Palestinians and, from time to time, Lebanon. So much hangs on a river that in strictly hydrological terms is so small. From its sources in the Golan Heights to its former end point in the Dead Sea, it is barely three hundred kilometres long. It drains an area the size of New Jersey and, as Mark Twain once observed, "is not any wider than Broadway in New York." But throughout human history its waters have been vital in this region, and the current battle over who controls them is in deadly earnest. Here, when the river runs dry, war looms.

In all real senses, the River Jordan is now two rivers. One begins amid the snowy slopes of Mount Hermon on the Golan Heights—which is legally in Syria but since 1967 has been occupied by Israel. Its main source here is the River Dan, which bubbles to the surface in a spring amid glades of laurel, ash and fig close to the ancient Phoenician city of Laish. Two other streams, the Banias and the Hasbani, which begin life in Lebanon, join before it crashes down through a narrow gorge into the Rift Valley and the Sea of Galilee, and then passes into the netherworld of the National Water Carrier. The true end point of this river today is the Negev town of Mitzpe Ramon, a desolate hilltop outpost housing East European migrants, where the Carrier itself ends. Its water is at this point 1,100 metres higher than when it left the Sea of Galilee.

The second River Jordan is the former tributary known as the River Yarmuk. It rises in Syria and enters the bed of the Jordan ten kilometres downstream of the Sea of Galilee. The bed is at this point empty, but for a trickle of saline water from salty springs on the shores of the sea that Israel does not want to pollute its Carrier water. But the Yarmuk too is a shadow of its former self. Syria grabs half its flow in dozens of small dams on the headwaters. Jordan diverts much of what is left into the 100-kilometre King Abdullah Canal, which passes down the Jordan Valley on the east side of the river, irrigating fields as it goes. Even Israel takes some water from the Yarmuk, extracting it from the spot where the river joins the Jordan—a military outpost it grabbed in the final hours of the Six Day War in order to demolish a half-completed Jordanian dam there.

The Jordan Valley of biblical legend once carried more than a billion cubic metres of water a year to the Dead Sea. Now it carries less than a tenth as much. Most of it is sewage diluted with occasional winter storm flows out of Syria. The spot where John is supposed to have baptized Jesus is now a sewage seep behind the barbed wire of a military fence. And soon the dilution could be gone. In 2004, Syria and Jordan announced plans for a joint dam, dubbed the Unity Dam, to capture most of what remains of the Yarmuk's water. That, says Bromberg, "will probably take the last of the Jordan's regular flow"—the last of a river holy to Jews, Christians and Muslims alike, that has watered civilizations for ten thousand years.

And the Dead Sea? It is famously the saltiest large body of water on the planet. And the lowest. With next to no water entering it from the Jordan Valley, it is becoming saltier and lower. Its surface is at the time of writing 417 metres below the level of the world's oceans, and 25 metres below where it was half a century ago. It is falling by a metre every year. A third of the sea's surface area has gone and it has divided in two. Meanwhile, the retreating shoreline is leaving behind mud and quicksand that makes it unsafe to walk much of the shore. And thousands of sinkholes, some bigger than a car, have opened up as salt layers dry out along the shore and cavities collapse. Roads are buckling and bridges giving way. An area around the town of Engedi has been effectively abandoned. Dead indeed.

But hydropolitics are very much alive. Israel remains petrified that if it withdraws from the West Bank or the Golan Heights it will be powerless to prevent its neighbours from cutting off or contaminating its water supplies. It fears Palestinians could ruin the western aquifer, and that Syria might poison or divert the waters of the Jordan before it leaves the Golan Heights. Because of these fears, Israel fights harder to defend water even than it does land. In 2000, Bill Clinton came close to persuading Israel to hand back the Golan Heights to Syria as part of a peace package. But the deal failed, say diplomats, over who should have control of the tiny streams at the head of the River Jordan. Two years later, Israel threatened military action to force Lebanese engineers to stop supplying a few villages with water from the springs at the head of the Hasbani during a drought.

Some in Israel will not give a cubic metre, let alone a cubic kilometre. "Implementation of proposed peace initiatives would [mean] authority and control over almost 70 per cent of Israel's water supply would be transferred to the Arabs," says Martin Sherman, an influential political scientist at the University of Tel Aviv and author of a book on *The Politics of Water in the Middle East*. "Either Israel has sole control of her national water resources or her very survival is threatened," as one US pro-Israeli pressure group puts it.

Survival? How so? Well, Israel sees survival in terms of preserving a Western lifestyle. Sherman put it like this: "Frequent showers, swimming pools, well-groomed private gardens and public parks all involve water consumption, without which adequate standards of modern life cannot be attained." Ceding water for peace is not, in many Israelis' eyes, an option because it would threaten that lifestyle. End of argument.

This rhetoric makes it sound as if war is inevitable, as if water is in such short supply here that peace over such a vital resource is impossible. But further water wars are not inevitable. And water is not really in such short supply. Israeli hydrologists, if not their political classes, know that they have other options beyond fighting with their neighbours for water.

In the past five years, Israel has embarked on a program of constructing desalination works to provide drinking water from the sea. The first opened in 2005. Its water costs little more than the water expensively pumped up from the Sea of Galilee. A national plan agreed in mid-2004 will raise production of desalinated sea water to half the country's current water demand by the end of the decade, according to water commissioner Shimon Tal. Israel also has plans to increase substantially the amount of sewage that it recycles to irrigate its farms. Even so, Tal continued to maintain in 2004 that the country's water needs would rise steeply and that "redistribution of existing water resources [to Palestinians] is not a solution."

Many of his hydrologists disagree with him. They say no such rise in demand need occur. It is patently ridiculous, they say, for Israel to use two-thirds of its water to irrigate crops that generate less than 2 per cent of the country's GDP, even exporting "virtual water" in the form of oranges and tomatoes. If, to take an extreme option, Israel shut down its agriculture altogether, it could provide large amounts of water for Palestinians while improving its own hydrological security—with barely a blip in its own economic well-being. If it wants to maintain agriculture, they say, it can develop desalination further for drinking water and aim to use that water a second time by recycling treated sewage onto farmland. End of problem.

I talked about all this with Arie Issar, a man steeped in the history of Israeli water. More than half a century ago, before there was a Jewish state, his father sold ice with Arab friends in Jerusalem. As a young scientist in the new state of Israel, Arie helped green the Negev desert by finding new sources of water beneath the sands. He says there are still more to be found. But he has always preached careful use and sharing of the region's water.

We met one hot summer's day in Jerusalem. We looked out over the arid Jordan Valley, which his fellow hydrological engineers had emptied, and north to where Israeli soldiers prevent Palestinian villagers from sinking wells to meet their most basic human needs. An old Zionist idealist, he clearly mourned the new belligerence of the modern Israel. He confided that it had been in some respects a disaster for his people when they won the Six Day War.

"After that, we stopped developing the Negev, which was largely empty, and began to occupy the West Bank, which was already populated by the Palestinians. Now we are fighting over land and water in the West Bank when we could be developing the land and water in the Negev. We need to get back to that idea.

"People talk about water wars, but water can also be the basis for peace," he said. "And I think it can be so here. We Israelis use too much drinkable water for irrigation when farming is no longer important for our economy. We do crazy things like turning fresh water into oranges and exporting them. The Arabs need that water. They should have it."

23

SWORDS OF DAMOCLES

Southern Doda in Indian Kashmir is bandit country. Pakistan claims the region, and Muslim youths regularly cross the border into Pakistan for training, returning as guerrillas to fight Indian security forces. The war has been going on for more than a decade, with an estimated 50,000 dead. It usually only hits the headlines when foolhardy Western tourists get caught up in it. But some people believe that the world's first nuclear exchange could one day be triggered between India and Pakistan because of events up here in the foothills of the Himalayas. If so, it may not be over guerrillas or terrorists or even border incursions by regular soldiers. It could be over water, for Kashmir is the gateway through which Pakistan receives most of its water along tributaries of the River Indus.

Pakistan's 150 million people would be in trouble without the Indus. It runs the length of their country. Its waters irrigate most of their crops and generate half their electricity. But the Kashmir gateway is an Achilles' heel. India and Pakistan have been in armed conflict three times since the two states were formed on British withdrawal from the subcontinent in 1947, and the first conflict arose when India intervened in Kashmir to cut the flow of tributaries of the Indus on which Pakistan relied. Some in Pakistan fear that India may be about to do the same again.

After a decade of negotiations and skirmishes following the first conflict, the World Bank brokered the 1960 Indus Waters Treaty between the two countries. It bound them to share the flows of the river, with each taking the water from three tributaries. The flow of the River Chenab was among those going through Kashmir that were given to Pakistan, and it has since been the biggest source of water for Punjab, the breadbasket for Pakistan. But geography dictates that India always has the potential to stop Pakistan's lifeblood. And now, in the heart of southern Doda, Indian engineers are building a dam on the Chenab.

Pakistan sees the 160-metre-high billion-dollar Baglihar barrage, rising from the bed of the Chenab just before it crosses the border, as a clear breach of the treaty. India denies any breach. The dam is intended only to generate hydroelectricity, it says. It will not remove any water from the river, only channel its discharge downstream through turbines. India says Pakistan will get all the water it should. But Pakistan says India could, in a future crisis between the two nations, use the barrage to hold up the river's flow during the critical winter planting season. It could create famine in Pakistan.

Since 1999, when India unveiled its plans, Pakistan has been demanding that the dispute goes to arbitration. At the time of writing, India has refused. Instead it appears to be rushing to complete the dam. They are still talking. But the Indians are still building. And nobody can forget that, since the last dispute over these waters, both sides have developed nuclear weapons. Could this beautiful spot be the flashpoint for the unthinkable?

The stakes are huge. The Indus and its tributaries make up one of the world's largest river systems. Most of the water rises in the rain-soaked mountains of the Indian Himalayas and the Hindu Kush in eastern Afghanistan, before flowing through Kashmir and reaching arid Pakistan. For almost four decades the Indus Treaty has been held up as a model for other countries with water disputes. But in truth it has been enforced largely at the insistence of the World Bank, which refused to give either country loans for new dams unless they signed up.

Even without the Baglihar imbroglio, tensions over the treaty have been growing. In 2002, during the most recent standoff between India and Pakistan over Kashmir, some nationalist politicians and commentators in India were so angered by terrorist incursions that they talked of unilaterally taking back those Indus tributaries currently allotted to Pakistan. Most vociferous were the Kashmiri politicians, who want the tributaries that flow through their territory for their own people. Jasjit Singh, former director of the Institute of Defence Studies and Analyses in New Delhi, threatened, "Under normal circumstances, India would have continued to fulfil its moral obligation of sharing its water with Pakistan. But unusual circumstances call for unusual action."

Pakistan finds itself in the classic position of the downstream state—at the mercy of others upstream for its most basic resource. But from the Indian viewpoint things look rather different. As they see it, Pakistan got an extraordinarily good deal with the Indus Treaty. Both Afghanistan and India contribute far more water to the Indus system than Pakistan, but take far less. It is not their fault if Pakistan has hitched its wagon so firmly to the river. Moreover, they grumble, Pakistan uses its share of the river with spectacular inefficiency, while suffering no penalty. Having got itself in a position of undue dependence on the river, the Indians suggest, Pakistan would be better off not raising the spectre of a water war—a war from which it could only lose in a manner devastating for its huge and fast-growing population.

The whole world needs to care rather a lot about this obscure hydrological battle in a part of the world where few dare go. Though tensions reduced after Indian elections in 2004, the rumblings of what could become of the modern world's second water war never cease.

The dispute over the Indus is just one of a series of confrontations surfacing round the world as water shortages increase along shared rivers. A quick look at the atlas suggests the geographical extent of the problem. Most big rivers are shared. A host of upstream nations threaten to grab the water before equal numbers of downstream nations can fill their cups. The River Nile passes through ten countries. The Danube, Rhine, Niger and Congo all pass through nine, and the Zambezi through eight. Almost half the world's population lives in international river basins. Two-thirds of these basins have no treaties for sharing their water. Each is the scene for a potential water war.

Many downstream countries are dangerously dependent on external water supplies. Egypt is even worse off than Pakistan. Virtually rainless, it gets 97 per cent of its water from its numerous upstream neighbours on the Nile. The country's leaders say they will go to war if any of them starts diverting the river's water. That probably means Ethiopia, where three-quarters of the river's flow begins. The current international treaty on the Nile, a relic of British rule on the river, gives the lion's share of the flow to Egypt, a modicum to Sudan and none at all to anyone else, including Ethiopia. Clearly that situation cannot last forever; but will Egypt concede any of its current entitlement in order to reach peace on the Nile? It has not as yet conceded anything.

Africa—a continent of haphazard boundaries mostly created in the chaos of imperial conflict and maintained because anything else would bring chaos—is full of countries dependent on their neighbours for most of their water. It has eighty transboundary rivers. The isolationist Islamic republic of Mauritania in West Africa gets 95 per cent of its water from beyond its borders, mostly from the River Senegal coming out of Guinea and Mali. Tiny Gambia receives 86 per cent of its water from Senegal. And another desert state, Botswana, relies on others for 94 per cent of its water. The Limpopo comes from South Africa, and the Okavango rises in Angola and passes through Namibia before draining into a desert delta, a wildlife mecca where tourists contribute a tenth of Botswana's GDP.

Outside Africa, the situation is little better. Bangladesh, like Pakistan, receives more than 90 per cent of its water from India, which has built a barrage on the Ganges right on the border. Meanwhile, Syria and Iraq rely for most of their water on the Tigris and Euphrates Rivers flowing out of Turkey, which is building dams on both. During the first Gulf war, Turkey considered shutting the Ataturk dam on the Euphrates to put a hydrological squeeze on Iraq, though it never followed through.

All told, more than twenty nations round the world get in excess of half their water from their neighbours. And many should by rights get more than they do. Mexico receives virtually none of the flow of the Colorado River out of the US. Most of the water in the River Jordan disappears within Israel and never reaches the country named after it. The Illi has shrunk by two-thirds by the time it leaves China for Kazakhstan. The Karkeh, flowing west out of Iran, rarely makes it to Iraq anymore. Iran, meanwhile, rarely sees the Helmand flow west over the border from Afghanistan anymore. Given the extent of the damage caused by such disruption to natural river flows, it is perhaps a wonder that there have not been more out-and-out wars.

Many water disputes are simmering in places that few people have heard of and, for the moment at any rate, even fewer care about. They are concentrated particularly among the fractured remnants of the former Soviet Union. Moscow had a notable enthusiasm for large engineering projects, especially dams and big water diversions. Many were built in fractious mountain regions held together only by Soviet military, economic and political might. In those days, Moscow had absolute control over who got what water, and when. But with the glue of Moscow rule gone, the keys to the sluice gates are in the hands of new upstream states, which have equally new downstream nations at their mercy. From Armenia to Tajikistan and the independent-minded Russian republic of Chuvash, which some see as the next Chechnya, nasty local disputes have involved threats of hydrological terrorism. Witness the Ruritanian chaos in the Caucasus Mountains, where a giant hydroelectric complex is at the heart of a long-running dispute between ex-Soviet Georgia and the breakaway republic of Abkhazia.

The Inguri complex, which was completed by Russian engineers in 1980, is 272 metres high, making it the world's third-tallest dam. It controls a river of the same name. It provides most of Georgia's electricity and is the only source of power for Abkhazia. But while the dam is on the Georgian side, the power plants are in Abkhazia. Through several years of armed conflict, engineers have managed to maintain electricity generation for the benefit of both sides—largely because Russia, which also takes a slice of the power, has insisted that its own troops guard the complex. In effect, the complex has been a small slither of the old Soviet Union sustained on the border between the new warring republics.

But the situation is perennially unstable. Tensions rose in mid-2004 when masked men abducted two engineers from near the plant. The Georgian authorities accused Russian special forces of unspecified subversive activities against its power industry. The question of whether Abkhazia becomes an independent republic recognized by the UN or stays within Georgia probably hangs ultimately on who gets control of the Inguri complex. Assuming it survives, of course. The complex has seen only sporadic maintenance since the breakup of the Soviet Union. And it happens to straddle a potentially active fault line that could trigger an earthquake at any moment. Write your own doomsday scenario.

Increasingly, too, rivalries over water between different parts of relatively stable countries are overflowing into violence. Karnataka and Tamil Nadu in southern India have been feuding over the Cauvery River for decades. The row began in 1927 when upstream Karnataka built the Krishnaraja Sagar dam, creating a 130-kilometre-long reservoir on the river. Tamil Nadu responded with the Mettur dam in the 1930s. Both states built extensive irrigation systems and encouraged their farmers to grow water-intensive cash crops such as rice and sugar cane, in efforts to cement their claims to the lion's share of the river's water.

Initially this was just economic one-upmanship. But the stakes have risen. Today both states have populations as large as major European countries. And on top of escalating rural demand, cities such as Bangalore, the heart of India's "Silicon Valley" in

Karnataka, are demanding ever more water for themselves. Estimated demand from the two states has now reached 25 cubic kilometres a year. Average flow on the Cauvery is only 20 cubic kilometres. Inevitably, the upstream state Karnataka is in the driving seat. Many years it refuses to deliver downstream the water that Tamil Nadu expects and demands. Below the Mettur dam, the Cauvery is virtually empty. Rice fields on the river's delta have no water.

During droughts, the conflict spills over into riots. In 1992, twenty-five water rioters died in Bangalore. In October 2002, after the worst drought in southern India for forty years, India's Supreme Court ruled that Karnataka must release water downstream. But farmers blocked the state's main highway to protest against the releases. The government responded by shutting schools and colleges, and suspending all train services. The state's business virtually ground to a halt as thousands of riot police broke up demonstrations with tear gas and surrounded the main dams to prevent angry farmers from invading them.

There are important reasons why warmongers with serious designs on power may stay their hand when it comes to dams. During two decades of guerrilla warfare in northern Mozambique in the 1970s and 1980s, fighters on both sides spared the giant Cahora Bassa dam on the Zambezi. The reason? They expected to win—at which point they would need the dam. But in the twenty-first century, many terrorists have little desire to take power and few prospects of doing so. So they have less reason to stay their hand. And they will know that there are few better ways of inflicting terror than threatening to attack a dam, and few better ways of causing chaos than carrying out the threat.

In September 2004, the Chinese military suddenly sent helicopters, patrol boats, armoured vehicles and bomb-disposal robots to the site of its giant new dam at Three Gorges on the River Yangtze. Nobody is sure what was in the minds of the Chinese authorities, but the action followed press stories about the risk of terrorists hijacking a large ship on the Yangtze, packing it full of explosives and ramming it into the dam. And it came only a few weeks after the Pentagon in Washington had reported that the Taiwanese military were considering just such an attack on the dam.

Three Gorges is the world's largest hydroelectric dam, holding back a reservoir 500 kilometres in length that will before long contain 40 cubic kilometres of water. Unleashing that water downstream would stand a good chance of creating the worst man-made disaster in history. It could dwarf the blasting of the Huayuankou dyke that released the full fury of the Yellow River in northern China back in 1938. Even a credible threat of such an action would cause panic among the 350 million people downstream on the Yangtze. If the reservoir were emptied to neutralize such a threat, the nation's war machine would be crippled by the loss of electricity.

When campaigner Dai Qing interviewed scientists opposed to the construction of the Three Gorges dam back in the 1980s, one military expert told her, "War is the key fact that determines whether or not we should construct the Three Gorges project. Are we going to make a sword of Damocles that will hang over the heads of future generations for decades to come?" They did.

PART SEVEN

WHEN THE RIVERS RUN DRY ...
CIVILIZATIONS FALL

24

ELISHA'S SPRING AND THE MYSTERIES OF ANGKOR

The first known permanent human settlement was on the west bank of the River Jordan. Jericho was constructed some 9,000 years ago as the last ice age faded and *Homo sapiens* began to prosper in the warmer post-glacial world. The settlement was modest enough. It covered barely four hectares and had a thick defensive wall. Inside were a few hundred people and a stone tower, which survives today as reputedly the world's oldest man-made structure. Close by was a spring, recorded in the Bible as Elisha's Spring. It was the reason for Jericho's existence. As the Book of Kings puts it: "The hand of the Lord came upon him. And Elisha said: make this valley full of ditches. Ye shall not see wind; neither shall ye see rain, yet that valley shall be filled with water." The spring gushed into ditches that distribute its water to the fields and orchards.

The original town was destroyed by floods in the valley about 8,000 years ago. Jericho has been rebuilt and destroyed several times since. But the spring and the farming that it sustained just kept going. The area around was vital to the development of modern farming. It was probably the first place to cultivate wild grains. By 6,000 years ago, they were growing peas and beans and olives and vines and figs. Soon the hills were carved into terraces that captured their own water from the rains. Today the spring still delivers water, at a regular 76 litres a second, into a small pool, as if nine millennia of human history had never happened. And the farms still grow crops in what must be one of the longest-lasting and most durable agricultural systems anywhere in the world.

During the thousands of years since the fields of Jericho first flourished, many grander civilizations have come and gone in the Middle East, many of them based on apparently more sophisticated methods of catching and manipulating water. These are the places where Western civilization is deemed to have begun. It was around 7,500 years ago that early Sumerians in the "fertile crescent" of modern-day Iraq constructed the first large irrigation systems using river water. They diverted water from the Rivers Tigris and Euphrates down long canals and erected earth defences against the spring floods. And they began to build great cities too, like Ur and Kish and Uruk, where the first writing was produced and the first sciences developed. Uruk eventually had a population of 50,000.

These first Sumerian cities fought the first water wars. Some 5,000 years ago, the king of Umma cut the banks on canals that neighbouring Girsu had dug to the Euphrates. The breaches spilled water across the plain and destroyed Girsu's ability to feed itself. But the kings of Girsu were not beaten. They dug a new canal to tap the waters of the Euphrates' twin river, the Tigris. That gave them a larger empire than their rivals, and they ultimately cut off Umma.

But the Sumerian fields gradually became blighted. The bumper wheat harvests began to fail. Wheat gave way to barley. Then the barley too waned. And with that, the fields became barren, the civilization foundered and the land returned to desert. When the British archaeologist Sir Leonard Woolley excavated Ur in the 1930s, he wondered at the contrast between the great civilization he was uncovering and the barren land around him. "To those who have seen the Mesopotamian desert, the evocation of the ancient world seems well-nigh incredible, so complete is the contrast between past and present. Why, if Ur was an empire's capital, if Sumer was once a vast granary, has the population dwindled to nothing, the very soil lost its virtue?"

Woolley's successors believe they have solved the riddle. The problem seems to have been tiny amounts of salt coming down the river and accumulating over the centuries in the fields, eventually poisoning soils and crops. Cuneiform tablets of 3,800 years ago describe a farm system in its death throes, recording "black fields becoming white" and "plants choked with salt." And that would explain why wheat, which is less tolerant of salt than barley, gave way first. Manipulation of the rivers made the Sumerian cities, but ultimately it destroyed them, too. Salt chased civilization through Mesopotamia as mercilessly as any barbarian horde.

While the fields of Sumer turned to dust, new cities grew up farther north, in the lands round modern Baghdad. These societies culminated around AD 500 in the Persian Empire, which constructed canals to carry water from the Tigris to irrigate fields for 300 kilometres either side of the river. This remaking of the landscape far outstripped the efforts of the Sumerians. Indeed, nothing bigger has been built in this region till today. It was "a whole new conception of irrigation which undertook bodily to reshape the physical environment," said American archaeologist Thorkild Jacobsen. In places the canals were 100 metres wide, and according to Sir William Willcocks, a leading Victorian engineer, "must have been capable of quite crippling the Tigris." The Persians in Iraq may thus have been the first to make a great river run dry.

The Persians had learnt to keep salt at bay by avoiding over-irrigation and planting weeds during the fallow to keep the water table low. But they faced a new problem with silt washing into the irrigation systems. They solved it by employing thousands of slaves to dredge the waterways. But when Islamic rulers took over from the Persians, the dredging was left undone and at some time in the twelfth century silt overwhelmed the irrigation works. Willcocks, who spent several years dreaming of reconstructing the system, wrote of a "terrible catastrophe which in a few months turned one of the most populous regions of the Earth into desert."

The lessons for modern times in the threats posed by salt and silt are clear. But for historians there is something else here that is, on the face of it, rather odd. Why cities? It is not obvious that rich agrarian societies should need them at all. And yet from Mesopotamia to the Nile in Egypt, and from the Indus in Pakistan to the Yellow River in China, a series of great civilizations grew up by irrigating arid areas from mighty rivers—and they all had cities.

One school of thought holds that cities were largely born because these agrarian societies needed new kinds of social organizations to collect, distribute and contain water on a large scale. They had to hire farmers or coerce slaves into digging and maintaining dykes and canals and watching for floods, and they needed to develop scientific skills like astronomy and mathematics to predict nature's whims. It was the American historian Karl Wittfogel who coined the phrase "hydraulic civilizations" to describe societies that are organized primarily around the need to manage water. He argued that societies often required cities to do this. "It is the combination of hydraulic agriculture, a hydraulic government and a single-centred society that constitutes the institutional essence of hydraulic civilization," he said.

Not all academics agree. But it remains remarkable how many great early civilizations emerged in environments where management of water was the first priority. Wittfogel contended that until the Industrial Revolution, the majority of human beings lived within the orbit of hydraulic civilizations. Ancient Egypt developed its water-management skills so well that it maintained population densities along the Nile that were double those of modern France. In the Americas at one time, three-quarters of the population lived in a few small centres of hydraulic civilization in Mexico and Peru.

Much of Europe did not need such sophisticated water management, because it could rely on rainfall to irrigate crops. But nonetheless it was those arid areas that did have to manage water that innovated and developed in other ways too. In the Middle Ages, Córdoba, the capital of Moorish Spain, sustained a population of more than a million people through irrigated agriculture, at a time when the largest city north of the Alps was London with a mere 35,000 people.

It was not just the desert civilizations of the ancient world that depended on sophisticated management of water. One of the most stupendous pre-industrial civilizations was centred on Angkor Wat in Cambodia. The Khmer civilization rose around AD 800, reached its height under Hindu kings in the twelfth and thirteenth centuries and crashed in the early fifteenth century. Its influence spread throughout Southeast Asia, and its great capital, one of the true wonders of the world, was set in jungle at the head of the Great Lake on the Tonle Sap, the reversible tributary of the Mekong.

Angkor is known today for its array of temples. But in the past five years, research has revealed that the Khmer were about much more than temples. They too were remaking their land-scape and again water was at the heart of their works. The temples that we see today were simply the ceremonial heart of a huge suburban landscape that, at its height, was "by far the most extensive pre-industrial city in the world," says Roland Fletcher, an Australian archaeologist working there. "It was like modern-day Los Angeles."

Satellite pictures show what is not so visible from the ground: huge networks of canals spreading out from the temples, linking reservoirs and rice paddies, ports and outpost suburbs. Homing in on areas identified from the air, archaeologists are digging up the remains of communities engaged in mining and boat-building, in weaving and manufacture of salt. And all this, it is increasingly clear, was dependent on sophisticated water management.

Visitors to the Angkor temples can still see huge moats and reservoirs dotted among the temples. The largest reservoir, the West Baray, is eight kilometres across and still holds water. Locals go bathing and take boats out to a small temple on an island in the middle. Others reservoirs, such as the East Baray, are now empty and encroached by jungle. And yet, huge as they were, these barays were only baubles. The new evidence is that the workaday job of keeping the hundreds of thousands of Angkor inhabitants and their fields watered was done by waterways connected to suburban pools and areas of rice paddy that grew three and sometimes four crops of rice a year. It was this that underpinned the wealth and the splendour of the rulers and their temples.

The Khmer civilization, arguably the greatest that Southeast Asia has ever seen, eventually faltered. What went wrong? The latest evidence points to an environmental catastrophe brought on by a failure of the water supply. Matti Kummu, a Finnish hydrologist who is interpreting the hydrology for an international team of archaeologists working in Angkor, says that the barays and ponds and canals and paddy fields all drew their water from streams draining from the surrounding hills into the Great Lake. The great urban centre was established beside the lake precisely to bag those waters.

The channels that collected the water and delivered it to the suburban complex were beautifully built and sometimes as much as forty metres wide. But they were also artificial channels and prone to break out of their allotted course. They required constant maintenance. Kummu says that over the centuries one of them, the Siem Reap channel, started to take more and more water. And as it did, it grew and began to cut its bed ever lower. In the end, the channel became so low that it could no longer deliver water to the barays and the ponds. The distribution network was left high and dry. (The west baray has water in it today, Kummu points out, only because it now gets it from another source.)

I found the Siem Reap channel in among the temples. It is still flowing and has indeed eroded a deep gorge some way from its original course, where several piers of an old stone bridge stand forlorn in the bush. Locals have rather elegantly installed a large waterwheel that scoops water out of the bottom of the channel and pours it into a pipe at the top to irrigate a small tree nursery. Farther on, where the channel skirts past the eastern Baray, it is twelve metres below the surrounding land and evidently could not fill the reservoir.

There are many unanswered questions about the collapse of the Khmer civilization. But it is increasingly clear that just as management of water made this quite mind-boggling civilization in the jungle, so too must failures of management have destroyed it.

And maybe that is what happened in the jungles of Central America where the ruins of the Mayan civilization, like those of Angkor, today emerge from regrown rainforest. Here, great pyramids loom amid the trees as a reminder of a culture that, starting some 3,000 years ago, cleared large areas of the forests and converted it into fields and cities and suburban areas that became one of the most densely populated regions on the planet. The Mayans created an urban society that established universities for mathematics and astronomy, pioneered the cultivation of maize, and built large reservoirs, viaducts and canals to grow crops all year round.

Reservoirs at Tikal, a Mayan city in northern Guatemala, could hold enough water to supply 10,000 people for up to eighteen months. At Coba, the Mayans built dykes to increase the capacity of a natural lake. The Central Peten region, the civilization's jungle heartland, may have had a population of more than ten million. But after two millennia of success, it suddenly and mysteriously collapsed in the ninth century. The collapse was so complete that, when the Spanish arrived in the region a few hundred years later, there were left roaming the jungle just 30,000 people, less than 1 per cent of the former population. And life was so poor that even expert looters and pillagers like Hernando Cortés and his army almost died of starvation there.

What went wrong? The most likely theory is that changing climate overtook the Mayans. Tree rings and lake cores reveal three catastrophic droughts in the final century of the civilization that peaked in AD 810, 860 and 910. The lakes all but dried out. Presumably the reservoirs suffered similarly. Perhaps there were brutal wars for what water remained. Perhaps disease and starvation overtook the parched cities. At any rate, a civilization that prospered for two millennia by taking advantage of the fecundity of the rainforest and its water supplies eventually succumbed when the climate turned against it and the rivers and reservoirs dried up.

What can we make of all these tales of collapse? Two things. First that civilizations built on intensive use of water often find themselves highly vulnerable to climate change or to insidious and destructive elements in their own systems of water exploitation like salt and silt or the eroding power of artificial water channels. And second, perhaps, that less intensive and less grand uses of water—such as those employed round Jericho—can be more flexible in the face of change, and so more long-lasting. Jericho never grew as big as the famous hydraulic civilizations round the Middle East. But while those civilizations fell long ago, farmers still make a living there. That too may offer lessons for our management of water today.

25

LOSING THE WEST

The big question is this: how vulnerable are our modern societies to hydrological breakdown? When the rivers run dry, will our own civilizations buckle? Is salt waiting to turn our best endeavours to dust? One place to look is the American West, where the epicentre of the coming water crisis may be Phoenix in Arizona.

With a population now well past three million, the metropolis of Phoenix is one of the fastest-growing urban areas in the US. It sprawls across the Sonora desert with no apparent limit. In the mid-1990s, it was believed that Phoenix was growing by almost a hectare every hour. It is scarcely less now. Metropolitan Phoenix covers more than a thousand square kilometres so far—by chance, roughly the size of the old Angkor urban zone.

Phoenix is as profligate with water as it is with land. The residents of private estates in smart satellite suburbs such as Scottsdale and Paradise Valley water their lawns and fill their swimming pools as if they lived anywhere but a desert. Private lakes are blossoming. Developers compete to offer the greenest golf courses, the most luxuriant gardens and the tallest fountains. In Fountain Hills, one of the outer suburbs, they have installed the world's highest shooting fountain. It spurts 180 metres into the air for thirty minutes in every hour throughout the day. In such ways, Phoenix contrives to be among the biggest urban water users on the planet. Through the summer, residences in some suburbs consume around 4,000 litres of water a day.

There used to be a river flowing through Phoenix—the Salt River. In pre-Columbian times, Hohokam Indians used it to irrigate fields. But dams have long since dried up the river down here. They built the Phoenix red-light district across its old bed. Phoenix and its suburbs grew increasingly reliant on underground water pumped from beneath the desert. But water tables have been falling fast. Arizona now pumps up more than twice as much as the sparse rains can replenish. Even projects in Scottsdale and elsewhere for recycling water back underground have not been able to make up the difference.

The end for Phoenix's profligate water use would have happened by now if it had not been for the city fathers, who as early as the 1950s began lobbying Washington for cash to bring in water from out of state. Like California, Arizona saw its future in tapping the great waterway of the American West, the Colorado River. After twenty-five years of persuasion and the installation of an Arizona senator as chairman of the House Appropriations Committee, pork-barrel politics delivered the goods, and in the 1980s the Bureau of Reclamation built for Arizona one of the world's largest and most expensive water-delivery systems.

The Central Arizona Project takes almost two cubic kilometres of water a year out of the Colorado River—about as much as flows down the Thames—and pours it into a concrete canal 500 kilometres long that zigzags across the desert to Phoenix and its smaller sister Tucson. The project cost $3.6 billion to build and another fortune to run, as well as losing to evaporation 7 per cent of the flow en route. In recent times, the canal has been taking more than a fifth of the entire flow of the Colorado—much more in dry years. Its hydrological bounty unleashed the latest real estate boom in Phoenix. But it could be the final straw for the beleaguered Colorado River. And it could take down the American West with it.

It is a truism that water won the West. The 2,300-kilometre Colorado River, which drains a twelfth of the US, is the lifeblood of seven states, delivering its water to fast-growing cities, feeding irrigation projects and generating hydroelectricity. Since the 1930s, many of its heart-stopping canyons have been flooded to make reservoirs. So much water is captured that the amount making it to the sea has fallen to all but zero, leaving the Colorado delta to shrivel in the sun. A once rich landscape, where jaguars and beavers roamed, has not seen fresh river water since 1993. And no river water means no silt to maintain the delta, which is growing ever more vulnerable to tidal erosion.

Nature has been sacrificed to the demands of Uncle Sam's farmers. But now, the river itself is faltering. And from the snow-covered mountains of Wyoming and Colorado to the desert cities of California and Arizona, the beneficiaries of the Colorado are getting worried.

There are two giant reservoirs that control the flow of the middle reaches of the Colorado and ensure supply to the lower states. The first, Lake Mead, was filled in the 1930s behind the Hoover dam in Boulder Canyon. Then, in 1964, the Glen Canyon dam drowned a series of spectacular gorges to create Lake Powell, which was named after John Wesley Powell, a one-armed Civil War hero who in 1869 made the first boat journey by a white man down the river.

The two reservoirs collect water when snowmelt in the Rocky Mountains fills the river, and distribute it to cities and fields during the long summer growing season. Having more than four times the capacity of the river's average annual flow, they can also even out fluctuations between wet and dry years.

While urban areas are taking an increasing amount, most of the water abstracted from the river still goes for irrigating some 1.5 million hectares of fields in the river valley and in Arizona and California. America has always subsidized farming in the west, and today perhaps a billion dollars a year is poured into keeping farmers irrigating crops that they would not otherwise grow. And subsidies encourage waste. Every year several cubic kilometres of water evaporate from reservoirs, farm ponds and flooded fields, while much of what does get to crop roots is used to grow low-value crops like alfalfa. Even in dry years, the presumption is that a wet year will be along soon. But that presumption looks increasingly foolhardy.

The Colorado is both legally and hydrologically one of the most regulated rivers in the world. But it is becoming increasingly clear that the legal and the hydrological no longer mesh. A century ago, more than 25 cubic kilometres of water flowed unimpeded to the Gulf of California every year. When in 1922, on the eve of the dam-building era, lawyers shared out the river's waters between the states, they gave 9.25 cubic kilometres to the upper basin states of Colorado, Utah, Wyoming and New Mexico, and another 9.25 cubic kilometres to the downstream states of California, Arizona and Nevada. With another 2 cubic kilometres assigned to Mexico, that added up to around 20.5 cubic kilometres.

That should have left water to spare, but, ever since, flows have been diminishing. Since the compact was signed the average flow has been 16 cubic kilometres. From 1999 to 2003, the average sunk to 8.7 cubic kilometres—worse by far even than the dust-bowl years of the 1930s. In 2002, it fell to just 3.7 cubic kilometres. The US Geological Survey says the Colorado hasn't seen a drought like it in five hundred years. Whether the cause is cyclical or a result of global warming is unclear. But the Survey says it can see no end in sight. The wet years that refilled the reservoirs have simply vanished.

Lake Powell was full to the brim in 1999. But by the end of 2004, after several years of drawing down the reserves, it stood three-fifths empty. Its 270-kilometre-long reservoir could, if the drought continues, be empty by 2007. Lake Mead was scarcely better off. It is, of course, quite possible that between this being written and you reading it, the drought will have broken. Wet years can be very wet. The reservoirs could be full and the crisis could be over. Better rains in early 2005 brought some relief, but the crisis continued and the Bureau of Reclamation said in early

2005 that, at average river flows, it would take the reservoirs ten years to refill. If the drought persists, the whole region is in deep trouble. And even if it breaks, most climate forecasts suggest that it will soon return with even greater force.

So in 2005 the states were starting to prepare for the worst. Since there was no more water, they deployed lawyers instead. The lower states, their briefs contend, have a guaranteed entitlement, regardless of the state of the river: their share has to be provided from the reservoirs. If Lake Powell falls much lower, then the upper states will have to give up their share, emptying their own small reservoirs and halting abstractions from the river to meet downstream commitments. The upstream states understandably disagree. Colorado is not happy at being required to export three-quarters of the snowmelt from its mountains when its own farms and cities are running low. Denver and Colorado Springs don't quite see why they have to shut off their sprinklers so Phoenix, Las Vegas and Los Angeles can keep theirs on.

The upper states say they may contest certain downstream uses. That would include Arizona's Central Arizona Project. They argue that as the last user to come online, the canal to Phoenix and Tucson should be the first to give up access to the river in a crisis. In late 2004, interior secretary Gale Norton appeared to agree with them. As one Denver newspaper put it with what sounded almost like relish: "It could stack up as the biggest water war in the West. Arizona could get shut off completely." Because there has never been such a crisis before, the differing interpretations of Western water law have never been contested. They soon may be. It could happen in 2006. But at the end of the day, if there is no water, there is no water. As campaigners from WWF say, it is now "not a matter of if, but *when* the Colorado River plumbing system collapses."

Environmentalists meanwhile chose the moment of maximum decline in Lake Powell to resume a long campaign for the Glen Canyon dam to be dismantled in order to "bring back the old canyon to its former glory," as founder of the campaigning Glen Canyon Institute, Richard Ingebretsen, put it. The drought, he says, shows that the reservoir serves so little purpose it could be removed. Others say it shows why the reservoir is needed, to catch water in the infrequent wet years. With the reservoir increasingly empty, it seemed a rather academic argument. As Ingebretsen put it, either in hope or expectation, "It's gone. It will never fill again."

Most observers of the hydropolitics of the Colorado believe that the days when most of the waters of the mighty river could be used to irrigate crops cannot last much longer. Cities are demanding an increased share of the cake. And the size of the cake is declining. But if water shortages don't see off the farmers, salt may be the apocalypse awaiting the great American agrarian civilization. Salt could kill off parts of America as certainly as it did Ur and Urek. As Arthur Pillsbury, the doyen of water resources academics in the American West, put it to me before his death: "The Colorado basin will eventually become salt encrusted and barren, because of salt." The only question was when.

All down the river, more and more salt is clogging up the system. It is flowing downstream from the headwaters in the Rockies. It is also being washed from soils and bedrock in irrigated areas like Paradox Valley in Colorado and Wellton-Mohawk in Arizona. The river and the extensive man-made irrigation and drainage networks that circulate its waters have also become a vast system for collecting and distributing salt. Each year about nine million tonnes of salt enters the system, but virtually none reaches the ocean.

Almost all the water flowing down the Colorado leaves the river several times to irrigate fields and return via drains. At each step it both loses water volume, through evaporation, and picks up salt from local rocks. So the concentration of salt in the water increases as it travels downstream. At its headwaters, the Colorado contains about fifty parts per million of salt. By the time it reaches the last dam, near Las Vegas, it contains more than 700 milligrams. Tens of millions of dollars are spent on farms every year trying to minimize the problem, but, even so, crops losses from salt are currently estimated at $330 million a year.

Outside Yuma, Arizona, just upstream of the border with Mexico, is the ultimate technical solution to the salt problem. There lies a giant $300-million desalination plant. It was built more than a decade ago to clean up the briny flow from the Wellton-Mohawk irrigation district, the last in the US, as it returns to the river close to the border. The idea was to deliver the cleaned-up flow to Mexico as part of the US treaty obligation to supply two cubic kilometres of usable water annually for irrigation over the border.

The Yuma plant has never been used. The desalted water would cost ten times more than its value to farmers. So instead, through the wet 1990s when there was water to spare, the US supplied Mexico instead with water from the main river. It sent the untreated Wellton-Mohawk brine down a canal to the Colorado delta, where it is the only water the delta gets.

But as the reservoirs upstream empty, the desalination plant may be dusted down and prepared for use.

Phoenix is so called because it rose from the ashes of the Hohokam civilization—a society that probably ran the most extensive irrigation system north of Mexico. Why did it die? We don't know for sure, but it looks like salt brought it down. Of course, whatever happens, the American West won't be destroyed in quite the same way as Mesopotamia or the farming culture of the Hohokam. Even if its lifeline to the Colorado is cut, Phoenix won't disappear as completely as Ur or Urek. But the lessons from the past are potent nonetheless. Rivers can run dry. Salt can tighten its grip. Great cities can fall as a result. And even if the cities keep going in the American West, desert farming does seem doomed in the many places where it currently relies on the water of the Colorado.

RUSSIA

0   350 km

200 m

K A Z A K H S T A N

Sor
Donyzlau

Akespe
Shomishkol'   Aralsk
Akbasty

ARAL SEA

Vozrojdenie

Uch-sai

Muynak

Kanlikol   Chimbai

Nukus   UZBEKISTAN

Dashoguz   Khorazm

Tashkent

TURKMENISTAN

Bukhara   Samarkand

Karakum
Desert

Amu Darya

Ashkhabad   Karakum Canal

IRAN   AFGHANISTAN

Syr Darya

26

ARAL SEA: THE END OF THE WORLD

About five kilometres out to sea, I spotted a fox. It wasn't swimming. For the sea as marked on the map is no longer a sea. The fox was jogging through endless tamarisk on the bed of what was once the world's fourth-largest inland body of water. In the past forty years, most of the Aral Sea in Central Asia has turned into a huge uncharted desert. For the most part, no human has ever set foot there. This new desert is adding dry land the size of a small English county every year. It cannot be long before someone decides that it should be protected as a unique, virgin desert. At present, though, such is the scale of what has happened here that the UN calls the disappearance of the Aral Sea the greatest environmental disaster of the twentieth century.

Till the 1960s, the Aral Sea covered an area the size of Belgium and the Netherlands combined and contained more than a thousand cubic kilometres of water. It was renowned in the Soviet Union for its blue waters, plentiful fish, stunning beaches and bustling fishing ports. Most atlases still show a single chunk of blue. But the new reality is very different. The sea is broken into three hypersaline pools, containing only about a tenth as much water as before. The beach resorts and promenades lie abandoned. The fish died long ago. As the fox and I peered north from near the former southern port of

Muynak, there was no sea for 150 kilometres. It felt like the end of the world.

What has caused this environmental Armageddon? The answer lies in the death of the two great rivers that once drained a huge swathe of Central Asia into the Aral Sea. The biggest is the Amu Darya. Once named the Oxus, it was as big as the Nile. In the fourth century, Alexander the Great fought battles on its waters as he headed for Samarkand and the creation of the world's largest military empire. It still crashes out of the Hindu Kush in Afghanistan. But, like its smaller twin, the Syr Darya from the Tian Shan Mountains, it is largely lost in the desert lands between the mountains and the sea.

During the twentieth century, these two rivers were part of the Soviet Union. And Soviet engineers contrived to divert almost all their flow—around 110 cubic kilometres a year—to irrigate cotton fields that they planted in the desert. This was one of the greatest-ever assaults on major rivers. Perhaps nowhere else on Earth shows so vividly what can happen when rivers run dry.

This chapter records my journey to discover how this disaster happened, to talk to its victims and to find out what can be done now that Moscow's rule has ended. It was a deeply depressing journey. I found a landscape of poison, disease and death in what was once one of the most prized areas of the Soviet Empire. I found mismanagement of water on an almost unimaginable scale—a scale that has turned a showcase for socialism into a blighted land. More disturbing still, I found that in the aftermath of the collapse of the Soviet Union, nobody seems to have the vision or the will to rethink how this land and its rivers might serve the people living here better.

After the Russians went home, the governments of the region did set up an International Fund for Saving the Aral Sea, and protested their desire for the sea to return. Soon afterwards, I went to the region and heard their hopes at a big conference. But when I returned in 2004, the situation was worse than before. Even less water was reaching the sea than in Soviet times. In fact, most years now, no water at all makes it all the way down the

Amu Darya, and the Syr Darya has less than a quarter of its former flow. And that is deliberate policy. I discovered that there is
no plan to save the Aral Sea. Whatever the public statements, the
engineers today, as in Soviet times, regard water flowing into the
sea as wasted. Their policy is to keep the water back and allow
the sea to dry out forever.

First, a little history. Central Asia has a long tradition of using
the waters of its two great rivers to grow crops. In the days when
Alexander the Great and the Mongol conqueror Tamerlane
invaded these lands, when cities like Samarkand and Bukhara
flourished on the Great Silk Road, the people used the land and
water carefully. Much of the region was covered in orchards and
vineyards and grain fields. Then the Russians came. The czars in
the nineteenth century first saw the potential for planting cotton
in the desert. They realized that the combination of near constant summer sun and water from the great rivers could produce
cotton harvests to rival those in the US. But it was the Bolsheviks
who got down to business, turning ambition into action with
socialist fervour.

Lenin in 1921 lectured the southern republics of the new
Soviet Union that "irrigation will do more than anything else to
revive the area, bury the past and make the transition to socialism
more certain." Under his successor Stalin, the region's farms were
turned into Moscow-run "collectives," growing cotton for the
textile mills of European Russia. "Commissar Cotton" had
arrived. An ever-growing network of irrigation canals supplied
water to billions of cotton bushes planted each spring on millions
of hectares of fields. Nations of nomads and cowboys and
orchard tenders were turned into a near-slave society of cotton
pickers. Dissent was not tolerated. "You cannot eat cotton," the
prime minister of Uzbekistan complained in 1938. He was swiftly
executed for "bourgeois nationalism."

By 1960, after several decades of obedience to Commissar
Cotton, the canals were removing a staggering 40 cubic kilometres of water from the rivers. But the Aral Sea remained full,

partly because the rains had been good and partly because the irrigation systems eventually returned much of the water to the sea as drainage. But Moscow demanded more. Between 1965 and 1980, the area of irrigated land more than doubled. Central Asia became one of the largest irrigated areas on the planet, with some eight million hectares of fields criss-crossed by canals that could stretch to the moon three times over. By its own lights, all this was a dramatic Soviet success story: central planning at its finest, with everyone yoked to the common purpose of clothing the Soviet Empire.

By the 1980s, 85 per cent of all the fields in the Aral Sea basin were growing cotton. Orchards and vineyards, vegetable patches and wheat fields, even sports fields were given up. Almost every citizen was seconded to pick cotton. They began picking in searing summer heat that could reach 50 degrees Celsius, and ended in November when frost froze the fingers. Prisons and mental asylums and schools were emptied, factories and offices were shut and herds of animals were abandoned for the duration. Buses were halted by police and the passengers were allowed to continue their journeys only after they had stripped a field of its cotton. Nobody was excused: not nursing mothers, not students, not doctors, not their patients. Only government officials remained at their desks, counting cotton.

But this marvel of organization carried the seeds of its own destruction. The newest canals were delivering water to the driest areas with the poorest soils. Farmers poured two metres of water onto these fields each year, whereas the earlier fields required just one metre. And increasing amounts of water never returned to the river in drainage water. It accumulated in waterlogged soils, evaporated from fields or drained into the desert, where new lakes formed. The Aral Sea was not so much disappearing as being broken up and dispersed.

Much the biggest reason for this dispersion was the creation in the early 1960s of the Karakum Canal, which tapped the Amu Darya as it poured out of the mountains and took much of its flow west for some 1,300 kilometres across the desert of

Turkmenistan. Turkmenistan was the driest, emptiest, least populated republic in the Soviet Empire. The canal was the longest and biggest irrigation canal in the world, and it turned Turkmenistan into the empire's biggest and most profligate water user. And it was the death knell for the Aral Sea.

In its first forty years, the canal has taken approaching 500 cubic kilometres of water from the Amu Darya. Crucially, it has taken that water right out of the basin of the Aral Sea. None of it ever returns, even as drainage water. It was after the completion of the Karakum canal that the Aral Sea began to empty in earnest. By 1990, when the Soviet Empire imploded, the sea was receiving a tenth of its natural flow. Its volume was down by two-thirds.

Many have called the emptying of the Aral Sea a classic Soviet blunder. Russian geographer Grigori Reznichenko in 1988 made a marathon expedition across the lands of the Aral Sea to help expose the tragedy, and said afterwards, "Everything happened as it would in a fairy tale, where everybody acts without being aware of the final result. In the end, tens of millions of tonnes of cotton outweighed and overwhelmed the Aral Sea." But the truth is more chilling. The draining of the Aral Sea was in fact perfectly deliberate. In a museum at Nukus on the Amu Darya delta, I found a series of maps drawn by Soviet engineers in the 1970s depicting the planned demise of the sea. By 2,000 they expected it to be almost empty. Economic development plans once decreed that the seabed itself should be converted to cotton production as it dried up.

Today, Commissar Cotton is gone. But his legacy remains and, as I discovered, his engineers are still in business. Since 1990, the new governments that rule the Aral Sea basin have increased the area of land under cultivation by a further 12 per cent, and water abstractions from the rivers are up by a similar amount, to roughly 80 cubic kilometres a year. That is considerably more than the 60 cubic kilometres that, after evaporation, the rivers themselves once provided to the Aral Sea. The difference is made up by the drainage water that does return to the rivers, contaminated with salt and farm chemicals. But these days, not even drainage water gets to the sea.

Some things have changed down on the farm. A market economy has emerged for some crops like wheat, rice and sunflowers. But cotton remains easily the region's biggest export. Today in Uzbekistan, the biggest producer, the government is still the only purchaser, and meeting cotton production targets remains a national obsession. During the harvest season, cotton employs a staggering 40 per cent of Uzbekistan's workforce, including hundreds of thousands of schoolchildren. Every province, every canal network and every farm has its production target. Even as the old collective farms are privatized, the targets persist, and farmers and officials can lose their land and jobs for failing to meet them. And cotton still consumes most of the region's water.

In October 2004, during my visit, the government declared that Uzbek cotton production had exceeded 3 million tonnes for the first time in several years. Ministers brimming with pride were interviewed standing in cotton fields on the TV. Officials that had seemed uptight and nervous suddenly relaxed. The bottles of vodka came out. Nobody cared that in the process the ratchet on the Aral Sea had been given one more turn.

The amount of water used here is simply insane. Today the countries around the Aral Sea—Uzbekistan, Kazakhstan, Turkmenistan, Tajikistan and Kyrgyzstan—occupy five of the top seven places in the world league table of per-capita water users. Turkmenistan and Uzbekistan, the two countries that take their water from the Amu Darya, use more water per head of population than any others on Earth. The Aral Sea basin is very far from being short of water. The problem is the simply staggering level of water use.

I travelled through Uzbekistan, the heartland of the old Soviet cotton empire, from its capital, Tashkent, in the far east, along the old silk road through Samarkand and Bukhara, and then north following the Amu Darya through desert towards its delta and the final, fateful destiny with the bed of the Aral Sea. What struck me was not the Soviet single-minded determination to convert water into cotton, but the sheer chaos that had resulted.

I drove first through the arid Hungry Steppe west of Tashkent, where around a million hectares are cultivated on one giant treeless cotton farm. All along the road, broken water channels leaked their water into the ground, and a salty white residue on the top of the newly harvested fields revealed massive over-irrigation and poor drainage. Maintenance of the irrigation network has largely broken down since the Russians left, said my guide, Iskandar Abdulaev, from the Tashkent office of the International Water Management Institute. Cotton yields have halved in the salty soil. The Stalinist dreams of the sixties are over. "The farmlands here are coming back to where they once were," he said. "They are returning to desert."

Beyond Samarkand, we passed through Bukhara. Its ancient mosques are a major tourist attraction. But it has also been a centre of irrigated agriculture for four thousand years. Iskandar grew up round here. As a child, he picked cotton every summer, and later wrote his Ph.D. on the state of the irrigation system. As we sped past more waterlogged and salt-encrusted fields, he explained the extent of the hydrological chaos here. The fields were for a long time irrigated from the local river, the River Zarafshan, which drained into the Amu Darya. But by the 1960s so much water was taken from the Zarafshan that it dried up for the last 200 kilometres. So Soviet engineers dug a new canal and pumped water back uphill from the Amu Darya to Bukhara.

Yet still the water is wasted. Some 40 per cent of all the water pumped uphill to these farms spills into the ground, collects in ponds or seeps into the desert. Waterlogging has brought the salts in the soils to the surface, where they form a toxic crust after each harvest. Half the fields of Uzbekistan are salinized; in Bukhara the figure rises to 80 per cent. The only practical way of removing the salt is to apply yet more water each spring to wash the salt into the drainage ditches that surround every farm.

So farmers are stuck on a treadmill, applying more water to grow their crops, which poisons the soils with ever more salt that can only be removed with yet more water. In many areas more water is now used for flushing salt from soils before the cotton is planted each spring than for irrigation itself. But still the salt accumulates. Now the drains can't cope. So huge areas of land are being abandoned. Cotton yields are crashing on the fields that struggle on. So incomes are falling, too. Nothing you see here is new. Everything is old Soviet-issue. What cars are on the road are mostly old Ladas from the Soviet era. The world that Commissar Cotton created is crumbling.

We drove on, now following the Amu Darya through the empty desert. Watering this landscape proved too much even for Stalin's engineers. But somewhere off to the west, the Karakum canal was all but emptying the river into neighbouring Turkmenistan. My first sight of the Amu Darya showed that it still contained some water. But little of it was clean mountain water. Most of it was by now briny drainage water returned to the river from places like Bukhara. Then, over a ridge of sand dunes, I saw a giant reservoir. The Tuyamuyun reservoir, built in the 1980s, catches this briny wastewater and diverts it one last time to keep in business the fields of the last two provinces on the river: Khorazm and Karakalpakstan. The most obvious thing about this reservoir is how shallow it is: a few metres deep at best. The water is smeared across the desert, evaporating in the sun. Another piece of chaos.

And so to the Amu Darya delta. Politically, the delta is the autonomous republic of Karakalpakstan. Until the arrival of Commissar Cotton, the Karakalpaks were a nomadic cattle-herding and fishing race, whose name means the "black hat people." Many of them still wear black hats, though usually peaked caps made of cheap Russian leather. The Soviets and Uzbeks have treated them with disdain, using the republic for developing biological weapons and housing the notorious Jaslyq concentration camp. Even the ubiquitous security roadblocks give out here. Nobody, it seems, can imagine these beaten people causing trouble. This, their land, is the end of the line: the last stop before the Aral Sea. Its population of 1.5 million occupies the cockpit of a human crisis that is afflicting the region in the wake of the disappearance of the sea.

Here I met officials in overcoats and black hats, sitting in drafty offices, their cold fingers leafing through huge ledgers as they attempted to manage the ramshackle irrigation systems and divide up the salty drainage water delivered to them by their upstream neighbours. I met some who had trained in Moscow, even the US. They need never have come home to this brackish backwater. But they did, out of patriotism to Karakalpakstan. They were trying to make the best of a very bad job indeed, and were proud to take me on a tour of their crumbling empire.

Things were not good. Each year there are fewer tractors and more donkeys. The giant tractor-parts factory at Kanlikol, with its railway sidings waiting to bring in fresh raw materials from across the Soviet Union, has long since closed. One telling statistic: diesel sales in Karakalpakstan have halved since the Russians went home. Children as young as eleven years old are still shipped out for months of cotton picking, working ten hours a day for a dollar or so to bring in the harvest on which national salvation apparently depends—though it increasingly seemed to me that cotton was the curse rather than the saviour of the nation.

While most of the Soviet-style central planning has been kept in place, Soviet cash is not available and the Soviet-built system is in a bad state of repair. Canals leak. Sluice gates are broken. Drainage ditches are silted up and filled with weeds. Fields are not levelled, so water ponds up uselessly in depressions. Many corrugated fields are wasting 30 per cent of their water as a result. Some 60 per cent of water intended for farms here, in the most water-short region of Uzbekistan, does not reach the fields.

One senior official told me, "Twenty years ago Karakalpakstan produced more than a million tonnes of crops a year—cotton, rice, wheat and vegetables—but now we produce less than 300,000 tonnes." The precious waters of the Amu Darya are being used to less and less effect. Allowing for losses along the canals, farmers now take between 15,000 and 20,000 cubic metres of water to irrigate a single hectare of land—equivalent to flooding every field to a depth of two metres. Half of that water is needed to leach the previous year's accumulation of salt from the soil. Even with this profligate use of water, farmers in many areas get just one tonne of cotton, a fraction of the old crop. Two-fifths of all the fields of Karakalpakstan—200,000 hectares—have fallen out of use since the 1980s, partly from want of water and partly because the soils are clogged with salt. Half that loss has been since 1999.

We drove past miles of abandoned land and empty farmhouses. The state farms have mostly gone bankrupt and even the government's privatization program, which essentially gives the land away free, has failed to tempt many. Why take on land that will never grow anything again? Tamarisk scrub now grows amid the salt left behind by the last irrigation. Much of the land looks indistinguishable from the old seabed. It is returning to desert. That evening, local TV proudly announced that Karakalpakstan had met its cotton target for the first time since 1993. What the newsreader forgot to mention was that the government target had been halved since 1993. Failure was dressed up as success.

Poverty is spreading like a disease. And there are fearful memories of the drought that overtook the republic in 2001 and 2002. Karakalpakstan received less than 30 per cent of its water entitlement. Parts got no water at all, not even drainage water. Relief agencies put out famine alerts round the world. But the world was preoccupied with Afghanistan and Saddam, and nobody took much notice.

These days, even drinking water is becoming hard to come by—this in a country with the second-highest per-capita water use in the world. On one former state farm west of the republic's capital, Nukus, they drink from the briny, chemicals-laden water scooped from the irrigation canals. When the drought dried up the canals in 2001, they did not have even that. "I had to walk three kilometres to get drinking water for my family," one old farmer told me when we met in a drafty outbuilding.

On my visit, two years after the end of the drought, I saw women and children queuing with buckets at a hand pump, one of five thousand installed by the World Bank at the height of the drought. But they were fearful. Two-thirds of the pumps had gone dry. It turned out that they had mostly captured water percolating from irrigated fields. But as the fields have been abandoned, the pumps have nothing to tap.

All this is a staggering development for a people who once thought they were part of the socialist revolution. All the billions of dollars and trillions of roubles invested over decades across this landscape have left many people little better off than the inhabitants of rural Africa. This is not a disaster that grabs you as you walk down the streets of Nukus or Muynak or the countless fly-blown towns and villages across the delta. The people are too familiar in their pullovers and shabby black jackets and flat caps. And there are no refugee camps or soup kitchens. But probe a little and you find it is a blight that cuts right through a society that once prided itself on its order and ability to provide for all. And it affects everyone.

Nobody can escape the deteriorating climate. Once, the Aral Sea moderated the harsh desert environment here—cooling summers, warming winters and ensuring rainfall. Since it disappeared over the horizon, the summers in Karakalpakstan have become shorter and three degrees hotter; the winters colder and longer. Every farmer I spoke to said that they used to plant their cotton in March, but now it was May or even June. "It's not warm enough to grow cotton anymore," one told me.

Rainfall has declined, too, and the region is increasingly ravaged by dust storms. An estimated seventy million tonnes of dust from the seabed blows across the landscape every year, carrying with it an alarming cocktail of farm chemicals brought to the sea in past decades in drainage water and now carried by the winds. They include long-lasting pesticides like lindane, DDT and phosalone. Traces have been found in the blood of Antarctic penguins and in Norwegian forests. But most of the poisoned dust falls close to the former sea, deposited on fields, inside houses and, worst, down the lungs of children. An average year now has fifty days of dust storms.

Alarming though the spread of pesticides on the wind may be, most researchers believe that there is a still more devastating threat in the dust storms—salt. The stuff is everywhere in Karakalpakstan. There is no escape. It comes on the wind, down the irrigation canals and through the pipes carrying drinking water from reservoirs; it is in the vegetables the Karakalpaks grow in their gardens and the fish and birds they catch out on the delta; it is left behind on the soil surface by the irrigation process itself. Salt destroys the perilous productivity of the land, uses up precious water in flushing it out of soils, creates poverty and ultimately kills the people themselves. Salt is the true tragedy of this land. Worse than the poverty, worse than the water shortages, worse than the pesticides, the land and its people are being poisoned by salt.

Sixty per cent of the rural population of Karakalpakstan drink from wells dug into the salty underground reserves beneath the desert. In many villages the water is so salty that milk added to tea instantly curdles. Mothers in some villages say their children will not take their breast milk because it contains too much salt. And salt is a relentless silent killer.

I talked for a long time to Oral Ataniyazova, a gynaecologist and campaigner for the health of her people. Oral grew up on the delta, where her father was first secretary of the local Communist Party. International acclaim for her work here has included the Goldman Environment Prize awarded in 2000. She could have fled this blighted land but decided to return to work full-time for her people. Salt, she said, has turned Karakalpakstan into a nation of anemics.

Among the 700,000 women in the tiny republic, 97 per cent suffer from the condition, five times the rate in the early 1980s, three times that elsewhere in Uzbekistan, and probably the highest rate in the world. "All of our women are sick—and so are all our newborn," she said. Anemia causes a disturbing number of pregnant women to die from hemorrhages during pregnancies and childbirth; and 87 per cent of their babies are born anemic.

Aigul Aspanova at the maternity unit of the Kanlikol hospital told me, "The children are slow and get sick a lot. We also have lots of birth defects, especially of the mouth, legs and hands." One in every twenty babies is born with a defect. Infant mortality, at seventy-five children per thousand births, is the highest in the former Soviet Union. Karakalpakstan also has the highest rate of cancer of the esophagus in the world, among the highest rates of TB and unusually high rates of other cancers, immunological disorders, kidney and liver diseases, allergies and reproductive pathologies, said Oral. Half of all deaths here are caused by TB and pneumonia. Average life expectancy in these border regions round the Aral Sea has fallen by thirteen years from sixty-four to fifty-one.

"The entire population of Karakalpakstan has been chronically exposed to salt and farm chemicals for a long time," said Oral. "We have examined the literature but can find no research into a health situation like this anywhere in the world."

I talked about this later with a group of farmers meeting in Chumbai, one of the towns on the delta. These aging, weather-beaten men in shabby jackets, pullovers and hats against the encroaching winter chill told me nobody escapes the salt. "We get salty water, put it onto salty land; and then the winds bring another layer of dust as well." These men had lived tough lives. They were certainly not experts at diagnosing medical conditions, but when I asked if they saw any health effects among them and their families from this toxic environment they all nodded.

My interpreter tried to shut off the conversation. It was too difficult for them to talk about, he said. But the manager from a state farm rose slowly to his feet as if pronouncing at a funeral. He clutched his hat in front of him and looked me in the eye. "You can see it in the faces of everyone living here," he said. "We are all affected. There is a lack of good blood. All the women have it and it is worse in pregnancy. Many children are born deformed here. In the drought years, lots of people died,

especially the children. My daughter and son were both in hospital for six months. Every family has someone like that."

There was more nodding, but nobody would say any more.
This was private grief among old men with sick wives, sicker children and grandchildren, failing crops, growing poverty and a
poisoned land. I wondered if these farmers were the last of their
kind. Was I meeting the last farmers of Karakalpakstan? The last
to live and die by the Soviet dream?

This delta certainly seems to be a place where things end. Back in
1972, somewhere near Chumbai, the last tiger in Central Asia—
the final wild member of the Caspian tiger species anywhere in
the world—was hunted down in one of the last forests on the
delta. A few decades before, the last remnants of a rebellion
against Soviet rule in Uzbekistan make their final stand here on
the delta, finally meeting their end in a hail of bullets at a place
called Blood Lake.

These days, it seems to be the entire landscape and entire population that is reaching the end. The 7,000-square-kilometre delta
was once a rich natural ecosystem with dozens of lakes and
woodlands full of wild boar, deer and huge numbers of fish. As
late as 1960, hunters took 650,000 muskrat pelts from the
delta—a quarter of the muskrat-fur production for the whole of
the Soviet Union. But today the woodland has gone, most of the
lakes have dried up and there are fewer than a thousand muskrats
left. And now the farming system that killed nature is in its turn
being destroyed.

As you get closer to the Aral Sea, the proportion of abandoned fields increases until you see that almost nothing grows.
But as salt and water shortages have destroyed the fields here, the
authorities have plans to rehabilitate the delta by diverting the
upstream drainage water that once irrigated fields here into a
series of new lakes. The bulldozers and earth-moving machinery
that once dug canals are now remaking the delta once more. In
his office in Nukus, I met the smartly suited Ashirbekov
Ubbiniyaz. As a first secretary in the republic's government in the

1990s, he had helped prop up the system that created the current crisis. As local boss of the International Fund for Saving the Aral Sea, he was now in charge of the lake-making project. He dismissed my suggestion that the water should be allowed to flow on into the sea. "We can't recover the Aral Sea," Ashirbekov told me. "We need to use to the maximum the water we have from God."

You could see the superficial logic, and the locals were grateful. I met a fisher, Mohammed, on his way to the largest of the new man-made lakes. "When there is water flowing into the lake, like this year, there are plenty of fish," he said. By some counts two or three tonnes of fish emerge from the lakes on a good day now. The prices are pitiful—we paid less than $3 for a five-kilogram fish in the market at Muynak—and less than $2 for a large, freshly shot pheasant. Heaven knows what they contain in the way of chemicals. But that is the least of the concerns of the locals. As one asked me, "What should we do? It's not just the fish. We are all polluted."

A few fish cannot hide the increasing poverty and suffering of the people of the area. The lakes can only keep a minimal population active. There is already an alarming rate of migration out of the delta. A fifth of the people have left, and that seems bound to accelerate. The delta could one day be as empty as the Aral seabed itself. But not necessarily.

People trying to find a way forward here say the first thing to do is forget both cotton and the old Soviet ways of servitude. Oral is appalled at the passivity of her people in the face of a crisis that threatens their very survival. "It's important to get people to speak up. If we keep silent, our mentality will kill us," she said. Ecologically, she said, the real need is to retire irrigated land and revive the old ways of herding livestock and tending orchards and growing vegetables. "We don't need cotton; we need fruit and vegetables." Then, both the people and the sea could recover too.

It is easy to forget that most of the people in Karakalpakstan were nomads and cattle herders before they became cotton pickers. They have always kept a few animals; it was one of the few areas of life that neither Moscow nor Tashkent wanted to interfere with. And now that the state has so comprehensively failed them, the Karakalpaks are building their herds again. The abandoned fields provide new pasture. Almost every family has a cow or two. Most people told me that if they got any extra cash they would buy more cattle. An adult cow is money in the bank— fetching about $150 in the local markets. Morning and evening, the delta roads that once hummed with tractors going home from the fields are now full of cattle coming home from grazing on the abandoned cotton fields. The old ways are coming back.

And so to Muynak. Back in the 1950s, when the sea still lapped the shores of Muynak, Soviet filmmakers portrayed the heroism of fishing fleets on the Aral Sea. The ships caught 44,000 tonnes of sturgeon, carp and bream each year. Ferries sailed from Muynak to Aralsk, its companion port on the north shore in Kazakhstan. But there is more sand than sea between Muynak and Aralsk today. Muynak last saw the sea in 1968. The last trawler set sail in 1984. And the corroding remains of the trawlers stranded on the seabed in Muynak harbour have become one of the totemic images of the sea's demise.

Another is the crumbling fish-processing factory at Muynak. It was once the largest fish factory in the Soviet Union. It employed thousands of workers and produced 6,000 tonnes of fish products a day. It had its own power station. When I first came here in 1995, they were still canning fish caught in the delta and, ludicrously, brought by train from the Baltic. It was a dark, Dickensian operation, with pasty-faced women in cheap scarves chopping and gutting fish on wooden benches and spraying the unwanted entrails across the floor. But at least it was in business.

This time, the same manager greeted me at the same grandiose factory gates. But all he could show me now was a dirty and dingy shed where, two or three days a month, a handful of work- ers clocked on to convert the smelly remains of a couple of tonnes of fish bought in the local market into dry, powdered fish meal for sale as cattle fodder. The rest of the factory stood derelict. The manager dreamed of spending half a billion dollars to revive the plant. He said the government had drawn up a plan. But this seemed pure delusion. Where would the fish come from? Where would the money come from? The sense of decay was as pungent as the lingering smell of fish.

Muynak still bravely keeps its fish insignia. The mayor's office has a map showing the old sea lapping the town's shores. Paintings of the heroes of the trawlers still cover the walls of shuttered offices in the fish-processing factory. It is a town living on memories. Once, the townsfolk remember, the balmy climate meant they could go swimming in the sea in November. Now they have their overcoats on before the end of October. The population back in the sixties was over 40,000; today, after a mass flight of what might be called ecological refugees, it is around 10,000. The sole income for many families is the pensions of their senior members.

Muynak seems like the end of the line. But beyond it is Uch-sai, or "tiger's tail," a name it got because it sits at the very end of a peninsula that once jutted out into the Aral Sea. If Karakalpakstan is the end of the line for the Amu Darya, Uch-sai is the end of the line for Karakalpakstan. Back in 1995, I found it one of the most depressing places I had ever visited. On my return, it was even worse, like a ghost town out of the Wild West. Its population had fallen from 10,000 to 1,000. And few of these ghostly, emaciated people stayed for any reason other than lethargy and lack of an alternative.

The town's one source of employment, a fish-smoking yard that limped on in 1995, had closed down two years later. Worse, on the day it shut, the piped-water supply for the town was cut off. Nobody there now seems to know why. It just happened. A couple of days later, a water tanker began twice weekly visits from Muynak. It is Uch-sai's only source of water. Every family buys about 200 litres a week—about what the World Health Organization says is the minimum water requirement for a day—at a cost of about 20 cents, which is all they can afford.

I met two elderly schoolteachers in the town's only street. "The sea left here in 1961," one of them remembered. "It came back in 1966 and 1968. But that was the last time we saw it." For a while the trawler crews, which included both the teacher's parents, followed the retreating sea. But as it disappeared over the horizon they gave up. The last trawler returned, with empty nets, in 1981. Now they have only the sand and the salt. When I first came here, the workers at the fish-salting plant had told me that they expected the sea to come back one day. "It has dried up before and returned," one told me. Not now. The women said it was gone forever.

A couple of boys played football in a listless way in the road. I asked them what they would do when they left school. "We will go to Kazakhstan to find work," they said without enthusiasm, before sidling off, totally uninterested in who we were or why I was there. "Most of our children are sick here," said one of the teachers. "They have anemia. You can tell. They are weak and slow and cannot study well." She blamed the sand and the salt in the air, the poverty and the lack of fresh fruit and vegetables— "We used to grow vegetables in our gardens when we had piped water. But we can't do that now."

There were epidemics of TB and birth deformities in Uch-sai. "During the drought many children died here." Had they received any assistance from the outside world? One of the teachers remembered that the World Bank took a look, but nothing came of it. I later discovered that none other than the president of the World Bank, James Wolfensohn, one of the most powerful people in the world, had touched down for a few minutes in Uch-sai during a helicopter ride over the Aral Sea back in 1995. But they were right: nothing came of it.

You could be forgiven for thinking that the government in Tashkent had no interest in this forgotten corner either. Except that, half a kilometre down the road, I spotted a gas flare. The state company Uzbek Gas has been drilling for gas beneath the Aral seabed and, right outside Uch-sai, had built a gas-compression station. But its large fenced-off complex brings no benefits for the people of Uch-sai. "They never stop; they don't talk to us; they fill our town with gas smells and give us no compensation; they don't even buy things in our shop," the teachers complained. "But their trucks are destroying our road. When the snow falls in winter the water tanker won't be able to get here. Then what will we do?"

On the way back from the end of the world, as we bounced and swerved through the potholes along the isthmus from Uch-sai, we drove past the notorious ship's graveyard, where rusting hulks are blasted by sandstorms. For many, this scene has become a symbol of the disappearing Aral Sea. But for me the symbol is now the betrayed people of Uch-sai. Once almost surrounded by water, they now line up in the main street with old milk churns, awaiting the water tanker. When the river ran dry, the tide really went out for them.

27

A GOLDEN CENTURY LOOMS

F ountains are everywhere in Turkmenistan, the closed desert
state of Central Asia where President Saparmurat Niyazov, a
former Communist Party boss, rules with a mixture of old-time
Soviet authoritarianism and an eccentricity that must make even
Colonel Gadaffi weep. Water gushes from every hotel and public
square. Fountains festoon the front of the president's palace in the
capital, Ashkhabad, and line the road from the airport. They
have become "a mandatory attribute of administrative buildings
and multi-storey elite apartment buildings," says the news agency
TASS, another Soviet leftover. Profligate use of water is the ultimate status symbol here. If you have it, you flaunt it. In that
respect, if no other, it resembles Phoenix, Arizona.

Turkmenistan may be one of the driest states on Earth—a
vast, flat stretch of desert extending north from the mountains of
Iran deep into the wasteland of Central Asia. It has no indigenous
rivers to speak of, and few underground aquifers. And yet,
preposterously, it has equipped itself with so much water that it
has far and away the highest per-capita use of water in the world.
The 4.5 million cotton-farming subjects of president-for-
life Niyazov—who has ruled since 1985 and calls himself
Turkmenbashi, or father of all Turkmen—get through five million
litres of the stuff each in a year. That's enough to flush a toilet
twice a minute, night and day, all year. It is also twice as much as

the world's second-most profligate user, which just happens to be its neighbour and partner in the destruction of the Aral Sea, Uzbekistan.

How can Turkmenistan get its hands on so much water? The answer is the forty-five-year-old Karakum Canal, a Soviet-built artery through the Karakum desert that annexes the flow of the Amu Darya—the Nile of Central Asia. The river itself passes through Turkmenistan for only some 200 kilometres, and receives virtually no runoff while it's there. But during that short passage it is looted of up to half its water.

The Karakum Canal runs almost the length of southern Turkmenistan, delivering water all the way. Up to a kilometre wide, it is the largest irrigation canal in the world and the third-biggest waterway of any sort in Central Asia, carrying between twenty and thirty cubic kilometres of water a year. Combined with two much smaller canals draining the Amu Darya, it provides more than 90 per cent of the country's water, filling irrigation canals and watering cotton fields across the desert country. But it is also a decaying relic of Soviet times, increasingly silted up and losing half its water to seepage and evaporation. The waterway leaks so much from its bed that the desert for ten kilometres either side is waterlogged.

Turkmenbashi runs a paranoid, megalomaniac regime. In recent times he has renamed the days of the week after members of his family; shut down the Academy of Sciences and reduced a world-famous desert research institute to three staff; banned young men from growing beards and anyone at all from sporting gold teeth; cut higher education by 90 per cent; uprooted the state botanical garden and prevented all access to the World Wide Web. Turkmenistan is a virtually closed country. So the cause of the crash in its cotton harvest in 2004, when three-quarters of the expected crop failed to grow, remains a matter of conjecture. Disease, poor agrochemicals, low prices to farmers and bureaucratic incompetence have all been suggested. But water shortages were not mooted.

Turkmenistan became the world's biggest waster of water thanks to a generous share-out of the Aral Sea's waters between different republics of the Soviet Union a generation ago. Moscow decreed that the Amu Darya racing out of the hills of Tajikistan should be shared equally between the two downstream nations, Uzbekistan and Turkmenistan. They each got 22 cubic kilometres, even though the Turkmen population dependent on the water is only a little over a quarter that of its neighbour. When the Soviet Union broke up, the nations of Central Asia decided to stick with their existing shares. But the Uzbeks are growing increasingly jealous of Turkmenistan. Preposterously, the world's second-biggest water waster looks on with envy at the world's biggest waster.

Every farmer in Uzbekistan's Amu Darya delta blames Turkmenbashi for the drought they suffered in 2001. Every hydrologist in Uzbekistan believes that Turkmenistan takes much more water even than its allotted share while the river is flowing through the country. "They can divert as much of the Amu Darya's flow down the Karakum Canal as they want. And they do. It takes twice as much water as it did in Soviet times. We think they take thirty cubic kilometres," one told me.

But Turkmenbashi is undeterred. He has ever more ambitious plans to make the most of his, and perhaps Uzbekistan's, water. He announced in 2004 that he would create a twelve-kilometre man-made river through Ashkhabad, surrounded by parks, lakes, waterfalls and yet more fountains. He wanted it, he told his people, to remind him of his days as a student in St. Petersburg. But that is nothing compared with his latest master plan to, as he modestly puts it, "change the destiny of Turkmen people for generations to come," by creating a new civilization in the desert. He wants now to create a vast new sea in the middle of the Turkmen desert. Not content, it seems, with his major role in destroying the Aral Sea, he would like to create a new one on his territory.

Turkmenbashi's planned Golden Century Lake would cover around 3,500 square kilometres and contain some 120 cubic kilometres of water, making it about as large as the current Aral Sea. He plans to spend $9 billion, most of it from his country's oil revenues, on the project. And he says it will be used to irrigate

4,000 square kilometres in the north of the country—enough to grow an additional half a million tonnes of cotton.

Where will the water come from? There is the rub. Turkmenbashi says it will come from draining the waterlogged cotton fields and drainage sumps along the Karakum Canal. He is already building a network of canals across the desert from the fields to the site of the planned new lake. But suspicious Uzbeks say a sea of the size he plans can never be filled from drainage water. They fear the scheme is a ruse to deprive them of yet more water from the Amu Darya.

It is hard to be sure where the truth lies. Turkmenistan does seem to be digging the drainage network that would be needed to fill the lake from waterlogged fields. The combined capacity of the drains, apparently almost as great as the Karakum Canal itself, could certainly deliver a huge amount of water. But, equally, both the long drainage canals and the lake will lose water on a vast scale. The drains will be unlined and will leak as much as the Karakum Canal. Up to half the water entering them is likely to disappear before it reaches the lake. And the lake, if its surface area ever gets as big as promised, will evaporate around seven cubic kilometres of water—almost a third of the water that Turkmenistan is currently entitled to take from the Amu Darya.

So, there must, at the least, be a serious risk that Turkmenbashi will need to top up his lake from the Amu Darya. One senior official in Karakalpakstan told me, "If the Lake of the Golden Century is built, we will be left without any water." He might not be wrong. A thousand years ago, the Amu Darya emptied all its flow into a large lake in the deserts of modern-day Turkmenistan. The Aral Sea then was all but dry. Soon, Turkmenbashi's medieval dreams of empire may see that ancient drainage system resurrected.

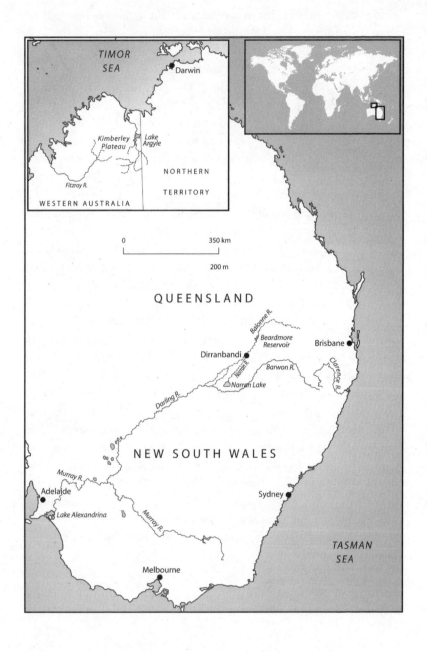

28

MURRAY: UP A GUM TREE

The giant river red gum trees tell of the death of the Murray River. In their thousands. These trees, lining riverbanks and creeks and congregating across river flood plains, are totems of outback Australia. You can carve a canoe from their deep maroon bark, as Aborigines have done for millennia, and they still recover. Koalas eat their leaves. The trees live for up to a thousand years, hunkering down during droughts and then spreading their seeds after floods. But if the drought goes on too long, they die.

By some estimates there are a quarter-million of these trees on the Murray. They provide shade and food and cover for everything from cormorants and pelicans to rare squirrel gliders and carpet pythons, which glide through their branches. But since the mid-1990s a combination of poor rains and abstractions of water by the river's managers have created the longest and deepest drought on the river since records began in the 1890s.

The Murray River is the source of water for one of the world's largest irrigated regions. And to satisfy the rapacious demands of the irrigators, the managers of the Murray system have virtually ended the inundation of the flood plains. They have emptied the backwaters and billabongs to water fields of cotton. Since 1993, there have been no floods on the Murray River. "The Murray is Australia's most important river and it is on its last legs," says the head of the environment agency in Victoria, one of four states in the basin.

And the loss of the nation's wellspring is touching a deep emotional cord. In Australia, water is the most valued resource, and the Murray in particular has a special place in the country's history. Don Blackmore, boss of the government's Murray–Darling Basin Commission, says Australia may be "on the cusp of a catastrophe...a character-changing event for the whole nation." If the Aussie swagman cannot camp by a billabong, what future for Australia?

The river and its huge network of tributaries, which include the River Darling, drain a seventh of the continent. The basin stretches from Queensland to South Australia and includes most of Victoria and New South Wales. The rivers catch their water on the mountains that fringe the eastern side of the country, and then make a long westward journey through the low, arid interior, eventually forming the single River Murray and reaching the sea through Lake Alexandrina close to Adelaide.

Before Europeans arrived, Aborigines lived here in large numbers. From their riverbank villages they harvested fish and mussels, as well as the kangaroos, possums, tortoises, fruit and grubs that prospered on the river's wide flood plain. In Aboriginal dreamtime, the creeks and waterholes are sacred, the physical embodiment of creation itself. But today, Europeans have harnessed the waters to create what they like to call the "economic powerhouse of rural Australia." The basin contains two-thirds of the country's irrigated lands. Its rice paddies, cotton fields, vineyards, wheat prairies and cattle pastures produce 40 per cent of the country's agricultural output, valued at A$10 billion a year.

It is not just the declining volume of water coming downstream that is killing the river and its flood plains. It is the timing of the flow too. Once the river ran free over the flood plain in winter and dried up in summer. The huge variability in flow between seasons and years shaped the ecology of the basin. But modern agriculture wants a different regime. The winter flows are held back to provide a steady supply of irrigation water in the summer. And levees down the main river channel ensure that, except in the wettest of years, the water is kept in the river for abstraction downstream. The river is prevented from spilling over onto the flood plains.

Official reports claim that a fifth of the Murray system's water flows to the sea. But in many recent years, virtually no water has made it. The Murray's mouth has become choked with sand as the last flow forms a small, increasingly saline pool within the once huge lagoon of Lake Alexandrina. Only a $9-million dredging program has stopped the lake's link with the sea being broken altogether.

This demise of the Murray is an ecological tragedy for a huge area of Australia. It is also a growing economic tragedy. For, as the Murray–Darling Basin Commission puts it, "The extensive wetlands perform essential hydrological, biological and chemical functions that support and maintain the productivity and health of the river systems." And as the river runs dry, it threatens to undermine Australia's rural powerhouse. The heart is being ripped from the Australian heartland.

Salt is a big part of the problem. The subsoils of Australia have always been full of salt. But the salt has been kept from reaching the surface by natural vegetation, which kept down the water table by sucking moisture from the surface. No longer. As the trees are replaced by crops, and the crops are irrigated with water, the water tables are rising. And as the water comes to the surface it brings with it billions of tonnes of salt. Some 25 million hectares of irrigated land across the Murray basin are drowning in the stuff. Increasing amounts are getting into the river in drainage water. And without dilution from floods, the river's salinity levels have been rising for years.

A $100-million engineering program to intercept salty drainage water and pump it into evaporation basins has kept Murray water drinkable in Adelaide. But lack of water and the accumulation of salt are slowly killing the Murray system. And the dying red river gums are its most visible sign.

Despite being an industrialized nation, Australia insists on using huge amounts of water to irrigate crops and cattle pastures. It acts like a third-world nation prepared to sacrifice its most basic natural resource to make ends meet. Around 85 per cent of the total water captured from nature is delivered to farms. Australia is among the top three exporters of virtual water on the planet. Rice, cotton and sugar—three of the most water-thirsty crops—account for a third of the country's water use. As one commentator put it: "The Murray is dying so that Australia can export rice to China."

So who are the villains? The most visible culprit is the Cubbie Station, former forest land 600 kilometres west of Brisbane in Queensland that has been converted into a vast cotton farm. The 140-square-kilometre farm can claim to be the largest private irrigation project in Australia. It requires an Olympic-sized swimming pool of water to grow one bale of cotton out here, and to irrigate its land Cubbie Station has the country's largest private reservoir—27 kilometres across and storing approaching half a cubic kilometre of water. That is more water than there is in Sydney Harbour. It would also be enough to irrigate the fields for two years if it weren't for the fact that an estimated 40 per cent of it is lost to evaporation. Cubbie Station, incidentally, has been paying just $4,000 a year for the licence to catch—and lose—that much water.

The water for this orgy of irrigation comes from the headwaters of the Balonne River, a tributary of the Darling, including the state-run Beardmore reservoir. Altogether fellow cotton farmers on the Balonne River can store 1.2 cubic kilometres. They strip the river of three-quarters of its water. "When the irrigators turn their pumps on, they can virtually make the river flow backwards," says the local environment council. Most years, there is little water left by the time the river crosses the state line into New South Wales, where it once filled the Narran Lakes. Listed under the Ramsar Convention as of international importance, the lakes are surrounded by coolabah trees and fill with duck and ibis whenever they flood—which, these days, is infrequently.

Cubbie Station director Tom Siddins defends the cotton operation. He says the local town of Dirranbandi was dying before
cotton came along. But much else is dying because it did. The
Queensland government called on the federal government to buy
up the station and shut it down. Canberra refused. The local cotton kings are big political players too these days.

But something will have to give. In 2004, the government
announced a Living Murray program that would retire a
modest amount of farmland and save perhaps half a cubic kilometre of water—less than 5 per cent of existing water
abstractions and, coincidentally, roughly the content of the
Cubbie Station reservoir. That won't wash with conservation scientists who declared that to rescue the Murray system requires
keeping at least an extra 1.5 cubic kilometres of water every
year in the rivers. Without it, they say, the red gum will die, the
fish will disappear, the land will turn to dust, farms will clog
with salt and the tap water of Adelaide will turn to brine. Unless,
of course, the irrigators find another source of water. Cue mega-
engineering?

They talk big in Western Australia. Always have. And now that
the province is facing a potentially catastrophic water crisis, big
water is the name of the game.

Their crisis is real. Runoff into the dams that supply Perth, the
capital of Western Australia, has fallen by two-thirds since the
1970s, as the rains have repeatedly failed. To keep the taps running, the city is draining underground fossil reserves and is
building a $350-million desalination plant. But it is economic
madness to grow crops with desalinated sea water. And climatol-
ogists warn that Western Australia faces permanent reductions in
rainfall because of global warming.

So its leaders want to dig what would be by some way the
world's longest canal. It would bring water 3,500 kilometres
from the remote Kimberley Mountains in the tropical far north of
the province, where monsoon rains sweep in off the Indian Ocean
and deluge the hills.

The idea had been proposed before. Back in the late 1980s its biggest backer was the larger-than-life Aboriginal representative for Kimberley, and then Western Australia water minister, Ernie Bridge. Bridge, who was almost as famous for his country-and-western singing prowess as his politics, proposed a Y-shaped pipeline, with one half going from Kimberley to Perth and the other half striking out east and south for Adelaide and the Murray basin. It was an Australian replica of Gadaffi's Great Man-made River, though tapping surface water. As in the Libyan desert, a pipeline was thought essential because a canal would lose most of its water to evaporation on the long journey south. But when the costings were done, it proved to be even more expensive than desalinating sea water and was abandoned.

The new plan would revert to the cheaper canal idea but prevent evaporation by covering the canal water with a plastic membrane. It could, according to the first blueprints, take water from the River Fitzroy, which carries nine cubic kilometres of water from the Kimberley Mountains to the sea each year, five times the flow of the River Thames through London. Or it could tap the existing Lake Argyle, a giant reservoir on the north-flowing River Ord that was created in the 1970s as part of an irrigation project up there.

Looking at the map, it is easy to imagine the Kimberley canal becoming the start of a vast continent-wide water grid. Australia is a land inhabited round the edges but largely empty in the normally arid interior. But in the tropical north there are permanent crocodile-infested rivers that carry two-thirds of Australia's regular river runoff. Most still run free. Most are untapped for irrigation. What a waste, you can hear Bridge and his fellow dreamers say. Australians have mined the country's mineral resources to become one of the world's richest nations. Why not go after water now?

And during the most intensive year of drought, 2002, backing for the idea of grabbing the country's tropical rivers grew on the east coast too. Cotton farmers and cattle barons began a campaign to get their government to divert all manner of these northern rivers south to the Murray basin and elsewhere. It would "drought-proof" the country, said a gallery of larger-than-life characters backing the scheme.

Besides the Kimberley project, other proposed diversions involved sending water from the Clarence River, which currently flows east through Queensland, into the Murray–Darling river system, and tapping the Burdekin and Daly in Queensland and the Northern Territories, respectively. The farmers gave the mega-plan a down-home feel by setting up an organization called the Farmhand Foundation and recruiting talk-show hosts to the cause. "All the rivers can be turned inland," declared shock-jock Alan Jones with disarming simplicity. The Farmhand Foundation reckoned A$40 billion could do the job.

River scientists and biologists were horrified. They formed their own organization, the Wentworth Group, named after a town near the confluence of the Murray and Darling Rivers. "What we really need to do is myth-proof Australia," says John Williams, head of the government's main research agency into land and water. "It isn't the drought that is our problem, it is our delusions. These are not solutions, but recipes for disaster."

It did not help the Farmhand cause that some of the scheme's backers were swiftly identified as being among the most profligate water users on the Murray–Darling basin—the very people responsible for the water crisis.

Australia likes to call itself the driest continent. But it is not really short of water. It has three times more per head than the UK. In Europe, only Russia and Norway have more. At the World Water Forum in Kyoto in 2003, Australia was derided as the world's "water waster" in chief. Back in Canberra, a Senate environment committee report the same year said, "It is clear that urban centres in Australia are using water in ways and in quantities that are not sustainable." Personal consumption of water in Australia was around 350 litres per person per day, one of the highest in the world. With reservoirs serving Sydney at a twenty-year low in 2004, the government introduced legislation to cut water use in toilets and promised new rules for dishwashers, washing machines and shower heads.

It was a start. But modest savings in the domestic sector won't solve a problem caused largely by an agricultural sector that uses 85 per cent of the nation's water. The Wentworth reformers say Australia's farmers are stuck with a supply-side obsession, when what they need is demand-side solutions. The reformers want to force change by taking water from farmers and cattle barons and giving it back to the rivers. They say this will ultimately be for the benefit of the farmers as well as the environment because, without water in the rivers, salt will accumulate and their fields will eventually become useless.

Several states are considering trumping the federal government's plan for a 5 per cent reduction in water use. In Victoria and New South Wales, they have been talking about 20 per cent. If they win, then maybe the billabongs and coolabahs and river red gums will be saved after all. Australia may be about to become a test case for whether engineers opt for large engineering solutions to the kind of problems being raised by climate change, or whether they choose a more environmentally sound route to salvation.

PART EIGHT

WHEN THE RIVERS RUN DRY...
WE GO LOOKING FOR NEW
WATER

29

TAKING THE WATER TO
THE PEOPLE

It is the world's largest civil-engineering project and aims to
remake the natural hydrology of the world's most heavily populated nation. But it began rather inauspiciously, one morning in
Beijing in April 2003, when the city's vice-mayor, Niu Youcheng,
accepted a bottle from a visiting local official. The bottle was
filled with water from a reservoir on the Yangtze River 1,300
kilometres away in the south of the country. Its handover sig-
nalled the start of China's south-to-north transfer project, which
is intended to be the ultimate solution to the desiccation of the
Yellow River and the North China plain.

Some people see the scheme as an exercise in engineering
hubris and a disaster in the making. But Chinese leaders say it is
a logical extension of the grand schemes of great societies down
the ages to remake their hydrology. Ancient Mesopotamia and
Egypt both harnessed their rivers to feed their people. The
Romans were famous for their aqueducts. Persian empires were
built around laboriously excavated tunnels that delivered water
from deep underground. But even at their greatest extent, these
ancient works were mild modifications to natural drainage patterns. Today's engineers have bigger ambitions, diverting entire
rivers onto distant plains. And China's scheme is the most ambitious ever to have got under way. It will, we are told, enable the

"Middle Kingdom" to carry on feeding itself as it has done for thousands of years. Maybe.

The south-to-north scheme will divert part of the flow of the Yangtze, the world's fourth-biggest river, to replenish the dried-up Yellow River and the tens of millions of people in megacities that rely on it. The price tag is $60 billion, more than twice the cost of even Colonel Gadaffi's fantasy-world Great Man-made River Project. And it aims to deliver twenty times more water than Gadaffi's pipedream.

Some of the water will come quite soon. In Beijing they should be drinking Yangtze water regularly in 2007. Certainly it will be there in time to fill the swimming pools and pretty the streets with fountains as Beijing hosts the Olympic Games in 2008. Some of the water will take rather longer. But within twenty years, say the planners, the project should be siphoning north annually three times as much water as England consumes in a year. The costs may be colossal, but China says the south-to-north project cannot be allowed to fail.

The project is actually three separate diversions. Two of them are already under construction. The first one will enlarge the existing Danjiangkou reservoir on the Han River, a major tributary of the Yangtze, and bring its water north. The reservoir is already Asia's widest artificial expanse of water; enlargement will flood another 370 square kilometres and displace a quarter of a million more people. The canal north will be sixty metres wide and as long as France. As it crosses China's crowded plains, it will span 500 roads and 120 railway lines and tunnel beneath the Yellow River through a giant inverted siphon.

The second will take water from near the Yangtze's mouth to the Shandong province on the North China plain and the megacity of Tianjin, which has suffered chronic water shortages since the 1990s. Part of it will use the 2,500-year-old Grand Canal, which was the world's largest artificial river in pre-industrial times and the first to have lock gates. Today it is a sump for effluent from China's burgeoning industry, but there are plans to clean it up.

The third, western route is the most ambitious. It alone is expected to cost $36 billion. It will take water from the Yangtze headwaters amid the glaciers of Tibet, and push it through tunnels up to a hundred kilometres long into the headwaters of the Yellow River. There is no firm route yet, but several tributaries will be tapped and there is talk of building the world's highest dam. This western route will be the only one to deliver water directly into the Yellow River. The other two are intended to relieve pressure on the river by supplying water for cities and farms on the North China plain that currently take ten cubic kilometres a year from the river. But altogether the plan is to send some forty-five cubic kilometres of water a year from the Yangtze to northern China.

China's leaders love megaprojects. Modernism lives on in their souls. With the World Bank claiming that China has already lost $14 billion in industrial production from water shortages, the scheme seems to them like a sound investment. But even as the first sods were dug, fears were growing about escalating costs. And academics and water planners I met in Beijing in 2004 raised a range of concerns.

The middle route, they said, could cause an ecological crisis on the Han River, taking a third of its water and worsening an already serious pollution problem. Wuhan City, a busy river port with a population of three million, could become a stink-hole overnight. What, they wondered, about the cost of relocating refugees from the Danjiangkou reservoir? Could the filthy and decrepit Grand Canal really be cleared of pollution? Is the engineering intended in Tibet more than a figment of someone's imagination? And, since China is trying to move to more realistic pricing for water, won't the transferred water be far too expensive for the intended recipients to buy?

China has a vibrant anti-dam community, which honed its arguments over the Three Gorges Project. It sees the scheme as another megalomaniac folly and wants the billions to be spent instead on improving Chinese water efficiency. Ma Jun, a journalist and campaigner in the mould of Dai Qing, says, "Chinese factories use ten times more water than most developed countries to produce the same products. Chinese irrigation uses twice as much." Even old-fashioned Chinese toilets use much more water than their Western counterparts. The US has been able to grow its economy for the last thirty years without increasing water use, he says, and so can China. And in the long run, he argues, it would be easier to shift the focus of Chinese food production from the northern plains to the south—where the water is.

But they lost the argument over Three Gorges, and they seem set to lose this one, too.

Already, China's scheme is being taken as a template for an even larger project in the world's second most populous nation, India. During 2003, as Chinese earthmovers embarked on their south-to-north project, politicians in Delhi were queuing up to back plans for what is known as the River Interlinking Project. It would redraw the hydrological map of India in a quite breathtaking way by harnessing the great monsoon rivers of the north, like the Ganges and Brahmaputra, and sending their water south and west to the parched lands where the droughts are worst and the underground water reserves are sinking fastest.

The Indian scheme is far more complex than the Chinese plan. It would build dozens of large dams and hundreds of kilometres of canals to link fourteen northern rivers that drain the Himalayas. And it would pump their waters south along 1,500 kilometres of canals, aqueducts and tunnels and through 300 reservoirs to fill a second network, linking the seventeen major rivers of the country's arid south. These rivers include the Godavari, Krishna and Cauvery that have each been diminished by heavy over-abstraction for irrigation.

The transfer would involve moving forty-seven cubic kilometres a year, and would be very similar in scale to China's scheme. But with so many more rivers and links, the price tag would be two to three times higher, with official estimates ranging from $112 billion to $200 billion, or around 40 per cent of the country's GDP. While the Chinese project sounds doable, whatever the pitfalls, the Indian scheme sounds like a great leap into the unknown.

Even so, the River Interlinking Project did not come out of nowhere. It has a long history. The legendary British engineer Sir Arthur Cotton first conceived of something similar in the mid-nineteenth century as a means of improving the country's transportation by linking rivers with canals. His scheme was dashed when the British decided to build railways instead. But the fantasy never quite died. For a while it was poetically described as providing India with a "garland of canals." But it took a drought across India in the summer of 2002 to bring the idea back to the fore.

The spectre of famine returning to India after more than a decade in which the country has had food to spare, was a profound shock. Southern India, like northern China, seems to be on the verge of a hydrological crisis. And with water tables tumbling and the country's population predicted to increase by 50 per cent within the next half-century, overtaking China to reach a staggering 1.5 billion people, there is a sense that a hydrological holocaust might not be far away. Surely, say many Indian politicians, the only answer is to replumb the nation.

In 2003, the president and prime minister, most state governments and the Supreme Court—agencies that in India's complex democratic system spend much of their time in internecine warfare—united to promote the River Interlinking Project. Government scientists said it could provide enough water to increase irrigated farmland by more than 50 per cent, and to power 34,000 megawatts of hydroelectric capacity. On closer inspection, though, the blueprints show that as much as a third of this power would be needed for pumping water round the scheme's network of canals and tunnels.

Will it happen? There were plenty of objections. The rampant pollution in most northern rivers would result in a grand interchange of sewage down the canals. One estimate was that an area of land the size of Cyprus would have to be flooded for the various structures, leaving three million people homeless. Even engineers in the states that apparently stood to gain the most were skeptical. Karnataka, one of the driest, is also one of the highest—often more than 600 metres above sea level. Engineers there doubted that the water from the north would ever reach them.

A former head of the national water ministry, Ramaswarmy Iyer, calls the whole idea "technological hubris." India already has half-complete water projects that have cost billions of dollars that should be finished first. He says that across arid India, three-quarters of the monsoon rains still evade dams and wash into the sea. Better to try to collect that rain as it falls onto fields, rather than trying to carry water across the country. "The answer is to harvest our rain better," he says.

Bangladesh objects too. It sits downstream of India on both the Ganges and Brahmaputra. Bangladesh may fear the rivers' monsoon floods in summer, but it also relies on those rivers to irrigate its crops and recharge underground aquifers. It complained angrily in 1974, when India built the Farakka barrage on the Ganges close to the border, diverting valuable dry-season water flows into Indian irrigation canals. It blames the barrage for dried-up fields, disease and a salty invasion of sea water into the Sunderbans mangrove swamps in the Ganges delta. In 1996, India promised not to reduce the flow further. Yet now it is talking about doing precisely that.

Like China, India is in a bullish mood at present, with annual economic growth of around 8 per cent. Its engineers have always thought big, and now its politicians want to turn their dreams into reality. So it could happen. It is at least possible that, within two decades, the two most populous countries in the world—with the two fastest-growing economies—will have spent a quarter of a trillion dollars on redirecting their rivers and remaking their hydrology.

And the urge to build big seems to be spreading. Spain spent 2003 lobbying the European Union to fork out most of the $10-billion bill for its own north–south project. It wanted to build a thousand-kilometre canal from the Ebro, the biggest river in the wet north of the country, taking as much as three-quarters of its water to Murcia and Almeria in the country's increasingly arid south. There, it was earmarked to irrigate half a million hectares of desert where they once filmed spaghetti westerns, and to water golf courses at new tourist resorts.

"Our problem is not water security; it is over-development," Julia Martinez of Murcia University told me as we toured the region in the summer of 2004, charting the new holiday villas and swimming pools and hillsides covered in plastic greenhouses. "Some of the aquifers round here are completely exhausted or filling with salt. A lot of the irrigation is illegal but the regional government is not even interested in applying its own laws on water. Everyone is trying to get rich with water, and then they call on the government to bail them out with water from the north."

The bailout scheme bit the dust late in 2004 when a general election brought in a new government that had listened to critics of the plans like Martinez and Pedro Arrojo-Aguda, an economist from the University of Zaragoza. "It's clearly crazy," he told me just before the plug was pulled. For one thing, he said, it would wreck the Ebro delta. The twenty-kilometre tongue of sandbanks, lagoons and reed beds protruding into the Mediterranean is one of southern Europe's most important wetland nature reserves, as well as Spain's largest rice-growing area and an important fish nursery. This land of flamingos and paella is already starved of water and silt from the river by upstream dams. The sea is eroding it. The transfer would seal its death warrant, he said. And for what? The golf courses and tourist resorts might be willing to pay for the new water. But the farmers could never pay. "The water will cost more than a dollar for every cubic metre—twice the current cost of the desalination of sea water. By the time it is delivered, few farmers will want it."

For Spaniards like Martinez and Arrojo-Aguda, the Ebro transfer seems like a return to the bad old days of General Franco, the fascist dictator who gave Spain more dams than any other similar-sized country. Perhaps that is why, in the heady days of their campaign, angry villagers from valleys in the Pyrenees that would be flooded for new dams for the scheme joined irate farmers from the Ebro delta, city environmentalists and political activists in probably the first-ever protest to go to Brussels demanding that the EU close its purse. The new government, sworn in in 2004, heard the protests, assessed the economics and opted to build desalination works instead. But the scheme still has powerful backers and after the drought of 2005, the worst in fifty years, calls to exhume the transfer grew once more. It is, in all probability, just one general election away from a revival.

Europe has other such schemes in the pipeline. The Greek government wants to take water out of the country's largest west-flowing river, the Acheloos, and pump it through a tunnel to irrigate tobacco fields on the eastern plains. It would partly destroy the Messolonghi delta, one of the last surviving untouched deltas on the Mediterranean.

Even in Britain, government agencies have proposed using the eighteenth-century canal system, dug to ship industrial goods around before the age of the railways, to create a national water grid able to ship water from the wet north and east to the drier south and east. And London's water engineers have long dreamed of tapping the River Severn as it runs out of Wales and through the West Country to pump its water over the Cotswold hills and into the headwaters of the River Thames.

Back in the days of heroic Soviet engineering, there was a plan to tap great north-flowing rivers of Siberia like the Ob and Yenisei and send their water south to refill the canals of the Central Asian cotton industry and, just possibly, to help revive the Aral Sea. First proposed by the czars back in the late-nineteenth century, and revived by Stalin in the 1930s, the scheme became a serious proposition in the early 1980s. Thousands of scientists and engineers were recruited to help bring it about. But in the end it fell foul of a mixture of romantic Russian nationalists who did not want to give up their rivers to Muslim states far to the south and the reformist pragmatism of Soviet leader Mikhail Gorbachev.

But you cannot keep a bad megaproject down. And in 2003, Igor Zonn, director of Soyuzvodproject, a Russian government agency in charge of water management and ecology, told me, "We are beginning to revise the old project plans. The old material has to be gathered from more than three hundred institutes." It had won vocal support from ambitious politicians like Moscow's mayor, Yuri Luzhkov, a possible successor to Vladimir Putin as Russian president. If for no other reason, that link makes it a project to be taken seriously again.

The proposal would be roughly equivalent to irrigating Mexico from the Great Lakes, or Spain from the Danube. It would drive a 200-metres-wide canal southwards for some 2,500 kilometres, from where the Ob and Irtysh meet, to replenish the Amu Darya and Syr Darya Rivers near the Aral Sea. The canal, according to blueprints shown to me by Russian scientists, would carry 27 cubic kilometres of water a year. Though this is just 7 per cent of the Ob's flow, it would be equivalent to half the natural flow of the two Central Asian rivers into the Aral Sea.

Down among the "stans," they have always loved the idea. "Although it seems ambitious, it appears to be the only tangible solution to the ecological and other problems caused by the drying of the Aral Sea," says Abdukhalil Razzakov of the Tashkent State Economic University in Uzbekistan. And early in 2004, Luzhkov visited Kazakhstan to promote the plan. He said that this time round, there would be no handouts from Moscow. Central Asia would have to pay a realistic price for the water. But behind the scenes, Moscow is starting to see the scheme as one of the water projects that could rebuild its political and economic power in the region.

Madness? Certainly. But as Nikita Glazovsky, a leading Russian geographer and former deputy environment minister under Boris Yeltsin, told me when we met in Moscow in 2001, the region's engineers "still find it easier to divert rivers than to stop inefficient irrigation."

In North America, the parched Western states of the US have their eyes on Canada's water. It is not very surprising. Canada has some of the largest rivers in the world. When the spring snowmelt gets going, around a tenth of all the water in all the rivers in the world is gushing through British Columbia and Yukon and the Northwest Territories into the Pacific and Arctic Oceans. And the Great Lakes, on the border between the two countries, are one of the largest freshwater reserves on the planet. Meanwhile, only a few hundred kilometres to the south, the High Plains are parched, the reservoirs in the Colorado River sit two-thirds empty and California imposes restrictions on its lawn sprinklers.

In 2003, George W. Bush raised hackles in Canada by calling for talks about private US companies buying some of Canada's water to fill taps in the American West. It could become the ultimate fulfilment of the old maxim of the American West that "water flows uphill to money." Exactly how the water would be shifted economically was not made clear. Bush was less interested in the engineering than in establishing that NAFTA, the North American Free Trade Agreement, could cover the continent's water reserves. But for many north of the border, the issue is highly emotive.

The idea also has unpleasant echoes of vast schemes devised in past decades. One would have drained part of the Great Lakes into the Mississippi. Another, dreamed up back in the 1960s by Donald McCord Baker, an official in the Los Angeles water department, would have captured the waters of the Columbia River in the US, and then, in south to north order on the map of Canada, the Fraser, Liard, Skeena and finally the mighty Yukon and Mackenzie Rivers.

Its backers, who included Ralph Parsons, head of one of the world's largest civil-engineering companies, envisaged building dams up to 540 metres high in the canyons of British Columbia to funnel water into the Rocky Mountain Trench, a natural depression that would have been turned into a 840-cubic-kilometre reservoir—that is, one with three times the total capacity of all the man-made reservoirs in the US today. The scheme would, so the blueprint proposed, carry south 140 cubic kilometres of water a year—three times the capacity of China's entire south-to-north project.

That particular plan is dead and buried. But Canadian water officials say the pressure is growing to allow small water exports, especially from the Great Lakes. And they fear that once a precedent has been established, the likes of California and Arizona could come calling. Everything has its price under NAFTA. And if the current drought in the American West persists, and if climate predictions prove right that there is worse to come, then who knows?

Africa already knows a bit about harnessing great rivers. The Nile is today as dammed as it could be. Its waters power Egypt and supply its irrigators. Barely a drop reaches the sea in most years. But the continent's other great river—the world's second-largest river through the world's second-largest rainforest—is a new target. The Congo River runs undiminished throughout the year and has ten times the flow of other major sub-Saharan rivers like the Zambezi. Veteran British colonial water engineer Henry Oliver, the man who built the Kariba dam on the Zambezi, called it "one of the greatest single natural sources of hydroelectric power in the world." He would love to have got to grips with it, he told me after he retired to South Africa.

And now his post-apartheid successors say the great river through what Joseph Conrad called the "heart of darkness" could soon be lighting up Africa. South Africa's state-owned utility Eskom is leading a five-country project to upgrade a small and largely moribund hydroelectric plant on the river at Inga and turn it into a dynamo that runs a pan-African electricity grid.

At Inga, just downstream of the Congolese capital Kinshasa, 42,000 cubic metres of water a second rush down a series of rapids. Eskom's engineers say the force of this staggering volume of water at this point could generate 40,000 megawatts of power.

That's twenty times more energy than comes from the Hoover dam, ten times as much as Africa's current largest hydroelectric dam, the High Aswan on the Nile, and more than twice that of China's Three Gorges scheme. It is "enough to light up Africa and export to Europe as well," according to the company's adviser on project developments, Ben Munanga.

The proposed $50-billion Grand Inga hydroelectric project would not even require a large dam, because, unlike the Nile, the river is guaranteed to run strongly all year round. So there is no need to store water. Most of the money would be spent connecting this vast power source across Africa's jungle, bush and desert to the continent's main population centres. The first power lines would link it to South Africa via Angola and Namibia, a distance of 3,000 kilometres. Next, pylons would strut across 4,000 kilometres of rainforest and swamp in the Central African Republic and Sudan to Egypt. Nigeria also wants to take Inga power to West Africa. Its power might even straddle the Sahara and enter Europe via Spain.

The plan is backed by South African president Thabo Mbeki, who hopes that it could become the flagship project of NEPAD, the New Partnership for Africa's Development, which is being promoted by the G8 governments in Europe and North America as a new Marshall Plan for the continent. It could just happen.

There is a surprisingly strong political push too behind another megaproject to harness the Congo. This time the idea is to send the water itself north to irrigate the fringes of the Sahara and refill Lake Chad. In 2002, a huddle of governments met in the rainforests of Central Africa to sign an agreement on sharing the waters of the Congo. They said they wanted to raise $5 billion for a dam that would barricade one of the river's major arms, the Ubangi River, at a sleepy river port called Palambo in the Central African Republic, and send the water north.

The Lake Chad Basin Commission, representing Nigeria, Niger, Chad, Cameroon and the Central African Republic, fleshed out the plan in 2004. The dam should, they said, divert 100 cubic kilometres of water a year over a narrow watershed into the headwaters of the north-flowing River Chari, and down its wide flood plain, before ending up 2,400 kilometres away in Lake Chad. The survival of more than twenty million people in the lake basin depended on the Lake Chad Replenishment Project, the commission claimed. It could rehabilitate huge irrigation projects round the lake, such as the South Chad Irrigation Project, that were built in wetter times but are now unused.

"If nothing is done the lake will disappear," claims Adamou Namata, water minister in Niger and chairman of the commission. But the project would be "an opportunity to rebuild the ecosystem, rehabilitate the lake, reconstitute its biodiversity and safeguard its people." In late 2004, Nigerian president Olusegun Obasanjo agreed to pay $2.5 million for a feasibility study of the project.

On the Logone and Hadejia Rivers, in Cameroon and Nigeria, the poor farmers quake at the thought. For them, large engineering projects to remake the rivers have only ever brought trouble. Wherever the promised water went, it never reached them. Generally it was their lot to lose water as it was corralled and privatized and sent uphill to money. They want and need very different solutions to their water problems, ones that go with the flow of nature rather than against it.

30

SEWAGE ON TAP

I advise against eating vegetables bought in the markets of Vadodara, a large industrial city in southern Gujarat in India. Most likely they will have been irrigated with neat industrial effluent from the town's numerous chemical works. The effluent pours down a drain that runs for sixty kilometres from the city's industrial zone to the sea. The drain is a river that "never runs dry," one farmer told me. "You can get as much water as you want, when you want it. It's an assured supply of water, unlike the wells here." (The wells, I need hardly mention, run dry because chemicals companies are emptying underground water reserves.)

The drain is not something you would want to go near. I peered beneath one of the drain's concrete covers, which have everywhere been broken by farmers trying to get at the liquid. There was a tarry scum on the surface. It was jet black, though I was told that at different times it took different colours, depending on the effluent of the day. The stench was sometimes unbearable—a mixture of solvents and paints and much else I couldn't recognize. But all along the road beside the drain, for tens of kilometres, there were plastic pipes trained across the pot-holed tarmac, siphoning the toxic treacle onto fields and into villages. Legally, pumping from the drain was banned. But "during droughts especially, some of the officials of the company running the canal turn a blind eye," said my guide, a local investigator called Vaibhav Bhamoriva.

Dozens of firms, from the giant Hindustan Petrochemical Corporation to backyard outfits like the Shree Bitumen Company, dump their waste into the drain. Some eighty million litres flow down it to the sea each day. And, said Bhamoriva, tens of thousands of people in more than forty villages rely on it to grow their crops. It is the basis for a vibrant local economy. After interviewing hundreds of farmers, he has calculated that the total output of crops from effluent-irrigated fields here is worth half a million dollars a year. Some farmers use it to grow rice; more grow sugar cane or millet. Most frighteningly, a lot grow fruit and vegetables that are sold in the city market. "The sellers mix the vegetables grown from effluent with all the other fruit and vegetables. So we all eat it," one farmer told me. "We farmers know about it, but in the town nobody knows what they are eating."

What is the health effect of all this? In truth, nobody knows. Officially, the farmers are not allowed to use the effluent, so officially there is no problem. I dropped in at Chokari, a village of 1,500 people living either side of the toxic canal. The villagers told me that they had no other source of water except a pump a kilometre away that they use for drinking. The contents of the drain were used to irrigate fields of rice and millet and vegetables. Farming with the stuff was not pleasant work. "Sometimes the smell when we are watering our fields is unbearable," one told me. "We avoid getting the liquid on our bodies, because sometimes it burns the skin. We watch the water and, if it changes colour, sometimes we stop irrigating." They knew nothing about any longer-term effects on their bodies. But they said that it killed their soils. After three or four years, the chemicals destroy the soil's fertility, leaving behind a cake of salt. They had to abandon the fields then. Eventually there would be no fields left, and perhaps no healthy farmers. But for now they made a living.

By a perverse irony, the drain in places runs less than a hundred metres from a canal built to carry clean water from the newly dammed Narmada River in the south of the state. But while the drain runs black and full, the canal has sat empty for some years. I spoke to one farmer who lost most of his land twenty years before, to make way for the canal. He was resigned to the black humour of his situation. "Last year, during the election campaign, they released some water down the canal," he said. "But we've had none since." The toxic effluent, however, was always available.

Water should be recycled. Most of us would instinctively agree with that—until, perhaps, we realize what that means sometimes. So should dirty water be recycled? Nobody should countenance using neat industrial effluent to water crops. But sewage may be another matter. After all, even in Europe the concentrated muck created at sewage works is sometimes packaged up and sold as fertilizer for farmers. And in high-tech Singapore in 2003, they announced plans to add volume to the city-state's main drinking-water reservoir by topping it up with a 2.5 per cent dose of recycled sewage effluent. But that is small beer compared with London, whose inhabitants—me included—drink water that has been drunk and excreted several times as it makes its way down the River Thames, being extracted and returned by towns such as Swindon, Reading and Maidenhead before it reaches the capital. The advanced water-treatment technologies in use at every step make it as safe as water anywhere, despite its unappetizing recent history. The water-treatment works have just become another loop in the water cycle.

But across the poor, developing world, raw sewage is being increasingly used for irrigating crops. Chris Scott of the International Water Management Institute has conducted the first global survey of the practice. He has come to the staggering conclusion that perhaps a tenth of all the world's irrigated crops—everything from rice and wheat to lettuces, tomatoes, mangoes and coconuts—are watered by the smelly, lumpy stuff coming out of the end of sewer pipes that empty the drains of big cities. Without it much of the world would go hungry. In many countries—India, China and Pakistan, to name just three of the biggest—there is very little sewage treatment, and yet a great deal of the sewage ends up being poured onto fields anyway, complete with disease-causing pathogens and sometimes laced with toxic waste from industry.

Scott estimates that more than twenty million hectares of the world's farms are irrigated with sewage. And business is booming. The practice is most frequent on the fringes of the developing world's great megacities, where clean water can be in desperately short supply in the dry season, while sewer pipes keep gushing their contents onto the nearest open land all year round. In Hyderabad, the Indian city where he works, "pretty much 100 per cent of the crops grown around the city rely on sewage. There is no other water available."

And, however much consumers may squirm, farmers like it that way. First, because the sewage is rich in nitrates and phosphates that fertilize their crops free of charge; and, second, because the supply is often much more reliable than for clean water from rivers or irrigation canals, which means farmers can grow high-value crops that need constant watering, such as vegetables.

For these reasons, farms hooked up to sewage pipes make bigger profits than their rivals relying on clean irrigation water. In Pakistan typical farmers using sewage for irrigation earn $300–600 more annually than those without the benefit of sewage, says Scott. In West Africa, he met one farmer who grows twelve crops of lettuce a year from his sewage farm. You can see the benefits in land prices as well. In parts of Pakistan, it costs twice as much to buy fields watered by sewage pipes than neighbouring fields irrigated with clean water. People downstream like the farmers too. They are essentially operating a free municipal waste-water treatment service that stops rivers and reservoirs stinking so much. And so, often secretly, do governments. It feeds the people. In Pakistan, sewage irrigates a quarter of the country's vegetables.

Many would say that the risks outweigh the benefits. They include disease among farmers and customers and environmental problems such as the buildup of heavy metals or unwanted nutrients in the soil and underground water reserves. "Right now," says Scott, "waste-water irrigation is in an institutional no man's land. Water, health and agriculture ministries in many countries ban the practice but refuse to recognize that it is widespread." But, he says, instead of trying to outlaw it, or pretending that it does not exist, governments ought to regulate it. "We need to recognize that sewage is a valuable resource that grows huge amounts of food. So instead we should help the millions of farmers involved to do it better."

That means keeping sewage effluent for irrigating non-food crops or crops that will be processed or cooked before being eaten. Obviously it is more dangerous to pour sewage onto a field of lettuce than a field of cotton, or even sugar cane. And ultimately it means working towards treatment to make sewage safe. In a handful of countries—most notably Israel, Jordan, Tunisia and Mexico—that is already happening. Sewage is treated to remove pathogens before being released to farmers. In these countries, recycling forms part of a national strategy for maximizing water use and making sure valuable nutrients are not wasted.

Mexico recycles enough treated waste water to irrigate around 250,000 hectares. I visited a giant new state-of-the-art sewage-treatment plant at Juarez, El Paso's twin city on the Rio Grande, that treats half the city's sewage and delivers enough effluent down a canal to irrigate 30,000 hectares. It is virtually the only source of water for crops downstream on the Mexican side of the river. Israel converts around 70 per cent of the waste water from its cities into treated effluent for irrigating export crops such as tomatoes and oranges. This is an effective addition to its national water supply of about a fifth.

This makes good sense. In urban areas, almost every drop of water brought to the city to fill taps eventually leaves again as sewage effluent or in industrial wastes. Where it can be made safe, it should not be wasted.

31

CLOSED BASINS AND CLOSED MINDS

The Salton Sea just happened. It was all the fault of Charles Rockwood, a land speculator in California's boom years at the start of the twentieth century. He and his buddy George Chaffey, who had already made a fortune planting orange groves in Los Angeles, dreamed of turning a desert depression close to the Mexican border into an agricultural boom town. They planned to do it by capturing some of the flow of the mighty Colorado River from Yuma in Arizona, a hundred kilometres to the east.

Despite the distance, it didn't look too difficult. The bottom of the depression they had earmarked for irrigation was seventy metres below sea level, the second-lowest point in the whole of the US. So once the Colorado bank had been breached, the water would flow downhill most of the way. And part of the way there was an old riverbed to channel the flow. So in 1901, Rockwood's California Development Company constructed a rickety wooden dam and canal to divert some of the Colorado's flow.

Rockwood and Chaffey did a swift bit of rebranding. Their desert depression had come at a rock-bottom price partly because it was known to locals as the "valley of death." It sounded much better when renamed the Imperial Valley. The soils were good, too, and settlers eager to make their fortune came thick and fast. Within four years, some 14,000 of them had staked out farms, dug irrigation canals and planted 120,000 hectares of fields irrigated with Colorado water. Traders moved in to service them. New towns such as Calexico, El Centro and Brawley sprouted. It was like a gold rush.

It seemed too good to be true, and it was. For with the water came silt. The Colorado is the second siltiest river on Earth, after the Yellow River, and by 1904 its muddy waters had clogged Rockwood's canal. The water dried up and crops were dying in the Imperial Valley. Facing down angry mobs of farmers, Rockwood cut a deal with a landowner over the border in Mexico ands dug another canal to Imperial Valley down an old creek known as the Alamo. But disaster struck again the following year. The Colorado was in full spate when it broke its banks near the new canal and began pouring into the desert. The floodwater soon found Rockwood's canal and by the end of autumn the entire river flow—40,000 cubic metres a second—was coursing into the Imperial Valley. There, having nowhere else to go, it created an inland sea.

As the floods subsided, the river stuck with its new course. It seemed to have permanently given up its old route to the Pacific Ocean and settled on a one-way ticket into the desert. It set about remaking the region's physical geography to fit its needs. There was a small waterfall where the new Colorado entered the new lake. It soon began to cut back upstream, eating up the soft soil bed of the new river. Such was the power of the river that, for a while, the waterfall was retreating through the desert at a rate of a kilometre a day. It gouged out a gorge 30 metres deep and 300 metres wide. It was as if a new Grand Canyon was being created before the world's eyes.

The federal government panicked. Farms were disappearing beneath the sea, and nobody was quite sure where the water would go when the river had filled the desert depression. With tens of cubic kilometres of water pouring into the valley there wasn't much time. So the government called in the Southern Pacific Railroad Company, which had already lost a chunk of its line from Los Angeles to Tucson. The company spent $3 million over eighteen months dumping 6,000 rail-car loads of rock, gravel and clay into the desert in repeated efforts to force the Colorado back onto its old course. Finally, on February 10, 1907, it succeeded. But while the Colorado flowed once again on its old course south into Mexico and finally to the ocean through the Gulf of California, it left behind a new sea in the Imperial Valley covering some 1,500 square kilometres.

If all the farmers of the Imperial Valley had departed, the lake would probably have evaporated to nothing by now. But the farmers were not done. They regrouped and lobbied for a more permanent canal to bring Colorado water to California. The All-American Canal, finally completed in 1938, was one of the first and largest major diversions of water from the Colorado. It was finished soon after the Hoover dam, which helped regulate the wilder flows of the river and prevent future disasters. The canal has since become the basis for a billion-dollar business in the Imperial Valley providing salad crops for sale across the US. The descendants and corporate successors of the farmers who stuck it out through the bad times have grown rich.

And the sea is still there, too, thanks to the large amounts of drainage water pouring from the farmers' fields. In its new role as a desert sump, the lake has gradually became more polluted and salty as pesticides and the salt brought down by the Colorado accumulated there. It soon became known as the Salton Sea. And the federal authorities had the idea of filling it with fish. First they tried striped bass; then salmon, halibut, bonefish, anchovies and turbot. All died. In the 1950s they tried thirty species of fish from the Gulf of California and some of these, especially orangemouth corvina, did much better.

Today, despite the accumulating toxins and occasional epidemics of disease among the fish, the sea is one of the world's most productive, home to an estimated 200 million fish. And the fish attract birds in large numbers. Strange to say, with the rest of California draining its wetlands for new real estate, the toxic sump has become the state's premier bird habitat, providing a home for 380 species, including egrets, cormorants, brown pelicans and various boobies. It is home to more species than the Florida Everglades, America's most famous wetland.

And it hasn't just attracted birds. In the sixties, before Las Vegas emerged as a desert oasis for the jet set, the Salton Sea was the place to be seen. Frank Sinatra came with his rat pack. And yacht clubs, beauty contests and nightclubs followed. Even the Beach Boys put in an appearance on a shore front that had everything except surf. Then nature intervened again. Heavy rains one winter flooded the yacht club and hotels and the jet set took off for pastures new.

Water is a precious commodity in California, however. And the Imperial Valley's farmers are legally entitled to three-quarters of the state's share of the Colorado. An annual dose of some four cubic kilometres of water into the valley ensured that they continued to prosper. But change is afoot. For years, California has been taking more than its legal entitlement of the Colorado's flow—6.2 cubic kilometres a year, rather than the allowed 5.4 cubic kilometres. And now, after years of drought on the river and with other states growing increasingly thirsty, Washington has ruled that enough is enough. On New Year's Day 2003, it began cutting flows to the sunshine state.

To avoid taps running dry, the state decided to cut its needs by persuading Imperial Valley farmers to give up almost a fifth of their share and to let it roll on down the All-American Canal to San Diego. The state plans to make things right with the farmers by lining the canals that distribute water through the valley and investing in more efficient ways of irrigating, such as drip irrigation. Reluctant farmers finally accepted the deal in 2003.

It seemed a neat solution. But there is a problem. If the farmers no longer flood their land, there will be much less drainage water flowing off the fields and into the Salton Sea. With inputs expected to fall by at least a quarter, the legacy of Rockwood's rocky engineering a century ago will start to dry out. The director of the Salton Sea Authority, Tom Kirk, is understandably anxious to save his charge. He says his sea may be a sump, but it is also "a rich and vital ecosystem of international significance." He fears that, with water that once filled his sea heading off instead to fill taps in San Diego, his sump will empty and within a decade all the fish could have died.

"On-farm conservation," as the irrigation engineers call it, would trigger "off-farm Armageddon." Rather than funding their increased "efficiency," Kirk would like the state either to divert other drainage water to the sea or start shutting down farming so that more water is left for the sea. But the farmers, now sold on the idea of trading their water rights, are talking about new sales—to Las Vegas.

Will Kirk get his way? Much may hang on how California chooses to classify its toxic oasis. Is it, as the Rockwood saga suggests, a man-made lake? If so, it has no right to protection under California's conservation laws. But if it were decreed to be a natural lake, the law would be very different. It should be entitled to its own allocation of water to ensure it survives.

Surprisingly, scientifically at least, the sea should have a case. It turns out that the sea is no one-off accident. Large bodies of water have occupied the "valley of death" before. And they too got their water from the Colorado. Probably four times in the past 1,500 years, the Colorado has changed course and poured its waters down the Alamo and other local creeks into the Salton depression. Each time, the wayward river soon choked on its own silt and resumed its old course. But often it left behind so much water that the lake was for a while bigger than the present Salton Sea. There are tide marks on mountains round the edge of the valley to prove it.

Maybe during the 1905 floods, the Colorado would have rushed into the valley without the help of Rockwood's rickety canal. We will never know for sure. But if so, then the sea is, in part at least, natural—and entitled to legal protection. It is now a century since the Salton Sea formed. Maybe now, before it starts to die again, would be a good moment to decide the matter.

The story of the Salton Sea may be somewhat singular, born of reckless engineering during reckless times. But it tells an important story of increasing relevance in river basins round the world. More and more rivers are becoming like the Colorado: rivers in which every last drop of water is utilized, sometimes several times over. In hydrologists' jargon, these rivers that no longer, or only barely, reach the sea are known as closed basins. The only water left for nature is often drainage from mankind's last use. And every effort to utilize the water better—whether building dams or lining canals or improving irrigation efficiency or even harvesting the rain—can have unintended consequences for downstream users.

François Molle of the International Water Management Institute tells the story of a small river basin in central Iran. The Zayandeh Rud basin covers an area the size of Wales, where some three million people live by irrigated farming. Until modern engineers arrived, they relied on a mixture of wells, old underground tunnels that tap water, known as *qanats*, and traditional diversions from rivers called *maadi*. These eventually took most of the water, allowing a small amount to drain to a swamp, the Gavkhouni, where the last of the river died. But farmers wanted more water. So engineers brought in a new tier of modern water structures: large dams and canals. They promised to provide more water. But, says Molle, "Basically, the new dams and canals redistribute the water that was once supplied by traditional *qanats* and river diversions." Some people got more water, but only at the expense of others.

Undeterred, the government tried another tack. It put money into lining irrigation canals to cut water demand. Saving water always sounds good. But as a result, less water percolated down through the soils. Water tables fell and wells emptied. The government responded with bigger electric motors to pump water from deeper underground. At that point, the *qanats* dried up.

Of course, there were winners and losers in this long process to grab every drop of water in the Zayandeh Rud basin. Bigger, politically better-connected farmers won. Small farmers and the age-old water distribution arrangements lost. The *mirabs*, traditional democratically elected water chiefs, lost their control and authority. But there was no more water. In fact, there was less. The growing volume of water held behind large dams increased evaporation. The endeavour was "costly and worse than useless," says Molle. "Dams and concrete disrupted what had been a nice, functioning system."

And that water, sitting in large reservoirs, set the stage for the next step—taking water out of the basin altogether. In the next valley, which contains the ancient Persian city Yazd, new bore-holes have started to lower water tables and destroy the *qanats* that traditionally supplied the city. So the new plan is to take water there from Zayandeh Rud. The lesson, says Molle, is that in closed basins "any change in water use or abstraction is likely to rob Peter to pay Paul. Or, in Iran, it will rob Yadullah's water to irrigate Saeid's garden."

There are dozens of similar examples from round the world of how efforts to save water can rebound. In our opening chapters, we looked at misguided water efficiency measures in the Rio Conchos in northern Mexico. Intended to provide more water for US farmers downstream on the Rio Grande, they are likely to lower water tables and deprive Mexican farmers of the under-ground water on which they increasingly depend. WWF's Hector Arias had it right there: the old idea that rivers are from Mars and groundwaters from Venus is dangerously misguided.

Yet water engineers, agriculturalists and even environmental-ists have proved slow to make these connections. They continue to promote the idea that if a hundred individual farmers "save" so much water by pouring less of it onto their fields, then the entire valley or river basin will have "saved" that figure times one hundred. But it isn't always so, because in many river basins most of the "wasted" water would actually have moved on through the water cycle, either returning to rivers, from where someone downstream would capture it, or percolating underground, from where the same farmer or his neighbour may later pump it back to the surface.

Saving water can often be good, of course. Drip-irrigation sys-tems and canal lining and the rest can all bring local benefits. And insofar as they reduce evaporation, they can provide victimless gains. But in closed basins, planners have to be very careful that water savings don't rebound to the disadvantage of others. One man's waste of water is often another man's source of water. The biggest danger occurs when farmers announce that some new water-saving technology will allow them to irrigate more fields or to sell the water for use elsewhere. This may not be so much water saving as water theft. It may simply be depriving someone else downstream of the use of their "wasted" water.

And at the global scale we need to be very careful not to conclude too easily that water saving, however locally beneficial, can solve the world's water problems. They will undoubtedly help, but only if seen as part of the wider water cycle. We can never separate one part of the water cycle for our attention, while ignoring other parts. Water is the ultimate renewable resource. But that only makes more critical the task of managing the water cycle prudently.

32

OUT OF THIN AIR

The dew hung heavy over the Sussex Downs near the ancient Roman city of Chichester. Peering through the swirling mist of a November morning, I spied a pond. It appeared almost magical, like an oasis in the desert. For, though the air was damp, this patch of water was far from any spring or stream, and too high to gather water from the surrounding pastures. And this was an unfailing pond. It had not emptied for decades, not even during the long drought of the mid-1970s, which had killed streams, dried up springs and turned fields almost to desert.

I was looking at a dew pond. Its secret was to capture unseen moisture from the hill air. Though largely forgotten today, dew ponds were once essential to the great sheep pastures that covered these chalk hills. They are a hidden mystery of the English landscape, only now being recognized and revived, out of nostalgia and a desire to provide water for wildlife.

For centuries, dew ponds flourished across southern England. Gilbert White, a famous eighteenth-century chronicler of the English countryside, wrote of a dew pond high above his home in Selborne in Hampshire. It was, he wrote, "never above three feet deep in the middle, and not more than 30 feet in diameter, and contained perhaps not more than two or three hogsheads of water, yet it is never known to fail, though it affords drink to 300 or 400 sheep and for at least 20 head of large cattle besides."

While the valleys dried up in summer, he said, the pond on the hilltop always kept its water.

Naturalists often imagine that dew ponds are prehistoric features. That is understandable: many of them still survive near ancient monuments. On the South Downs, I saw dew ponds near Iron Age forts at Cissbury Ring and Chanctonbury and close to the Celtic temples of Lancing Ring. In his poem "Puck of Pook's Hill," Rudyard Kipling talks of a time long ago "before the Flint Men made the dewpond under Chanctonbury Ring." And the celebrated war photographer Don McCullin hinted at the same antiquity when he opened and closed a book of his best photographs with ethereal shots of dew ponds close to Glastonbury Tor in Somerset, site of the first Christian church in England and reputed home of Camelot and King Arthur.

But most dew ponds are more recent. They were dug to provide water for the large flocks of sheep that grazed on the downs in the eighteenth and nineteenth centuries, but abandoned when the decline in sheep and the arrival of piped water in the twentieth century rendered them largely obsolete. One of the last diggers was a Mr. Smith from the Chiltern Hills. He advertised his craft into the 1930s, providing a phone number for free estimates in "a secret process handed down from father to son over 250 years." His ponds were "guaranteed to condense and retain beautiful clear water without the aid of pumping etc."

So what was the "secret process"? On chalk hills, water quickly slips underground through the porous rock. So the first requirement is a waterproof lining. Dew-pond diggers used local clay, "puddled" to make it watertight by driving teams of oxen through it. But that doesn't explain where they got their water. There is a ticklish mystery here. Some water comes from rain, to be sure. But their real trick is to capture moisture from the air, catching the tiny water droplets in passing clouds and fog, and encouraging more water vapour to condense onto the ground in the form of dew.

Here, the hilltop location is the key, because as air rises it cools, and cold air can hold less moisture. So the rising air creates water droplets that form cloud or fog. And at night, as the hill air cools further, more water condenses and dew forms. Martin Snow, a local historian, has been mapping dew ponds on the Sussex Downs for years. He says many of them are cleverly sited at the heads of dry valleys that channel mists and moist air uphill. The old sheep farmers, he reasons, noticed that fogs lingered at the heads of these valleys and the grass was often moist. "Creating ponds would have been a natural way to catch that water."

But the "secret process" guarded by the pond diggers was more than a matter of siting. Their trick was to create a pond that captured the maximum moisture by providing as cool a surface as possible on which dew would condense. They did this by putting straw beneath the clay and stones on top. The straw insulated the clay, keeping it colder than the soil beneath at night. The stones, which shed heat quickly at night, lowered the temperature further. Once a successful dew pond was created it would, in effect, generate its own water from the air.

Many dew ponds have been ploughed up in recent decades as pastures have given way to arable farming. Others are overgrown. On the hills above Worthing, residents still remember how shepherds would halt their flocks for a drink at the Tolmare Farm dew pond on the way to the Findon Sheep Fair. Today that pond is empty with a radio mast through its centre. At Cissbury Ring, military tanks have pierced the pond's clay crust. But a surprising number just keep on catching moisture from the air. And dew ponds have benefited from recent national efforts to restore and dig ponds of all sorts.

The National Trust renovated one on Bignor Hill in an ancient landscape of Bronze Age barrows crossed by neolithic causeways and a Roman road. The Sussex Downs Conservation Board dug a new one in the grounds of Sussex University in 2004. Sadly, says Snow, "Most of the renovators are more concerned with providing water for wildlife than in re-creating dew ponds for their original purpose." The Bignor dew pond is full of reeds and yellow flag and the pink-flowered amphibious bistort. A worthy aim, of course. But it is fenced off from the sheep that it was once dug to provide for.

Dew ponds do not, perhaps, stand comparison with other methods of catching moisture from the air such as rainwater harvesting. Their champions see them more as countryside curiosities than as a new paradigm of water management. But they do suggest that there is often water to be found from unexpected sources. Dew collectors, for instance, turn up on several Croatian islands in the Adriatic. The otherwise waterless island of Vis has paved surfaces on hillsides behind a Franciscan church that collect moisture from hot, dry summer air and channel it into cisterns. On the Canary Island of Lanzarote, few holidaymakers will have noticed that local farmers surround their crops with a mulch of volcanic gravel that condenses atmospheric moisture.

Perhaps the most bizarre discovery was made a century ago in the Crimea by Russian engineer Friedrich Zibold, who found thirteen pyramids of stones on hilltops in the forests around the ancient Byzantine town of Feodosia. Each was ten metres tall and thirty metres across. They looked like burial markers. But Zibold noticed that they were surrounded by broken terra-cotta pipes that went to the city. And locals called the pyramids "fountains." He concluded that they were dew-collecting machines, and proved the point by building one close by that turned out 130 litres of water a day for several years, before being abandoned after springing a leak.

So, can the air be harvested for moisture on any useful scale? The atmosphere contains around 13,000 cubic kilometres of water at any one time, six times more than all the world's rivers. Of this about 2 per cent has condensed into water droplets in clouds and will mostly fall as rain before too long. The remaining 98 per cent is still in the form of water vapour. It is a tantalizing prize and some outlandish machines have been proposed to capture it.

In the 1930s French meteorologist Bernard Dubos proposed building a chimney 600 metres high with a fountain at its base to create an updraft of humid air that would, he believed, saturate the air above and generate rain. The machine was never built. But military people have from time to time experimented with manipulating the electric charges in clouds to encourage the formation of raindrops. In the mid-1990s, I came across one such, a small Russian unit, doing just this in the badlands of Jordan, on the way to the Iraq border. Few results have ever been published. In the 1940s, South Africa's chief meteorologist, Theodore Schumann, proposed erecting an electric fence fifty metres high and three kilometres long on the top of Table Mountain outside Cape Town to ionize the air and condense millions of litres of water a day from the atmosphere. Again, it never happened.

Some have even suggested using sound to capture moisture from the air. On a cool, still night, the air can be so saturated with moisture that even modest air movements, such as sound waves, can condense the moisture and produce raindrops. In the mountains of Yunan in southern China, villagers have a tradition of yelling loudly in the hope that it will stimulate rain. The louder they shout, it is said, the more it rains. This gives interesting scientific credence to the African notion of the rain dance, once seen as the epitome of superstition.

An interesting new idea that demonstrably works is to condense moisture from hot desert air in a greenhouse, using sea water as the cooler. It works best where there is a handy cold offshore current that can be pumped to the greenhouse. Charlie Paton, a British engineer, has produced working "sea-water greenhouses" on Tenerife in the Canary Islands and in Abu Dhabi and Oman. The greenhouses require complex systems for heat exchanging to have the full effect. But they are, in essence, giant dew-making machines. The Royal Institute of British Architects called the design "a truly original idea which has the potential to impact on the lives of millions of people living in coastal water-starved areas round the world."

Paton's Abu Dhabi greenhouse has been growing cucumbers, tomatoes and flowers in the desert since 2002. It delivers forty litres of water a day for every square metre of greenhouse—that is more water than falls in the rain of an average rainforest. And, as well as producing water, the heat exchangers air-condition the greenhouse. So it makes cool air in the desert, too. As a result, the crops need much less water. In the Abu Dhabi greenhouse, this means ten times as many crops can be grown with the same amount of water.

And then there is rain-making. To many, seeding the clouds to make rain seems outlandish. But in fact scientists have been active in this business for more than half a century. The idea is to encourage the formation of raindrops by spraying into the clouds billions of tiny particles. These, so the theory goes, will form the necessary nuclei around which water droplets will form and coalesce to make raindrops. Nature does this mostly with tiny salt crystals from sea spray. Scientists mimic the process, usually with silver iodide crystals. Successes have been claimed, but proof is hard to come by. That is understandable. Who can predict what would have happened without the seeding?

But practitioners are convinced, and surprisingly large sums of money are spent on operational cloud-seeding. It is practised currently in twenty-four countries and in ten states of the US, from North Dakota to Texas. In North Dakota alone, planes spent more than 600 hours in the air spraying clouds in 2003. The Idaho state power utility invested almost a million dollars during the winter of 2004–5. It claimed the money was well spent. A previous operation had increased snowfall by 16 per cent, producing more spring runoff into the state's rivers. This in turn raised hydroelectric-power generation and reduced the utility's need to buy power from neighbouring states.

In Australia, New South Wales plans to seed clouds to produce snowfall in the Snowy Mountains and maintain ski runs. But Israel claims the most successful and long-standing cloud-seeding operation in the world. According to the country's rain-making guru Daniel Rosenfeld, it works especially well in winter clouds rolling across the north of the country, over the hills of Galilee. He claims spraying typically raises rainfall from clouds by 15 per cent, and produces 50 million cubic metres of water a year—adding 3 per cent to the country's overall water budget.

Cloud-seeding is good politics in a drought. As the planes take off and spray the sky, state authorities can at least say they are doing something to fill taps and irrigation canals. The Indian state of Karnataka is a cloud-seeder. So are the African governments of Morocco and Burkina Faso. All claim success. But the scientific basis for the claims is less clear.

While cloud-seeders suffer from an inability to prove success, they also suffer from public fears that they could be all too effective. For one thing, cloud-seeding can be an act of war. The US secretly seeded clouds over Laos and North Vietnam in the 1960s to waterlog the trails of human donkeys taking supplies for guerrillas south during the monsoon. And sometimes seeding has been accused of causing unwanted floods. Most notoriously, Operation Cumulus, a secret military rain-making experiment over southern England, may have triggered massive storms on Exmoor in the summer of 1952. A rush of water and mud hit the Devon village of Lynmouth a few hours after one spraying, and killed thirty-five people. The truth of cause and effect can never be known, but, according to documents unearthed years later in the Public Records Office, Operation Cumulus was abruptly suspended shortly after the disaster. Perhaps they knew enough.

There are other problems. Cloud-seeding, if badly done, can stop it raining. Too many crystals thrown into clouds will cause the moisture to form too many droplets, none of which become big enough to fall as rain. And even if seeding generates local rain, the question remains whether that will mean less rain falling somewhere else. Jordan, one of the driest and most water-stressed countries in the world, fears that Israeli cloud-seeding may be emptying rain clouds blowing east from the Mediterranean before they cross the Jordan Valley. Canada's prairie provinces have similar fears about US operations over the border in North Dakota.

China spent a quarter-billion dollars on cloud-seeding between 1995 and 2003 and, so its meteorologists claim, produced 200 cubic kilometres of extra rain—half the flow down the Yellow River in that time. As well as making rain, clouds were seeded to prevent hail formation, damp down forest fires, disperse fog and even to bring down summer temperatures. In 2003 alone, China employed 30,000 staff, 3,800 rockets, 7,000 shells and 30 planes in the task. But across the plains of eastern China, there have been dark warnings of rain theft. In the middle of another dry summer in 2004, Pingdingshan city sent up the planes to spray passing clouds. Some 100 millimetres of rain fell on the city. But 150 kilometres downwind, Zhoukou city received only a fifth as much. The city fathers concluded their neighbour had emptied the clouds of the rain that was rightfully theirs. Maybe so. But I was a few hundred kilometres away at the time and it was raining where I was, too, without the benefit of seeding. So who knows?

It looked like a volleyball court for giants: seventy-five large sheets of plastic mesh suspended along a remote hilltop in the Atacama desert of northern Chile. It does not rain here for years on end, but fogs roll in regularly from the cold offshore current of the Pacific Ocean, and the plastic sheets were getting wet by capturing the moisture from those fogs. Like giant sails pointing into the wind on the ridge, the polypropylene nets collected two-thirds of the moisture in the fogs.

Each sheet, measuring twelve metres by three metres, took 150 litres of water a day. Tiny droplets accumulated on the mesh till they formed single large drops that ran down into a trough that flowed to Chungungo, a small shell-fishing town of 350 people that previously depended for its water entirely on tankers driven from eighty kilometers away. The project provided an average of 15,000 litres of water a day.

After a seven-year research project, the nets on El Tofo ridge have been hailed as the first new method of providing drinking water in over a century. "Until we set up the water system, the town was dying," says Canadian Bob Schemenauer, who with Chilean researchers masterminded the technology in the 1990s and has since spun off his own organization, FogQuest, to develop it. "But with a secure water supply, people began to return, and new houses were built."

Well, that was what he said when we spoke in the 1990s. Five years later he was wiser. The town had indeed grown, so much so that the sheets could no longer meet its needs. There was plenty of room on the ridge, but instead of putting up more sheets, the government decided to install a pipeline to the resurgent town, at a cost of $1 million. After that, neither the local authority nor the townspeople maintained the sheets. The system is now defunct; the plastic sheets torn and abandoned.

But the idea is catching on elsewhere. All along the Pacific coast of South America, communities have put up fog-catching screens, usually to provide water for new tree plantations. Often, once established, the trees collect the fog for themselves on their foliage, re-creating fog-based ecosystems in the desert that flourished before settlers chopped down the forests.

Schemenauer has moved on. He has developed his fog-harvesting system for other arid lands from the Caribbean island of Haiti to Namibia, Nepal to the Yemen, and Guatemala to Eritrea. In Oman, where overpumping has wrecked groundwaters and desalination works are the main source of water, there are fogs on around eighty days every year. When Schemenauer put up nets there, he got ten times the yield that he managed in Chile. In Yemen, where the central plateau is set to run out of underground water by 2010, he wants to erect nets that could replenish ancient cisterns carved into the hillsides. Israeli scientists are experimenting in the Negev desert and on the Golan Heights. Other tests have been going on in the Peruvian desert and on Tenerife in the Canary Islands. Undoubtedly the technology works. But, if the experience in Chile is any guide, the problem is finding a way of encouraging locals to use it when governments, at the end of the day, will never let them die of thirst.

Nature is a good fog-catcher too, and may have some tips for would-be fog harvesters. On El Hierro, another Canary Island, people until a hundred years ago harvested fog droplets from the leaves of trees. Perhaps this practice was the origin of a report by Pliny the Elder, in Roman times, of a Holy Fountain Tree growing on the island. In Namibia, meanwhile, British zoologists recently discovered a beetle in the desert that has evolved a bobbly upper surface to its body with a pattern supremely efficient at capturing moisture from passing fogs. The hexagonal pattern of tiny peaks and troughs appears to push tiny droplets together to form larger droplets that then roll off the beetle's back and into its mouth. The scientists, headed by Andrew Parker of Oxford University, rigged up a prototype fog-catching surface based on the beetle's design, which captured five times more water than Schemenauer's netting. So they patented it, and several companies are vying to make fog-collecting devices that can be put on the roofs of buildings, or even tents.

Is desalination of sea water the answer to the world's water woes? Some say so. Distilling sea water by boiling it and collecting the water vapour is an age-old activity. But modern distillation technology was developed by the US Navy for operations on remote Pacific islands during the Second World War. Following that, large-scale distillation for public supply took off in the water-poor Gulf states, where they have plenty of oil to provide the necessary energy.

Today, global desalination capacity is approaching ten cubic kilometres a day—roughly 3 per cent of the global tap-water supply, though only a tenth of one per cent of total water use. Most of the global capacity is still in the Gulf states. Saudi Arabia alone accounts for one-tenth of world output, and in 2004 announced plans for six more plants costing a total of $5 billion. Holiday islands where summer tourists have overwhelmed local water supplies have until recently made up most of the rest. In Mediterranean Europe, Malta gets two-thirds of its drinking water from desalination. Greek islands like Mykonos have been doing the same for years, as have Caribbean islands such as Bermuda, the Caymans, Antigua and the Virgin Islands.

Four-fifths of the world's total desalination capacity still uses distillation. But, since the 1970s, an alternative technology has grown in popularity. Reverse osmosis forces water repeatedly through a membrane that filters out the larger salt molecules and lets through clean water. Both technologies require large amounts of energy, whether to evaporate the salty water or to force it through the filters. Until recently, it cost several dollars to produce a cubic metre of unsalty water—typically a hundred times more than conventional water supplies. But costs for reverse osmosis have come down and more cities are buying into the technology.

Tampa Bay in Florida and Santa Cruz in California have both taken the plunge and more reverse osmosis plants are slated for Houston in Texas, Cape Town in South Africa, and Perth in Australia. In Spain a new government elected in 2004 swiftly abandoned its predecessor's plans to pump water cross-country from the wet north to relieve the arid south, in favour of twenty reverse osmosis plants. They are expected to meet slightly over 1 per cent of Spain's total water needs.

The cheapest desalinated sea water is now in Israel, where one of the world's largest reverse osmosis plants has been built on the Mediterranean coast at Ashkelon. Israeli water economics are notoriously opaque, but the government claims to be able to deliver water at around 50 US cents per cubic metre, around a third of the production cost in Saudi Arabia. (More pertinently for Israelis, it compares with the 30 cents it costs to pump fresh water from the Sea of Galilee to Tel Aviv and the $2 to buy water by the tanker-load from Turkey.)

Such prices are encouraging cities in less extreme circumstances, and in cooler and wetter climates, to join the reverse-osmosis revolution. During 2004, China announced plans for a giant plant for Tianjin, the country's third-largest city, where water shortages have been endemic for years. Even more surprising, Britain's Thames Water announced that it wants to build a $400 million reverse-osmosis plant on the Thames estuary in east London to process water during droughts. It would be able to produce up to 150,000 cubic metres a day, enough to meet the domestic needs of almost a million people.

The boom in desalination is beginning to alarm environmentalists. One problem is what to do with the salt extracted from the sea water during desalination. It emerges as a vast stream of concentrated brine. Most plants, naturally enough, dump it back into the sea. But this salty waste water also contains the products of corrosion during the desalination process, as well as chemicals added to reduce both the corrosion and the buildup of scale in the plants.

Maybe this pollution can be fixed technically one day. But what can't be fixed is the huge energy demand of desalination. A typical reverse-osmosis plant consumes six kilowatt-hours of electricity for every cubic metre of water it produces. Most of the power, inevitably, comes from burning coal, oil and other fossil fuels. So while desalination could conceivably become a viable source of drinking water in coastal regions round the world in the coming decades, it would be at the expense of an extra push to climate change.

It is also hard to see desalination ever penetrating the agricultural market, where the majority of the world's water is currently used. So at the end of the day, desalination seems like an expensive high-tech solution to a global water problem that is overwhelmingly caused by wasteful use. Like mega-engineering projects for shifting water round the planet, it is a supply-side solution to a demand-side problem.

PART NINE

WHEN THE RIVERS RUN DRY . . . WE TRY TO CATCH THE RAIN

33

CATCH THE RAIN

Lian Jianmin is a smiling, worldly, chain-smoking raconteur. He was telling me his life story. "I was a seventeen-year-old just out of high school in Tianjin in the east. During the Cultural Revolution in the late 1960s, when students were sent to the countryside to learn about peasant life, I went to work in a village in the hills of Gansu in western China. I saw they all had these cellars under their houses, where they collected the rain from their roofs." Many of the cellars were very old and had silted up, he said. People preferred water from wells. But then there was a drought, and the wells went dry. Villagers without cellars had to walk for ten kilometres or more to find water. "Even the birds followed the water tankers," he said. And afterwards, everyone started digging out their cellars again.

The sandy hills of Gansu are one of China's poorest and most desolate regions. They have no rivers other than the Yellow River down in the valley, and the water in the wells is often salty these days, and prone to run dry. But they do have a little rain and a long tradition of catching it before it can run away. Some of their water cellars are said to be 800 years old. The tradition may go back 2,000 years. Lian said he had met a farmer who was eighty years old. "When he rebuilt his house, which he'd lived in all his life, he discovered a cellar underneath that still contained water. And the quality of the water was very good."

Lian was so captivated by the structures for harvesting rain that he decided to make their development his life's work. The city boy from the east has never left. Today, he sings the praises of the peasants of Gansu and their cellars to anyone who will listen. And these days that includes a large number of foreigners who have come to learn the wisdom of these hills. The world has come to him. Lian, now an engineer with the province's water resources bureau, entertains a growing galaxy of foreign water people. "We had people from thirty countries here last year," he told me.

This large arid province, straddling the middle reaches of the Yellow River, is solving its own rural water problems without waiting for any promised benefits from distant water delivered by the south-to-north river diversion—a scheme Lian sees as wasteful and unnecessary. And he and his fellow researchers practise what they preach. At the head office of the agricultural development research centre in Dingxi, where we talked, they have almost 900 underground cisterns that provide all the water for irrigating their greenhouses and research plots.

An estimated two million people in Gansu get most of their water for drinking and growing crops by harvesting the rain—a figure that is rising all the time. These days the basement cellars catching water for domestic use have been augmented by an increasing number of cisterns in the fields for growing crops. They usually have a distinctive bell shape and typically hold sixty cubic metres of water, big enough for a man to stand in. They are usually lined with cement, though some say the old cellars lined with mud bricks give better-tasting water.

Every household has at least one cistern. Travelling the villages round Dingxi I met sheep farmer Zhujia Zhuang. He had piped water, but kept a backyard cistern to water a small vineyard and a second hooked up to a solar heater in a shower cubicle. An Yueying, a woman farmer, showed me round her tiny but immaculate farmhouse. She relied on the rain for all her water. There was a cistern outside her house that caught water from the gently sloping yard, and another that collected water running off a hillside and down a small concrete channel. "I built them myself about twenty years ago," she said. She was growing alfalfa for her cattle in a field, and pear trees and vegetables in the yard. It was the end of the dry season, but there was still water in both cisterns.

Was the water safe to drink? Usually it was all right, she said. But to be sure, she boiled the water first. As we spoke, she filled a battered old black kettle with water from the cistern in the yard and hung it up above a giant shiny dish in the yard that was pointed towards the sun. I had at first taken this for a big TV satellite dish, but in fact it was concentrating the sun's rays to heat the kettle. A while later, the kettle came to a boil.

Later, over lunch, I met Zhang Zhenke, the chubby director of the Dingxi county water-conservancy bureau. Most of rural Gansu, especially in the east of the province, drank from cellars, he said. "We have 200,000 water cellars in this county alone. A quarter of them are privately built and the rest were initiated by the government." For farming, many people set aside small fields as a catchment area, laying plastic sheeting on the ground to ensure they lose no water.

In many parts of the world, local officials would be embarrassed to have only a tenth of their population connected to piped water. Here Zhang was proud of the achievement. "We already have more rainwater harvesting here than anywhere else in China, probably the world," he said. Cisterns, he declared, were the key to the future prosperity of the region. The policy now was for every household to have a concrete catchment of 100 metres square to fill two cisterns. But "Eventually we want four for every household," he said. "There would be one for drinking water for a normal year, one for a drought year and two for irrigating crops. We are very proud of what we have done here to survive. We have some of the worst conditions in the country. Without the cisterns people could not live here."

In China it was Chairman Mao and his Cultural Revolution that began the revival of the ancient tradition of rainwater harvesting. In India it has been a mixture of swamis and scientists, schoolteachers and even policemen. Haradevsinh Hadeja is a retired Indian police officer. He loves playing cricket for his village team. When we met, he had a broken arm after coming off second best against a fast bowler from the next village. But, win or lose at cricket, his village of Rajsamadhiya in the backwoods of the Indian state of Gujarat always excels at water.

His fellow villagers say Hadeja is a near-magical diviner of water. And you can see why. Round the village, he has transformed a near-desert landscape of desiccated fields and empty wells into a verdant scene of trees, ponds, full wells and abundant crops. With no piped water, most of the other villages in the area rely on water tankers to provide drinking water for much of the year. And they have little left to irrigate their crops. But here, says Hadeja, "We haven't had a water tanker come to the village for more than ten years. We don't need them."

He worked this miracle by catching the monsoon rains. Not, like the Chinese, in purpose-built cellars and cisterns—but in ponds. And they don't use the water directly from the ponds. They allow it to percolate into the soil to refill underground water reserves and replenish their wells. "There is no more rain than before. We just use it better. We don't let it wash away," Hadeja says. The village has twice as much water as before, and wells find water at only seven metres down where once the water had to be hauled up from more than thirty metres.

I went to look. The contrast between here and surrounding areas where water tables are falling is extraordinary. The heart of the village appeared conventional enough: a gaggle of single-storey houses leading from a small square out towards the fields. But on the paths there were thousands of fruit trees, where most villages are treeless. Under their shade were piles of mangoes and watermelons. And out among the small fields growing wheat and vegetables and groundnuts, there were the water ponds. Lots of them. "We have forty-five water-collecting structures altogether," said Hadeja, as we walked past a line of women washing clothes in a pond. "This one gets its water from land up to five kilometres away," he said.

The ponds are arranged along the routes that the monsoon water takes as it drains through the village. Rather than trying to get rid of the floodwater, Hadeja has redesigned the village's drainage to slow the water's passage long enough for it to collect in specially dug ponds. The water passes from one pond to the next in a slow cascade. From the ponds the water seeps through the soil to refill the aquifer all the way.

Hadeja's second innovation has been to manage how people use the water. As a former policeman he has some authority, and though all decisions are taken by the village council, his word has obvious force here. (In fact, he told me quietly, the police and the authorities never come to the village now. They leave it all up to him.) Under Hadeja's law, nobody is allowed to take water directly from the ponds. And farmers are banned from growing the thirstiest crops, like sugar cane. "There is no point in catching more water if we only waste it," he said.

News about this remarkable village has spread round India and beyond. One foreign scientist brought satellite images of the village that showed up hidden cracks in the geology through which water flowed. Hadeja slowed the flow by plugging the cracks with concrete. But mostly, as in Gansu, water scientists are coming here to learn about rainwater harvest, though the water diviner insists that there is little to learn. "I am an uneducated person. I saw that people were leaving the village and I wanted them to stay. That meant finding more water. So I tried to catch the rain."

And in truth, this is no miracle. Hadeja has tapped into an old tradition and developed it. In India, you can still see abandoned ponds and lakes dotted through the countryside and on wasteland in cities. Until the early nineteenth century, much of India was irrigated from shallow mud-walled reservoirs in valley bottoms that captured the monsoon rains each summer. The Indians called them *tanka*, a word the English adopted into their own language as tanks.

Most of the tanks were quite small, covering a hectare at most, and irrigating perhaps twenty hectares. Farmers scooped the water from the tanks, diverted it down channels onto fields, or left it to sink into the soil and refill their wells. The tanks served other functions, too. Some were stocked with fish. All were prized for the silt brought into them by the rainwater. Farmers guarded the slimy nutrient-rich mud in their tanks almost as much as the water. They dug it out to put onto their land, and turned silted-up former tanks into new farmland.

Overall across India, researchers reckon there are around 140,000 tanks, either still in use or abandoned. Tamil Nadu has the most, approaching 40,000, covering several per cent of the land surface of the state and still irrigating around a million hectares. Karnataka estimates it has 35,000. Every region has its own design. In the Thar desert of northwest India, they channel runoff into man-made desert depressions called *khadin*, creating wet soil for planting wheat or chickpeas.

The system thrived until the British took charge in India. Though full of admiration for some of the grand Indian water structures on rivers, British water engineers largely ignored the village tanks, apparently not realizing that they were how India fed itself. Tanks passed into a kind of forgotten underworld, used while they served a purpose, but unrecognized by officialdom and rarely repaired or cleaned out. As the British and later the Indian government itself promoted more modern water-gathering technologies, they gradually fell into disuse. But today, as the formal irrigation systems established on the Western model fail across the country, and as farmers are having to pump from ever-greater depths to retrieve underground water, the old tanks are starting to be restored.

All across India, groups are harvesting the rain either for direct use or to revive underground water reserves. Besides tanks and *khadin*, there are also check dams. These are barriers constructed in small streams and gullies to hold up the monsoon rain long enough for it to percolate underground. In Rajasthan, a government scientist, Rajendra Singh, gave up his job, taught himself traditional water-harvesting skills and went out to the edge of the Thar desert, where villages were dying for want of water. He encouraged them to install check dams. Now his movement has 4,500 of them collecting water in several hundred villages, forty-five permanent staff and a grant from the Ford Foundation.

Whole landscapes are being transformed. In Limbadia, a village in western Gujarat, the water table was 150 metres down and falling fast until villagers built a series of check dams. Soon afterwards several wells began spurting water at the surface. Tushaar Shah at the International Water Management Institute in Gujarat estimates that, across Rajasthan, some 6,500 square kilometres of land are being newly managed to capture the rains, "with dramatic impact on groundwater recharge and the revival of dried-up springs and rivulets." Water tables have risen so much in Rajasthan that five ancient desert rivers—the Ruparel, Arvari, Sarsa, Bhagani and Jahajwali—have returned to the map.

In Karnataka, on the plains west of Bangalore, I visited a group called the BAIF Development Research Foundation that has helped farmers dig 350 ponds across four valleys near the town Adihalli. Water flows from one pond to the next in a slow cascade. The result is more water in village wells, year-round farming of grains and improved yields of cash crops like coconuts and chilies, cashews and mulberries, vegetables and rice. Incomes have doubled and sometimes quadrupled.

"There used to be water on the land ten days a year; now they have it all year round," said the director of the project and Gandhi disciple G. N. S. Reddy. One local farmer told me with delight, "I can irrigate my vegetables from the pond once a week and afterwards there is still water in the pond." As Reddy and I walked back to the road, with birds singing in the trees, we met women goatherders who had walked several miles to the ponds. "Where we live, there is no water. So we come here. They let us use the water," one told me.

I met a husband and wife who a few years before had given up farming and become migrant labourers for much of the year— pretty much the bottom of the heap, even in India—after their 100-metre deep-borehole went dry. But now, thanks to the local network of ponds, the water table was back to forty metres and they were home again. When we dropped by, they were wielding a long hosepipe to irrigate rice and gherkins. Ratnama, the wife, said with a broad smile, "We used to steal fodder from other peoples' land for our animals. Now other people steal ours. We've built a new house and sunk another borehole. We are not begging anymore. We can even get loans."

Rainwater harvesting is becoming a widespread social movement, uniting many strands of Indian society. Pandurang Shastri Athavale—a Vedic scholar in western India known to his followers until his death in 2003 as Dada—preached a simple life, in which commonly owned resources such as water were revered, and their protection seen as an act of devotion. With this creed, Dada persuaded tens of thousands of villagers to construct low mud walls on their fields to divert the monsoon rains directly down their wells. Some 300,000 wells have so far been adapted to receive rainwater.

"Even cities can do it," says Sunita Narain, the director of the Delhi-based Centre for Science and the Environment, an outspoken advocate. "In parts of Delhi where old tanks and ponds have been cleared of garbage and refilled with water, the water tables are rising." Delhi could, if it got organized, obtain a third of its water from harvesting the rains, she says. In Bangalore, in India's "Silicon Valley," they are trying to boost the aquifers by rehabilitating the city's sixty ancient lakes. The city's water is among the most expensive in Asia because to keep its taps running, the city authorities pump half a cubic kilometre up 500 metres from the distant and drying River Cauvery. Bangalore architect S. Vishwanath says, "The city gets about a cubic kilometre of rainwater a year. We need to use that instead."

Vishwanath is part of a movement to revive the city's own water reserves called the Rainwater Club. I saw houses, offices, apartment blocks, schools, even a planetarium, that are catching water from roofs, gardens, paved areas and parks, thanks to its work. Vishwanath's own city eco-house captures enough water from the roof during the monsoon season to flush toilets and run the washing machine for most of the year. An evening's rain can be enough to run the house for a week. From the roof beside the cistern, he pointed down the street to a city water tower. "They supply water about every four days. But I have water from my roof any time I want it."

But, heartening though these individual initiatives are, the roots of the Indian rainwater-harvesting revolution lies in the communal rehabilitation of aquifers. Shah set up his groundwater research centre in Gujarat partly to learn the lesson of people like Hadeja, Singh and Dada. He says the vital factor in their success is that the initiatives happen at the village scale. Few individual farmers can successfully catch their own rain and store it underground; it would quickly dissipate into the wider aquifer. But when an entire village does it, the effects are often spectacular. Water tables rise, dried-up streams flow again and, with more water for irrigation, the productivity of fields is transformed.

Shah says the rainwater-harvesting movement is "mobilizing social energy on such a scale and intensity that may be one of the most effective responses to an environmental challenge anywhere in the world." It is, he points out, completely autonomous from government. "It emerged on its own, found its own source of energy and dynamism, and devised its own expansion plans."

By some estimates 20,000 villages in India are harvesting their rains. Not much, perhaps, in a country that boasts a million villages, but it is a start. And however the "social energy" is created—whether by the force of a personality like Hadeja, through religious devotion or a Gandhian ethos—some kind of communal water ethic seems to be the magic ingredient. That and a belief, whether expressed in religious or secular terms, that, as Dada put it: "If you quench Mother Earth's thirst, she will quench yours."

34

ON THE GRAPEVINE

There has never been a blueprint for catching the rain. You can catch it on rooftops, on agricultural terraces, by diverting flash floods into ponds, by blocking gullies or by putting up low earth bunds across hillsides or round individual plants. But harvesting the rain was once a worldwide technology on which hundreds of millions depended. Every locality had its own systems. Almost everyone did it. English country houses caught the rain from their roofs to water the flower beds. So did palaces from India to the Middle East. African villagers harvested water on the leaves of trees in their kitchen gardens. American Indians erected low stone walls and weirs made of brushwood across the Sonora desert to divert storm waters onto their fields. For small tribes and communities in particular, rainwater harvesting made much more sense than the larger river-diversion structures of "hydraulic civilizations."

Many countries, particularly in the Middle East, have almost apologetically carried on harvesting the rain in defiance of Western engineering norms. Jordan constructs earth dams in the desert to increase soil moisture for groves of olives, pistachios and almonds. Yemenis have captured floodwaters in wadis for centuries and exported the idea in the early twentieth century to the East African states of Eritrea, Ethiopia and Somalia, where it is now the dominant form of irrigation. Tunisia still grows 100,000 olive trees with Meskats, small rain catchments as big as tennis courts and surrounded by earth bunds, that channel water to a cropping area of about half the size. They tap rainwater and springs in the wet north and route it round precipitous hillsides and through tunnels, towards the sunny arid south, where the precious liquid grows bananas and grapes. A similar system continues to water orchards in parts of Afghanistan.

In the desert sands of Egypt, the ancient Bedouin technique of cutting cisterns into the rocks to catch and store water for drinking and irrigating vegetables has undergone a dramatic revival. Thousands of new cisterns have been cut.

The inhabitants of small islands surrounded by salty seas know better than most the perils of a finite supply of fresh water. Madeira, a holiday island in the warm waters of the Atlantic Ocean west of Morocco, has few rivers. But it does have a network of 2,500 kilometres of beautifully constructed stone water channels that cross the entire island. Known as *levadas*, the channels were constructed by African slaves under the last of the Portuguese sugar planters. The British territory of Gibraltar on the southern tip of Spain, which is politically if not quite geographically an island, has one of the most intensive rain-collection systems in the world, channelling water from collecting areas on the giant rock that dominates the enclave into tanks excavated into the rock. Across the Atlantic in Bermuda, new houses are required by law to include equipment for collecting rainwater from the roofs.

But if any moment was pivotal to the rediscovery of rainwater harvesting in the West it was when an Israeli archaeologist, the late Michael Evenari from the Hebrew University of Jerusalem, stumbled on hillside water channels in the Negev desert. Evenari had been excavating old settlements of the Nabateans, who controlled the caravan routes from Arabia to Rome via Mediterranean ports in Gaza around two thousand years ago, trafficking in gold, ivory, spices, frankincense and myrrh. This was big business, the ancient equivalent of running an oil pipeline. The Nabatean kings were probably the three kings of the Nativity story, and they ran six imposing desert cities— including the famous "pink city" of Petra in modern Jordan. But how, Evenari wondered, were their citizens fed and watered?

As he excavated, Evenari realized that these traders were catching the rain as it fell in occasional storms on the hills. Hydrologists estimate that a single hectare of Negev desert can capture as much as a thousand cubic metres of water over a year. Cleverly managed, this was enough to moisten the dry soil and grow olives and wheat and vines. It seemed to be a model of how to live in the desert. Evenari was so struck by the idea that he re-created an ancient Nabatean farm below the ramparts of Avdat, one of the ruined cities in the Negev.

When I paid a visit to the Avdat farm, it hadn't rained for six weeks. All around was barren wasteland. But on the farm the soil was damp, a field of wheat was growing, and almond and pistachio trees were in leaf. "We have tried to grow the crops mentioned in the Bible," said researcher Pedro Berliner. "And most of them will grow here in the desert if we harvest the rain." It was a stunning sight. And as I have spoken to practitioners of rainwater harvesting round the world since, I have discovered how important the Negev experience has been in their work.

Vedic scholars in India, it turns out, first learned of rainwater harvesting from the Nabatean work. Other Indian advocates made similar pilgrimages to Israel, back in the 1980s. It was around then, too, that Bill Hereford, a worker for the aid agency Oxfam, stumbled on Evenari's desert farm while on a sabbatical from Burkina Faso in West Africa. On his return, he encouraged African villagers to try and revive abandoned desert fields on the edge of the Sahara by laying low stone walls on the hillsides. It worked. The walls captured water long enough for it to soak in and nourish crops.

The news spread from village to village and eventually into neighbouring countries and across much of the West African bush. Thousands of hectares across the arid Sahel, which once seemed destined to turn to desert, now have crops and trees growing where before nothing grew. Where the rain has been harvested, there has been a 70 per cent increase in yields of local cereals such as sorghum and millet, as well as more trees for firewood and more grassland for livestock. Chris Reij of the Free University, Amsterdam, says rainwater harvesting is the leading cause of a widespread "greening" of the Saharan margins in the past fifteen years.

There have been other notable instances of the cross-fertilization of the rainwater-harvesting idea. In the Machakos district of Kenya, the Akamba tribe was in a bad way sixty years ago. A British administrator called the hills where they lived an "appalling example" of environmental degradation. "The inhabitants are rapidly drifting to a state of hopeless and miserable poverty and their land to a parched desert of rocks, stones and sand." But rather than accept their fate, the Akamba people sought out new ideas. Elders remembered seeing tanks and hillside terraces that catch water in India, where they had served in the British colonial forces during the Second World War. They decided to try it back home.

They have since dug ponds and terraced hillsides to such effect that today, despite a huge surge in the Akamba population, their farms are producing more, their people are wealthier and their landscape is greener. Researchers call this transformation the Machakos miracle. Desertification has been put into reverse through catching the rain.

Meanwhile, Oxfam has encouraged rainwater harvesting on the West Bank, where some 50,000 Palestinians catch rain on their roofs during at least part of the year. Such systems have a long tradition here. The Jordanians used to insist on it in towns like Ramallah when they were in charge prior to 1967. But now it is a means to get round Israeli restrictions on drilling new wells. Jad Isaac, director of the Applied Research Institute in Bethlehem, estimates that Palestinians take ten million cubic metres of water a year from rooftops in Gaza and the West Bank for both drinking and irrigation.

———

What is the potential? "Millions of hectares of the dry parts of the world were once used for water harvesting. In the twentieth century there has been a steady decline, but the twenty-first century is likely to see a huge revival," believes Dieter Prinz of the University of Karlsruhe in Germany. Social and economic conditions may have changed, "but the advantages of water harvesting remain valid and farmers in dry areas will have to use them if they want to be able to master their future."

Steve Halls, director of the UN Environment Programme's International Environment Technology Centre in Osaka, agrees. Two billion people across Asia could have their water shortages relieved by rainwater harvesting, he says. "You can take basic rainwater harvesting systems, which look small, and scale them up till they are helping millions of people. It is a technology that can be used right round the world, in urban as well as rural settings. As long as you have rain, all you need to do is plan where to build the holding tanks."

But many believe that the real potential for rainwater harvesting to transform lives lies in rural Africa. This is where unmet water demand is greatest, where huge areas have no clean running water, and where millions of women tramp for miles every morning to collect water from fetid pools and rivers or unreliable wells. It is where people go hungry for want of water to irrigate their crops. It is where the residents of squatter colonies in cities pay two dollars or more to receive water from lorries run by private vendors. Most of the increase in world demand for water in the coming half-century will be in Africa.

Johan Rockstrom, a Swedish hydrologist, calculates that conquering existing hunger and coping with an estimated three billion extra people will increase global annual water need by 5,600 cubic kilometres, or 80 per cent, by 2050. Where will that water come from? Extra dams cannot go anywhere near meeting that need, he says. There isn't the money. And even if there were, most rivers in farming regions are already running dry, and the good dam sites are mostly taken. At top weight, they could supply only an extra 800 cubic kilometres of water per year.

Meanwhile, most of the world's underground water reserves are ruled out because they are already overpumped. Their use should be scaled back rather than increased. Novel water sources like desalination may help in some places with drinking and industrial water—but not irrigation. So the future of the world's food depends on catching the rains. If Africa is to feed itself in 2050, it will have to increase rain-fed farming fivefold, Rockstrom says. "We need individual farmers to catch the rain," says David Molden of the International Water Management Institute. There is no alternative.

Hearing these words, I though of Jane Ngei, a poor farmer with a young family I met on a back road in Machakos in Kenya. She had never heard of the Machakos miracle, still less of her ancestors' visits to Indian terraces or a global movement in rainwater harvesting. Yet she showed me proudly how, with a wheelbarrow and a shovel, she had dug herself a pond to catch water that poured down the road by her smallholding after rains. She used the water to irrigate a kitchen garden of maize, vegetables and fruit trees. The extra money she got from selling her produce in the local market was paying for her children to attend school. It was simple. It had transformed her life.

Ultimately, the big numbers of the hydrologists come down to this. Africa needs millions of Janes if it is to remain fed and watered.

35

UNFAILING SPRINGS

Shallalah Saghirah is a small shabby village in northern Syria.
Its name means "little waterfall." But when Musa Oqlah came
here from the south in 1928, the land was deserted and dry, a frontier land of dry Bedouin goat pastures. When he planted barley,
the rains were not good enough and the crop died. He was on the
verge of moving on, until he noticed that in one spot the barley
grew round a seep of water. He started digging and found what
seemed to be a well. He stayed and drew water from the well to
irrigate his barley. The year is etched on the memory of everyone
in the village today as the founding date of their community.

A decade later, in 1938, Musa's well ran dry. Again he thought
of moving on. But first he did some more digging in the gulley
behind the village. What emerged staggered him. He found more
wells, and discovered that the wells were part of a chain, connected at their base by a tunnel 400 metres long, which tapped
underground springs up in the hills. They had discovered what is
known in these parts as a *qanat*. Musa and his sons cleaned out
the wells and the tunnel and constructed a stone surface channel
and reservoir to bring the water to the middle of the village. The
qanat has flowed ever since.

Shallalah Saghirah has about twenty households today. All
the seven elders of the village are cousins, grandsons of Musa.
They have no electricity and their only source of water is the

underground tunnel. Nobody knows how old the tunnel is. Ismail Hasoun, one of the cousins, says, "It is Roman; it is four thousand years old." But he doesn't know. At least 1,500 years seems a likely guess, say local researchers who took me there. It is, however, an unfailing spring. After a renovation in 2000, the village doubled the discharge of the system. Today, it pours into the small reservoir at a rate of about a litre a second, regular as clockwork, whatever the season.

Ismail is an elderly man now, his weathered face peering from beneath a keffiyeh scarf. But he clambered like a mountain goat up the gulley behind the village to show me the chain of seven wells along the tunnel's route. He pointed out the unlikely rocky outcrop from which the water first enters the tunnel from underground springs. He explored the tunnel for the first time during the recent renovation, and says that near the head it branches into several sections, apparently to tap more of the aquifer. He mimed how he had descended the wells and cleaned the tunnel. It was clearly hard work, but essential for the maintenance of this mysterious artery that sustains his village.

Ismail's grandfather divided up the water from the tunnel between his five sons. Each got a day of the water flow in turn. The fields are still owned by their descendants and the share-out continues much the same. Today, they grow figs and mulberries and vegetables and barley. As we talked, another cousin was ploughing the wet fertile soil with the village tractor. "The other villages in the valley have to buy water from tankers or the government wells," Ismail said. "And their water isn't as good as the water we get from the tunnel."

Researchers have mapped around 250 *qanats* across Syria. They remain the main source of water in a few dozen villages. But most have been abandoned either because they have filled with silt or because pumped boreholes have lowered the water table and dried them up. One tunnel, supplying Turkish baths in the ancient Byzantine city of Aleppo, is twelve kilometres long. But Shallalah Saghirah may be the only community where a *qanat* is the sole water source.

There are no other *qanats* in the surrounding villages in the Khanasser valley. Or that's what people told me. But the Bedouin had excavated underground cisterns up in the hills to provide water for their goats. Some still held water. The older men knew about them. I met Mohammed Al-Issa, who took me to see some cisterns up a long gulley near the town of Habs. It was a stumbling climb over rocky terrain, past abandoned shacks built by shepherds who once brought their animals up here. But every few hundred metres there was a hole in the ground leading into a water-filled cistern.

At last we stood at the top of the gulley, beneath a single olive tree where, Mohammed warned, snakes rested in the shade. He told me the cisterns were all connected by a tunnel. And as we returned to the road, he pointed out a beautifully constructed stone channel that followed the slope down to a nearby village. It was dry now. But it must once have delivered water from the cisterns. The system was, to all intents and purposes, another *qanat*. So Shallalah Saghirah was not alone, after all. But as we followed the channel, we noticed men loading pieces of its stone into a truck. They said they were taking it for building. They were, before our eyes, demolishing the *qanat*.

Qanats are one of the great engineering treasurers of the Middle East, central Asia and North Africa. In these arid regions, rain falls only sporadically and mostly in the mountains, where there is little flat land or soil for farming. From there the water swiftly percolates underground, accumulating in the stony slopes that flank the eroding mountainsides. If the water surfaces at all, it does so in small fluctuating springs on valley floors.

It was the Persians, in modern-day Iran, who first learned to excavate these springs, "chasing" the water back into the hillside by digging horizontal tunnels. They found that the farther they dug, the more water the springs delivered, and the more reliable the flow. What probably began as a smart idea to get through a dry spell turned into the wellspring for farming societies across a huge swathe of the old world.

Most textbooks on water technologies make little mention of *qanats*. Yet they are engineering marvels, dug straight and true, at a fixed gradient for their entire length, whatever the terrain above. And the scale of their construction is truly extraordinary. Syria is a minor outpost. In modern Iran, there are an estimated 50,000 *qanats*, mostly dug more than three thousand years ago during the heydays of the old Persian empires. The tunnels often extend for many kilometres into the hillside. Assembled end to end, they would reach two-thirds of the way to the moon. If these structures were aboveground, they would surely be regarded among the great wonders of the world.

Once, *qanats* were the main source of water in Iran. Until the 1930s, dozens of *qanats* supplied the capital, Teheran. One gushed into the grounds of the British Embassy. Tabriz, Shiraz and many other cities ran on *qanats*. One, supplying Isfahan, was more than seventy-five kilometres long. Some had such strong flows that the Persians built water mills along them to grind grain. As recently as the 1960s, their total discharge was around 600 cubic kilometres a year, equivalent to the flow of twelve River Niles. But modern water pumps have lowered water tables, drying up many *qanats*. The most recent estimate of productive use, made in 1998, was around ten cubic kilometres.

In many places, they are now little regarded and the skills that made them are dying fast. But in parts of Iran, they still form the backbone of water supply. The city of Irbil still uses *qanats* that were dug by slaves of King Sennacherib, 2,700 years ago. When an earthquake struck Bam in eastern Iran in late 2003, one of the first discoveries made by aid workers arriving in this remote town was that it was entirely dependent on *qanats* for water—and most of the tunnels had collapsed in the quake.

In the hot desert of central Iran, the ancient city of Yazd relies on *qanats* up to sixty kilometres long to bring water from the snow-covered Mount Sir and channel it beneath the city streets like a Metro system, supplying water to underground public water houses, called *ab-anbars*. Yazd is a city of tiled mosques and carpet shops and ancient Persian wind towers, which ventilate houses through turrets oriented towards the prevailing valley winds. Many of the water houses have wind towers attached. They are oases of cool air, cool water and well-being.

Wherever the Persians went, they took the secrets of *qanats*. The technology spread along the Silk Road to Afghanistan and China, where *qanats* are called *karez*; through Arabia, where they are *aflaj*; and along the north coast of Africa, where locals call them *fogarra*. *Qanats* watered Moorish Madrid and are still the mainstay of peasant agriculture in the Algerian Sahara, where the 20,000-hectare Ouled Said oasis grows dates watered from *fogarra* dug into the nearby hills. Recent excavations have found hundreds of *qanats* beneath the Libyan desert, relics of the ancient civilization of Garamantes. They lie abandoned not far from the green pipes of Gadaffi's Great Man-made River. In Kurdish northern Iraq, the great city of Sulaimaniya still makes heavy use of them.

One spring morning a few years ago in Cyprus, I interviewed a man who claimed to be the last *qanat* digger on the island. To prove the point, sixty-five-year-old Yannis Mitsis took me to the orchards near his village, where he assembled a large wooden tripod, attached a pulley and lowered himself down a hidden well into a tunnel that still fed water from the snow-clad mountains. The sun had already dried up the rivers in the lowlands, but his tunnel was running with water.

Yannis described how as a young man he had helped excavate new tunnels, which are locally called *laoumia*. It was an ancient family occupation. And a dangerous one. His father had died years before when a rope broke. In the old days, he said, "The tunnels were the source of water here, and water was power." Nobody had dug a new tunnel since 1954, but he was kept busy doing repairs. Many orchards still relied on them. There was nobody to take his place, however. "My son is a criminal lawyer in London," he told me. "When I stop work there will be nobody left."

In the hills of Palestine, there are tunnels very similar to *qanats* but shorter and excavated from hard rocks. They are known locally as spring tunnels, and most villages on the West Bank have one somewhere. Many have been mapped by an Israeli geographer from Tel Aviv University, Zvi Ron. But most are used only as a last resort by poor Palestinians such as Ahmed Qot, whose story we heard in chapter 20. "Most hydrologists don't know much about them," says Clemens Messerschmid, a German geologist with the Palestinian Water Authority. "But I collect data from one just outside Ramallah. It delivers only 1.5 litres a minute, but it is very reliable even in a dry summer, and the landowner still maintains it."

Almost everywhere, the *qanats* seem to be dying. And yet, they have hydrological qualities that should be in great demand. They are self-regulating because, unlike electric pumps, they tap the aquifer only up to the limit of natural replenishment. As a result, if properly designed and maintained, they are, as they call them in Yemen, "unfailing springs." They keep going in all but the worst droughts. And they are a source not of conflict, like many pumped wells, but of social co-operation. The tunnels often emerge from underground at the home of the most important family in the village, but thereafter everyone is entitled to water. Typically, *qanats* have many owners and the water is divided into hundreds or even thousands of time-shares. In Ardistan in central Iran, the division of waters at one *qanat* goes back eight hundred years to when Hulaga Khan, the grandson of Genghis Khan, ordered the share-out.

Can *qanats* make a comeback? It is difficult to see a revival of traditional, manual construction. While their hydrology is all right, their sociology is all wrong. In Iran a whole caste of people low down in the social pecking order had the task of excavation. It was dangerous and time-consuming work and nobody has yet found a way of making it safe. But some water engineers believe that *qanat* digging could be mechanized to provide new, cheap and permanent sources of water. Having seen ancient *qanats* in cliffs south of the Dead Sea, Israeli hydrologist Arie Issar has proposed developing mechanized *qanat*-diggers there. Tunnels could tap ancient water beneath the Negev desert that is uneconomic to capture any other way, even with modern pumps. The idea has never been tested in practice, he says. Somebody should try it.

But meanwhile, there is a good case for making better use of existing *qanats*; and for maintaining them and protecting them by placing restrictions on pumped boreholes nearby. And throughout the Middle East and beyond, there is a growing interest in making the best use of these remarkable subterranean structures. In Oman, the government has paid for extensive repairs to 6,000 *aflaj*, half the national stock. In the huge Turfan basin in the western Chinese province of Xinjiang, more than a thousand *qanats* dug during the Han and Qing dynasties were renovated in the 1990s. They provide a third of the district's water and take water up to twenty kilometres from beneath the snow-covered Bogdashan Mountains.

Aid agencies are also growing keen. Often, abandoned *qanats* are the most viable new sources of water to supply refugees in zones of conflict. Mustang Valley in the arid Pakistani state of Baluchistan was once watered by 260 *karez*. After the valley was connected to the electricity grid and locals began to drill boreholes for water, the water table fell and the *karez* were abandoned. But during drought in 2001, as Afghan refugees flooded across the border in the months after 9/11, teams of water engineers tapped the old *karez* to supply the refugee camps. In 2005, a US government aid program in Baluchistan earmarked more money for *karez* rehabilitation.

When American soldiers went to Afghanistan in 2001, they developed a deep suspicion of tunnels in the hills. Many believe Osama bin Laden escaped the US dragnet in Tora Bora in the final days of the war by fleeing down *karez*, many of which are wide enough to accommodate small companies of men. Certainly in the 1980s, the tunnels had made impenetrable hideouts for the US-backed mujahadin during their guerrilla war with Soviet occupiers.

But American engineers were amazed to discover that *karez* were indispensable to Afghan farming. They may water as much as a sixth of the country's irrigated fields. If anything, their importance has grown in the past decade, as drought has dried up rivers and springs and emptied reservoirs. In 2001, the aid organization Islamic Relief encouraged locals to renovate seventy-five *karez* in Helmand province, where the River Helmand had run dry. And since the removal of the Taliban, Western aid agencies have decided to carry on the work. The UN has proposed constructing small check dams in gullies to raise local water tables and bring *karez* back to life. In such inhospitable terrain at least, these mysterious tunnels could be ready for a comeback.

PART TEN

WHEN THE RIVERS RUN DRY...
WE GO WITH THE FLOW

36

LEARNING TO LOVE
THE FLOODS

Slavek the hippo enjoyed the worst floods in central Europe since the Middle Ages. He floated free from the Prague zoo and swam in the muddy waters that engulfed the heart of one of Europe's great cultural cities. He was happy, if a little hungry, by the time he was rescued as the waters of the River Vitava receded.

Nobody else much enjoyed the floods of autumn 2002. Central Europe is not the Mekong or the flood plains of Africa, where floods are good news, a necessary revitalization of vital ecosystems. In Prague, 40,000 people fled their homes and only a massive rescue effort saved the old town and its architectural treasures from total destruction. The cleanup bill was $2 billion. And there was worse damage downstream as the Vitava joined the River Elbe, where the German city of Dresden also suffered badly.

So what had gone wrong? The rains were, of course, intense. But this was not a one-off event. It formed part of a recent pattern of surges of water out of central Europe's mountains. Reports of hundred-year floods somewhere in central Europe are now almost annual events. The Danube has suffered two in eleven years, and three in fifty years. In March 2001, the rivers spilt over their banks in Hungary, Ukraine and Romania, followed in July by similar inundations in southern Poland. The year before it was eastern Hungary and Serbia; and in July 1999 much of the

Serbian capital, Belgrade, had to be evacuated as the Danube washed through it. In 1998 it was the Czech Republic, Poland and Slovakia in July, followed by Slovenia and Romania in November. In six years, flood damage in mainland Europe cost the continent $30 billion.

The summer rains are growing fiercer, owing possibly to global warming. Glacial melting adds to the flow. But something has also gone badly wrong with the way Europe manages its rivers. Engineering intended to prevent floods is, it increasingly seems, conspiring to create them. We saw in chapter 18 how the operation of large dams can cause floods. But this problem extends to the entire management of a river system. All the major rivers that flooded in 2002 had been engineered specifically to banish floods. Their wetlands had been drained and their meanders straightened. The rivers were held in check behind high levees and all impediments to the water rushing fast to the sea had been dynamited or chain-sawed from their path. But instead of eliminating floods, all this effort simply sped the water to the nearest bottleneck, where the floods became concentrated.

The strategy of rushing floodwaters to the sea, Europe's administrators were forced to conclude, has failed. "Flood peaks are higher and more damaging in places where wetlands and flood plains have been cut off from rivers, channelling more water into an unnaturally small space," Günther Lutschinger, a flood-plain ecologist for WWF Austria, told me as they cleared up the mess in 2002. At the same time, many of the continent's mountains had lost most of their forests, reducing their capacity to absorb heavy rains.

In a single day at the height of the floods of 2002, most of central Europe received more than 320 litres of rainfall for every square metre of land. Most of it surged within hours into the region's rivers, where 80 per cent of the rivers' flood plains had been barricaded off by a thousand kilometres of dykes, and where "improvements" had shortened the river's main channel by a quarter. The resulting floods came downstream in a great rush. And when the dykes failed, Prague and Dresden were engulfed.

The European Union is trying to improve forecasting of intense rainfall and to model better how such rains impact on river flows. That may help cities prepare evacuation plans. But it won't stop the floods. Europe's crowded flood plains are at constant risk of inundation. So is it time for a new approach—time to learn how to love the floodwaters, to embrace them instead of trying to get rid of them?

There are two ways of beating floods. You can get rid of the water fast, draining it off the land and rushing it to the sea down high-banked rivers that have been re-engineered as high-performance drains. Or you can encourage nature to hold on to it, letting it go only when the rains have stopped and the rivers are lower. Until recently, engineers preferred Plan A: the fast option. But however big they dug city drains, however wide and straight they made the rivers and however high they built the riverbanks to keep the river on its path, the floods kept coming back to taunt them. From the Mississippi to the Danube, the flood-free future has failed to arrive. Dykes turn out to be only as good as their weakest link—and nature will unerringly seek that out.

By trying to turn the complex hydrology of rivers into the simple mechanics of a water pipe, engineers have often created danger where they promised safety, and intensified the floods they intended to prevent. So now, more and more engineers are turning to Plan B. They are instead holding back the floods, capturing the water in fields and tearing down the banks and dykes and levees to give rivers back their flood plains. They are putting back the meanders and marshes to slow down the flow. They are even plugging up the drains on farms and in cities, encouraging the floodwaters to percolate underground. Rivers need room to flood, they say. And cities need to become more porous.

"The recent floods have provoked a completely new way of thinking," says Dutch hydrologist Piet Nienhuis of the University of Nijmegen in the Netherlands, a country that knows a thing or two about floods. "Rivers have to be allowed to take more space. They have to be turned from flood-chutes into flood-foilers."

Some call this soft engineering going with the flow of nature. Britain's Environment Agency, which was given an extra $250 million a year to spend after floods in 2000 that cost $1.5 billion, is an advocate. It says, "The focus is now on working with the forces of nature. Towering concrete walls are out, and new wetlands are in." The soft engineers want to go back to the days when rivers took a more tortuous path to the sea, and floodwaters lost impetus and volume while meandering across flood plains and idling through wetlands and inland deltas.

Take the case of the Rhine. Attempts to tame the river began in earnest in the nineteenth century, with "rectification" works undertaken by the German engineer Johann Tulla. Tulla's Rhineland rectification was the most spectacular of a series of great river-engineering projects across Europe. The very name "rectification" indicates the extent to which engineers' notions about re-creating the world in their own terms had taken hold.

Until then, the upper reaches of the Rhine took a tortuous, meandering path across a wide flood plain of woods and water meadows. Between Basel in Switzerland and the German industrial city of Karlsruhe, the river split into innumerable branches that continually moved, disappeared and re-formed. The islands between the branches were covered by flooded forests and wet cattle pasture. During each spring flood, the silty Rhine water slipped into the forests, meadows and fields.

It sounds idyllic. But the split channels and snaking meanders prevented the passage of all but the smallest boats, and building was difficult on shifting riverbanks. Even more disconcerting, the border with France, which followed the main channel of the river, moved whenever a flood passed. So Tulla forced the river into a single, well-defined and permanent channel. "As a rule," he declared, "no stream or river needs more than one bed." Nature never intended that this should be so, but Tulla's maxim has become the rule that almost every river engineer follows.

The rectification prepared the Rhine to become the great river highway of Germany. Along its banks grew industrial cities such as Mannheim, Koblenz, Cologne and Dusseldorf. More than two thousand islands in southern Germany disappeared, and most of the sluggish backwaters and shallow gravel reaches disappeared. The new, straight upper Rhine was about a hundred kilometres shorter than the old river and it flowed a third faster.

But this was only a halfway house to the modern Rhine. Tulla's plan kept high dykes well back from the river, so maintaining much of the flood plain. As time passed, however, farmers, villages and towns added their own dykes nearer the stabilized river with the aim of protecting buildings and turning seasonally flooded pastures into arable fields. And during the twentieth century, an entirely engineered channel, complete with giant locks and a series of hydroelectric plants, finally cut off the upper Rhine from 160 square kilometres of its flood plain, leaving just a tenth of the original area available over which the river could flood.

The faster river sped barge traffic to the sea, but also halved to just thirty hours the time it takes flood peaks to pass out of the Alps from Basel to Karlsruhe. After heavy rains, the peak flow on the Rhine itself now coincides with peak flows in tributaries such as the Neckar as they meet the main river. The resulting flood surge rushes downstream towards Bonn and Cologne, where peak flows are a third higher than before. Floods that previously were likely once every two hundred years can now to be expected every sixty years.

On top of that, the new faster river scours the river's bed and banks much more fiercely. This has been exacerbated because the artificial embankments on the remade Rhine prevent the river collecting silt from its former upstream flood plains. So the river is much more able to erode material from the river bed as it travels downstream. At Basel, the bed of Tulla's rectified river has fallen by seven metres; at Duisburg, it has fallen by four metres.

Tulla was known in his time as the "tamer of the wild Rhine." But his efforts helped turn the old, slow, silty stream that laid down alluvium as it went into a fast, silt-starved and eroding river. Almost two centuries of efforts to tame the Rhine have made it wilder and more unruly.

Similar stories are told round the world. Not least on the Mississippi in the US, which drains the planet's second-largest river catchment. The Spaniards who first arrived on the flood plain of the lower Mississippi in the sixteenth century thought better of building on it. They left great expanses of marshes and lakes to the Indians, who had long experience of coexisting with the floods. But the French settlers who followed felt no such constraints. They founded New Orleans right on the delta and called their marsh colony Louisiana, after their king.

New Orleans was always trouble. Water filled the basements of its buildings in the first months after its founding. Over the years, the French raised the natural levees ever higher in an effort to prevent floods. After an inundation in 1735, they built earthworks for seventy kilometres around the city. And after the US had bought the lower river as part of the Louisiana Purchase, slaves from dozens of cotton plantations, equipped with shovels and wheelbarrows, raised hundreds of kilometres of banks to speed "ol' man river" to the sea. But still it flooded.

In the mid-nineteenth century Congress stepped in with the Swamp Land Acts that handed ownership of unclaimed swamp to state governments. They were allowed to sell the land to raise money for further levee building. This brought to the Mississippi a land-drainage fever that had already taken hold in Europe. Louisiana sold off a quarter of the state to farmers, who drained the swamps for plantations. But in so doing, they undermined the effect of the levee construction that the sales were funding. For, in hydrological terms, the swamps were giant holding reservoirs for the river's natural floods. They spread the river's flow through the year, holding on to floodwaters during high flow and letting it seep back during low flow. Now barricaded off, they could do neither. The river floods grew higher and the levees broke with increased regularity.

Congress upped the stakes again in 1879, handing control of the river itself to the US Army's Corps of Engineers, through the Mississippi River Commission. The Corps' aim was to wage war on the river and finally "prevent destructive floods." But the river gave its reply by breaking the levees in 180 places in 1882. In 1927, despite ever-greater expenditure by the Corps, Mississippi floods submerged an area the size of Belgium, destroying 160,000 homes and every bridge for 1,600 kilometres upstream of Cairo, a small Illinois town with a name as presumptuous as the engineers' science. That year, New Orleans was saved only when, recognizing the river's unstoppable force, Corps engineers blew up a levee to draw off the river's flood.

Since 1927, some $7 billion more has been spent on raising levees. But separating the river ever more firmly from its flood plain has only increased further the flows during major floods. The 1993 floods demonstrated that. Much of St. Louis was submerged beneath water that rose fifteen metres above the normal level. The river rose over more than a thousand kilometres of levees. Nearly five hundred counties feature in a presidential disaster declaration, and property damage was put at $12 billion. And then came Katrina. The hurricane that battered New Orleans and the Gulf Coast at the end of August 2005 came from the sea, but its most lasting impact arose from storm surges into the Mississippi delta. Because the Louisiana wetlands have mostly been drained, the surge of water had nowhere to go. Water levels rose and breached New Orleans levees, engulfing a city of half of million people.

One of the river's nineteenth-century engineers, James Eads, uttered one of the great clarion cries of river engineering when he declared, "Every atom that moves onward in the river, from the moment it leaves its home among the crystal springs or mountain snows, throughout the 1500 leagues of its devious pathway, is controlled by laws as fixed and certain as those which direct the majestic march of the heavenly spheres...The engineer needs only to be insured that he does not ignore the existence of any of these laws, to feel positively certain of the results he aims at." In practice, the river has proved rather more intractable. Mark Twain was perhaps closer to the truth when he observed after the creation of the Mississippi River Commission that "ten thousand River Commissions, with the mines of the world at their back, cannot tame the lawless stream, cannot say to it Go here or Go there and make it obey."

These brutal lessons are being widely learned. Plan B is now up and running as governments try to fend off the huge costs and political difficulties that can follow major floods. To help keep London dry, England's Environment Agency is breaking banks and re-flooding ten square kilometres of ancient Thames flood plain at Otmoor outside Oxford. And further downstream its engineers have spent £100 million creating new wetlands to protect the boom town of Maidenhead, the ancient playing fields of Eton and the deer parks of Windsor Castle.

Meanwhile, in one of Europe's largest river restorations to date, Austria is letting the River Drava back onto sixty kilometres of flood plain as it exits the Alps. Its engineers are widening the riverbed and channelling the river back into abandoned meanders, oxbow lakes and backwaters overhung with willows. The restored flood plain, they calculate, can now store up to ten million cubic metres of floodwaters and slow up storm surges out of the Alps by more than an hour, so protecting towns downstream all the way to Slovenia and Croatia.

But the Dutch, for whom preventing floods is a matter of survival, have perhaps gone furthest. A nation built largely upon drained marshes and reclaimed seabed had the fright of its life in the early 1990s, when the Rhine twice almost overwhelmed it. In 1995, a quarter of a million people were evacuated. The resulting inquests concluded that the rivers had been straightened and the land had been built on so much that there was nowhere for the water to go.

Rob Leuven of the University of Nijmegen says, "Government policy is now to allow rivers to take more physical space." Rivers are being allowed back onto their flood plains, and overspill areas of low-lying land called "calamity polders" have been set aside to lessen the impact of major floods. The Dutch are caricatured as always having their fingers in their dykes; but now they have given soft engineers the go ahead to punch holes in dykes. They are making plans to return up to a sixth of the country to soggy nature in order better to protect the rest.

Similarly, since 1995, the Germans have given top priority to finding ways of lowering the floods on the Rhine. Their target is to shave more than sixty centimetres off the flood peaks by 2020. Nobody knows if this can be achieved. But for starters they plan to reinstate some of the 1300 square kilometres of flood plain lost on the Lower Rhine. Drained and dyked fields will be replaced by reed beds and water meadows designated to flood every winter. Just twelve months after the great floods on the Elbe in 2002, the German environment minister Jurgen Trittin announced legislation that will "give our rivers more room again; otherwise they will take it themselves."

In a crowded continent like Europe, giving land back to the rivers is easier said than done, says John Handmer of the Flood Hazard Research Unit at Middlesex University. A tenth of Europeans live or work on flood plains. That includes five million Britons. The pressure is growing to ban all new developments on flood plains. But protecting those already there is best approached by finding ways to slow up water before it reaches the rivers. That should mean using subsidies from the European Union's Common Agricultural Policy to discourage farmers everywhere from "improving" their field drains. Poor drains that hold on to water longer would be better for rivers. And, even more radically, it means redesigning our cities.

Modern cities could hardly be better constructed to create floods. They are concreted and paved and asphalted and culverted so that rains flow quickly into rivers. But the new breed of soft engineers wants our cities to become porous so that they can capture and store that water instead. In Germany, Berlin is leading the way. The city's massive redevelopment since the fall of the Berlin Wall has been governed by tough new rules to prevent its drains becoming overloaded after heavy rains. Harald Kraft, a city architect specializing in the new systems, says, "We now see rainwater as a resource to be kept rather than got rid of at great cost." Here is genuinely radical thinking. New ideas for flood protection begin to connect up to new ideas for harvesting the rain.

Take the giant Potsdamer Platz, a huge new commercial

redevelopment in the heart of Berlin. The city council has set a maximum limit for drainage from the site of just 1 per cent of the potential runoff during a big storm. If the project doesn't meet the target, the drains will back up. Simple as that. So architects have designed the buildings to capture rainwater from the roofs. The water will flush toilets and irrigate roof gardens. Meanwhile water falling onto the ground will go to fill an artificial lake or percolate underground through porous paving. All told, the high-tech urban development can store a sixth of its annual rainfall, and reuse most of the rest. It needs fewer drains. And it also needs fewer water-supply pipes.

New housing estates across Berlin are adopting similar technology. In the Zehlendorf suburb, rain from the roofs, gardens and driveways of 160 houses is collected to irrigate parkland. Not a drop of water leaves the development. Harzahn, a drain-free estate of 1,800 homes packed onto just thirty hectares, features roads built of cobblestones to allow rainwater to percolate through the gaps into the soil beneath. Could this be done on a citywide scale? The test case could be Los Angeles. This is where the benefits of combining modern thinking on flood protection and water supply could really pay big dividends.

L.A., as the songs says, is a great big freeway. With hard impervious surfaces covering 70 per cent of one of the world's largest cities, drainage is a huge task. L.A. has spent billions of dollars digging drains and concreting riverbeds to take the water from occasional intense storms to the ocean. And still many communities regularly flood. City engineers, locked in old thinking, want to spend a cool $280 million raising the concrete walls on the Los Angeles River by another two metres. Meanwhile, with terrifying irony, the desert city is shipping in more water by pipe and canal from hundreds of kilometres away in northern California and the Colorado River in Arizona to fill its taps and swimming pools and irrigate its golf courses. Is this sensible?

Like Phoenix, Southern California has a self-image as the desert region that can revel in water. It has the biggest swimming pools, the highest fountains and the most water-hungry agricultural crops. No problem. It prides itself on being able to pay. Marc Reisner titled his memorable book on the state's water politics *Cadillac Desert*, a phrase that summed up the mind-set. But this strutting hides a serious misreading of the state's own geography that sounds like bad planning. "In L.A. we receive half the water we need in rainfall, and we throw it away. Then we spend hundreds of millions to import water," says Andy Lipkis, an L.A. environmentalist. "We should be catching our own rain before trying to buy other people's."

Lipkis, along with citizens groups like Friends of the Los Angeles River and Unpaved L.A., want to beat the urban flood hazard, and fill the taps at the same time, by keeping the floodwater in the city. They call their dream the "porous city." They are working with schools and other places to convert asphalt areas into soft ground to soak up rain. And they believe it is a realistic proposition to do this across the city.

It could happen. City authorities have recently established a watershed-management division, and in 2004 they launched a $100 million scheme to road-test the porous city in one poor flood-hit community in Sun Valley. The plan is to catch the rains that fall on thousands of driveways and parking lots and rooftops in the valley before it gets to the drains. Trees will soak up water from parking lots. Homes and public buildings will capture roof water for irrigating gardens and parks. And road drains will pour water into old gravel pits and other leaky places that should recharge the city's underground water reserves. It's a direct replacement for a planned storm drain. The result, the city hopes, will be less flooding and more water for taps.

Plan B says every city should be porous and every river should have room to flood naturally. It sounds expensive and utopian, until you realize how much we already spend trying to drain our cities and protect our flood plains—and how bad we are at doing it. Plan B, going with the flow of the river, really is the better way. The question now is whether that can form the basis for a wider philosophy for managing rivers and the water cycle.

37

FREEING SADDAM'S CAPTIVES

In the aftermath of the first Gulf War in 1992, Saddam Hussein began draining the bulrush marshes of southern Iraq—home of the Madan, or Marsh Arabs, and sometimes described as the original Garden of Eden. Now, in the aftermath of the second Gulf War, wetland scientists are joining with Madan and Iraqi exiles in the US to rehabilitate the marshes. They are planning the largest and most ambitious recovery of a lost wetland ever attempted. The first phase of the rehabilitation was begun by returning Madan in the months after the toppling of Saddam; it cost little more than a few hours with a bulldozer. To complete the job might cost tens of millions of dollars. But if it could be achieved, it could be a model for reviving many other natural water reservoirs as the world fights to stave off water shortages and to remake other drying rivers. The world should be watching what happens down on the marshes.

When watching TV images of US forces crossing the desert of southern Iraq during the spring of 2003, few realized that, until a decade before, most of the land between Basra and the Euphrates bridges at Nasariyah had been marsh. Back then, the tank lanes had been covered in lakes and a network of waterways hemmed in by banks of reed beds. In this strange enclosed world, the great rivers Tigris and Euphrates nourished a flourishing ecosystem twice the size of the Everglades in the US. It sustained huge numbers of fish, large populations of birds and rare animals such as the smooth-coated otter.

But this was not a virgin wetland. It was also a highly productive natural factory that had given the Madan everything they wanted for five thousand years. Upwards of half a million people grew rice, caught fish, hunted otters and birds, gathered reeds and grazed their water buffalo in a world not so changed since it was immortalized in romantic simplicity by Wilfred Thesiger's 1960s book *The Marsh Arabs*.

But Saddam changed all that. In 1993 and 1994, he dug drains to empty the marshes of water, diverted the two great rivers away with huge canals, and raised embankments to prevent future flooding. By the end of the decade, more than 90 per cent of the marshes were gone. Their loss was "a major ecological disaster, comparable to the deforestation of Amazonia," said Klaus Toepfer, director of UNEP, the UN Environment Programme. It was also a crime against the Madan, and a major loss to people in Iraq who had never been near the marshes. Before the engineers moved in, the marsh waters had provided 60 per cent of Iraq's fish and much of its rice.

Saddam himself always insisted that his vast engineering works on the marshes were intended to boost farming. They would, he said, reclaim the land for farming and increase Iraq's crop production by up to a half. It was not a self-evidently preposterous claim. It was the same reason that most engineers and their political and financial backers have always given for draining marshes. And a similar fate for the Mesopotamian marshes had been proposed by British engineers fifty years before.

On a shelf in the Institution of Civil Engineers in London, I found a report called "Control of the Rivers of Iraq." It was published in 1951 by the Iraqi Irrigation Development Commission and written by a senior British colonial engineer of the day, Frank Haigh. In one chapter, Haigh proposed diverting the Euphrates into a "Third River" that would reach all the way from Baghdad to the Persian Gulf, bypassing the marshes. And he also proposed installing sluices to restrict the flow of the Tigris into the marshes.

Haigh's plan was to capture the water then "wasted" in the marshes and use it for irrigation. As I read the report, back in 1993 as Saddam's engineers were getting down to the job, I realized that Saddam's scheme was essentially a carbon copy.

In fact, construction of part of the Third River had begun under British supervision in the 1960s. "We did the early design work for the Third River," Bill Pemberton at the British consulting engineers Mott MacDonald later told me. "We built our bit, about fifteen miles. The rest they now seem to have done themselves." But, whatever Saddam's long-term aims for irrigation, and whatever blueprints he drew on, most agree that his immediate political purpose in draining the marshes was to empty them of the Madan, who had been prominent in the rebellion against him in the months after the first Gulf War.

And in that he succeeded. A marsh population of half a million was reduced to fewer than 80,000. Madan refugees were scattered across the Middle East, and their homeland was turned into a salt-encrusted desert, dotted with burnt-out villages and poisoned with the pesticides that Saddam's soldiers poured into the marshes to kill any remaining life.

Before Saddam, the marshlands were by some way the largest area of wetland in the Middle East. They comprised three distinct areas—the Hawr Al Hammar marshes south of the Euphrates; a large complex of permanent lakes and marshland between the Euphrates and Tigris known as the Amara marshes; and the Al-Hawizeh marshes that stretched east from the Tigris into Iran. The last of these survived Saddam's engineering the best because it was partly fed by the Karkeh River flowing out of Iran. But by the time of the second Gulf War that too was suffering badly as Iran filled a giant new dam on the river as part of a big agricultural development project.

The Karkeh's water rarely makes it across the border into the marshes anymore. According to UNEP's Hassan Partow, lakes that were permanent features as recently as 2000 have disappeared and the Al-Hawizeh marshes have become "a landscape of parched beds, withering reeds and sterile salt flats." The remaining wet areas are likely to disappear altogether before the end of the decade.

As the second Gulf War drew to a close, an unexpected defender of the Mesopotamian marshes emerged. Azzam Alwash is an Iraqi exile living in California, whose father had been an irrigation engineer helping outsiders grow rice on the edge of the marshes. On the face of it, you might expect Alwash to favour draining more of the marshes. But, as he told me in an interview as the US forces charged across his old homeland in the direction of Baghdad, he was a determined defender of the marshes, and wanted to form a scientific hit squad to bring back the water.

As a boy, he explained, he had gone duck-shooting with his father on the marshes at weekends. Now he wanted to rehabilitate them so he could one day go back. He and his American wife, Suzie, a wetland ecologist, gathered scientists from round the world. They called it the EdenAgain project, and it also had the support of the US State Department, UNEP, the World Bank's Global Environment Facility and eventually the interim Iraqi government.

But the scientists had a warning for anyone trying to bring back the water in a hurry. The desiccated soils on the former marshes were fragile, they said. They were caked with salt left behind as the marshes dried up in the sun in the mid-1990s. The danger was that as the marshes were re-flooded, the accumulated salt would flush through former freshwater marshes, poisoning them. The freshwater marshes were the most important ecological feature of the whole wetland, they said, being home to most of its rarest species. "The one thing we cannot do is just plug up Saddam's canals and let the water flow back into the marshes," said Tom Crisman, director of the University of Florida's Centre for Wetlands and a veteran of rehabilitation projects in the Everglades.

In fact, that was precisely what happened in the months after Saddam fell. Some of the Madan moved back and, with help from local engineers from the reconstituted Ministry of Water Resources, began tearing down embankments, breaking dams and opening sluices to allow water back onto the marshes. At the time of writing, it is not entirely clear whether the scientists' fore-bodings have proved correct. At the height of the spring floods in 2004, a quarter of the marshes had re-flooded. In places, reeds had grown three metres high, fish were growing among them, migrating birds had returned to nest among them, and some Madan were using them to rebuild their traditional houses. But in other places, there was little sign of recovery, perhaps because of salt problems.

The interim Iraqi government said it wanted to restore as much of the marshes as it could. At the Stockholm Water Symposium in late 2004, Iraqi water minister Jamal Rashid told me, "Maybe we won't be able to restore 100 per cent of the marshes, but 70 or 80 per cent would make me quite pleased." That is a big task. "The job can be done, but it will have to be a phased approach, starting with areas near the main rivers and then working into the centre of the marshes," said Crisman. And it could cost half a billion dollars.

Will it happen? That too is unclear. For one reason, after the first flush of environmental enthusiasm, other ministries with different agendas have been taking an interest in the marshes. There are competing demands, not least the possibility that large amounts of oil may lie beneath the re-emerging reed beds. But the big problem now that Saddam and his engineers have departed is water. Will there be enough to refill the marshes?

Like wetlands the world over, the Mesopotamian marshes are threatened by increasing demands for water upstream. And less and less water has been flowing down the Tigris and Euphrates in the years since Saddam sabotaged the marshes. Indeed, it is a moot point to what extent Saddam killed the marshes and to what extent new dams upstream did the dirty deed. Most of those dams are in Turkey, the source of most of the rivers' flow. Dams like the giant Ataturk dam on the Euphrates have cut flows on the two rivers into Iraq by a fifth. And, perhaps even more damaging for the marshes, they have eliminated the peak spring floods. It was these peak flows that inundated the widest areas of marshes. And, as on other great rivers, from the Mekong to the Logone, it was the flood season flows that sustained the greatest biological productivity, to the benefit of both wildlife and the humans who tap the natural resources.

"With more dams being built all the time, the whole region is in a water crisis," says Hassan Partow. Since the end of the war, UNEP has been trying to broker a deal among the nations on the rivers that feed the marshes, to share water among themselves and to engineer a spring flood pulse into the marshes. But the signs are not good. Turkey has been especially hostile. And Iran has refused to budge on its ambitions to take most of the water out of the Karkeh River before it reaches the Al-Hawizeh marshes.

In the short term, if Iraq wants to re-create the marshes, it may have to go ahead with what water it has. "Even with the present amount, it should be possible to do a lot," Partow says. "The key is to re-establish some flows of freshwater through the main marsh areas. After that there may be a choice between creating one large shallow saline wetland and sealing off some salty areas to create smaller areas of fresher water." But a full recovery will require a rethink on the management of the rivers by all four countries.

Meanwhile, Alwash is waiting and dreaming. "I used to go hunting and picnicking with my father on the marshes every week," he told me. "You could travel by kayak for hundreds of kilometres from my home in Nasariyah. My dream is that one day soon I will be able to go again with my own children." If that ever happens, it could be of huge importance for remaking the world's rivers.

38

MORE CROP PER DROP

Can the Pepsee save the world? Pepsees are small tubes made of light, disposable plastic and designed to encase individual ice candies—lollipops, or whatever you choose to call them. They are manufactured all over the world and are just about the most disposable product imaginable. In India they are made under the Pepsee brand name. Millions of roadside vendors across the land buy the polyethylene tubes, which come in long rolls that can be torn off at perforations stamped into the plastic every twenty centimetres or so.

Sometime around 1998, somewhere in the Maikal hills of central India, someone—perhaps a farmer with a sideline selling ices—started using Pepsee rolls for another purpose: for irrigating his fields. He had discovered that the rolls of plastic tubing made perfect cheap conduits for distributing water to plants. Shilp Verma of the International Water Management Institute in India says, "It is not very clear how and exactly where the innovation first started, but it spread among farmers like wildfire." The farmers took the rolls, laid them down rows of crop plants as near as possible to the roots, and poured water in at one end. As the water ran down the tubes, it dripped through the perforations to water the plants.

At the start, says Verma, there was one problem. Algae grew in the wet, sunny environment of the tubes. But Indian innovation was equal to the task. Wise to the new use for their product, the manufacturers produced an even cheaper version made of black recycled plastic and known to farmers as the Black Pepsee. Problem solved. Without light the algae dies. This startlingly successful exercise in lateral thinking has unlocked a holy grail for irrigation engineers. It has produced the first dirt-cheap method of providing drip irrigation for poor farmers.

Farmers across the world have traditionally irrigated their fields by pouring on water indiscriminately. Some water reaches crop roots; most does not. The result has often been waterlogged soils, a buildup of salt and growing water shortages. At a conservative estimate, two-thirds of the water sent down irrigation canals never reaches the plants it is intended for. Technologists early in the twentieth century got to work on the problem. First they came up with the sprinkler that doused fields in a fine spray of water from a central pivot. That saved the worst excesses of over-irrigation, but was equally indiscriminate and lost a lot of water to evaporation. It was also expensive and required energy to spray the water around.

The next advance was modern drip irrigation. Various people claim this idea for themselves. But credit is normally given to an Israeli engineer called Symcha Blass, who retired to the Negev desert in the early 1960s and, as he told it, one day noticed how a large tree grew in the desert because it was right next to a slowly dripping tap. He mused on the matter and subsequently invented a narrow tube that could deliver water under pressure and drip it close to the roots of plants. He filed a patent in Tel Aviv in 1969. The trick, as much as anything, was timing. His idea coincided with the development of modern plastics that made his system economic for the first time, and with the growing realization in arid countries like Israel that water was in increasingly short supply.

Drip irrigation can take many forms. Mostly, it is high-tech, with water pumped down pipes under pressure and sent into side pipes from where sophisticated "drippers" deliver it to roots. Such systems can include flow meters, pressure gauges and even soil-moisture gauges to optimize delivery and keep losses to a minimum. Today, large farms in California, Tunisia, Israel and Jordan specialize in such systems. In Jordan, drip irrigation has reduced water use on farms by a third, while raising yields. Israeli farmers have raised water productivity fivefold in the past thirty years through a mixture of drip irrigation and recycling treated urban waste water onto their fields.

The technology should have taken off. But it hasn't. It remains virtually ignored by the mass of small farmers in poor countries who face some of the worst water shortages. In India, for instance, despite strong government promotion and subsidies, drips irrigate fewer than 1 per cent of fields. "It is still largely seen as a technology for 'gentleman' farmers," says Verma. Which is perhaps not surprising, since the full kit can cost more than $2,000 for one hectare, and even stripped-down systems developed for poor countries cost at least $500.

Another reason is that most farmers in most places at most times get their water at heavily subsidized prices—a tenth of the real cost is typical everywhere from India to Mexico and Pakistan to California. And when farmers pump water from beneath their fields, they pay no more than the cost of a pump and electricity, which itself is usually highly subsidized. Except in an immediate crisis, there is little incentive to save water. So what will turn the tide? More realistic proper pricing of water would certainly help. But so too would appropriate technology. And that means going back to basics.

Drip irrigation, it turns out, is not a brand-new technology. At least two thousand years ago, Chinese farmers were making small holes in earthenware pitchers and burying them in the soil. They would go round their fields every few hours to refill the pitchers, which then simply leaked water into the root zone. This indigenous system is also known in India and parts of Africa and the Middle East.

Indian farmers also have a tradition of irrigating from hollow bamboo tubes, pierced with holes and laid out along fields. More recently they have adapted the bicycle inner tube, making a few extra punctures to allow a stead drip of water into the ground. But you can only get your hands on so many inner tubes. So now the Pepsee is spreading fast across India. No wonder it took off. A kilogram roll of the stuff can be bought for 50 rupees. Even allowing for the necessary plumbing to deliver water, the overall cost—around 2,500 rupees or $50 a hectare—is less than a tenth of that of even the cheapest conventional systems.

In the face of escalating water problems, agricultural researchers round the world are adopting a new philosophy of "more crop per drop." It is a huge turn around from the green revolution days, when the philosophy might reasonably be called "the more water the better." Raj Gupta, director of a large agricultural research centre run by the International Maize and Wheat Improvement Center in the heart of Delhi, says, "For the first time, we are starting to measure crop yields in terms of the tonnage produced for a given amount of water, rather than a given amount of land."

Gupta holds that cheap drip-irrigation systems like the Pepsee could just save India from running out of water. To go with it, he has a whole suite of changes to current farming methods. They include planting crops on raised beds, reduced ploughing and levelling the land to prevent waterlogging. Together, he believes they could reduce water use across northern India, the breadbasket of the country, by a third or more, and save millions of farmers in the south from penury as the groundwater bubble bursts. And what will work in India should work in China and Colombia, Mexico and Mali, Libya and Lesotho.

Rice is an early target for the "more crop per drop" crusade. The world's most popular grain consumes more water than any other food crop, typically twice as much as wheat for every tonne of output. More than a third of all the water abstracted from rivers and groundwaters on the planet goes to irrigate rice paddy in Asia. But with half of the world's rice grown in water-stressed China and India, that level of production cannot continue. Experiments in India and at the International Rice Research Institute in the Philippines show that rice can be grown with much less water. The trick is to abandon the traditional method of growing seedlings in nurseries and then transplanting them into paddy that has to be kept flooded. Much less water is needed if they are instead planted directly into muddy soil. Some varieties can already be grown this way. If those varieties were more widely adopted, they would cut water use by a fifth—and require less labour into the bargain. Other crops offer similar benefits from water-saving methods of cultivation.

Researchers say this new approach amounts to a "blue revolution" to follow the green revolution. The Washington-based International Food Policy Research Institute (IFPRI), which is part of a network that also includes the international water management and rice research institutes and Gupta's maize and wheat centre, says it is vital that technologies like drip irrigation are more widely adopted. Together, they could bring cost-effective global savings in water use of more than a fifth.

Already there are governments in water-short regions keen to take up the challenge. Parts of China are in the forefront. Unable to wait for Yangtze water from the south-to-north project, Shandong province on the North China plain—where the people get what water is left in the Yellow River after every other province has had its fill—responded to water riots in 2000 by agreeing to spend $6 billion on water conservation on farms.

Meanwhile, there is plenty to be done at plant-breeding stations. Most modern "high-yielding" plant varieties are hopeless water guzzlers. Only now are breeders turning their attention to producing varieties that use water efficiently. New rice varieties, the researchers say, could one day cut water use by as much as half. But another step is required. There has to be a rethink about where crops are grown. We need to fit the crops grown to water availability, rather than attempting to do things the other way round. Many parts of the arid world simply need to give up growing water-guzzling crops.

Cotton is perhaps the worst offender. The emptying of the Aral Sea is its most obvious victim. But most of the cotton-growing round the world is destroying rivers. The cotton growers of the Murray River and the Indus should be halted, too. Many researchers go further. Gupta says much of northern India should stop growing rice altogether, and switch to wheat and maize. Similarly the dairies of Gujarat should be weaned off cattle fed on alfalfa irrigated in the state. In China, many argue that the country should shift its entire farming effort from the arid north, where the Yellow River is running out, to the wetter south. Better that, they say, than spending tens of billions of dollars to bring the water north.

Mark Rosegrant at IFPRI says the effects of a blue revolution could be profound. Cutting water abstractions for agricultural irrigation water could leave an estimated thousand cubic kilometres of water in the world's rivers each year. "Many planned dams will be cancelled." From the Rio Grande to the Yellow River to the Indus and the Nile, dried-up rivers could resume their flows. A start could be made on reviving the Aral Sea.

Agriculture is, for most countries of the world, the biggest user of water and the biggest cause of water shortages. And that is where the big solutions lie. But we can all contribute. Take the lavatory. In most homes it is responsible for a third or more of all the water use. This need not be so. In the US, the amount of water used to flush the nation's toilets has been cut by three-quarters in the past two decades, thanks to bigger valves and S-bends that allow a shorter, faster and more efficient flush. The standard flush is now six litres rather than thirteen litres. (This ensured a substantial decline in indoor water use in US homes since around 1980 which, sadly, has been more than wiped out by increased outdoor use, especially for sprinkling lawns.) Similar savings can be made by redesigning everything from shower units and taps to public urinals and industrial processes.

Unfortunately, not all countries take this approach. One British water region found that modifying every toilet in London would save more water than could be provided by building a new reservoir on the River Thames. And it would be cheaper. But the company wants the reservoir anyway.

But water utilities that encourage their customers to save water would do well to put their own houses in order. In most of the world's cities—from London to Nairobi to Shanghai—between a third and a half of all the water put into the mains disappears through leaks before reaching its customers. In Africa, people in the countryside walk for miles to collect water while city water pipes leak half their contents into the ground. Yet cities with active programs to find and repair leaks have found saving water is cost-effective. Singapore, which has to buy most of its water from neighbouring Malaysia, has taken a tough approach and got its leaks down to 5 per cent—probably a world record.

If we take the trouble to use the water-saving technologies available, we can save water in the way we are learning to save energy and recycle waste—for the good of our planet as well as our pockets.

39

WATER ETHICS

The task of providing water for the planet's growing population is huge. Even basic needs for the existing population still go unmet. More than a billion people, in shanty towns and remote villages across the poor world, have no access to reliably clean drinking water. Most are in sub-Saharan Africa and South Asia. But we should not forget that there are hydrologically dispossessed even in the rich world; they include the inhabitants of *colonias* on the US side of the Mexican border.

The World Summit on Sustainable Development in Johannesburg in 2002 promised to provide for at least half of the dispossessed billion by 2015, to meet their basic human right to clean water. Fulfilling that promise will require making new water connections for 125,000 people every day. And even if the pipes can be laid and the pumps installed, nobody is sure whether there will be enough water to do the job—especially if the newly connected then all install lavatories that require flushing.

Optimist Tony Allan of the London School of Oriental and African Studies in London says, "The key to avoiding catastrophic water shortages is bringing people out of poverty." He has a case. By and large, the people who are short of water are the poor. Even in desert countries, those with money can get water. Sufficient money can almost always deliver sufficient water for immediate needs—even if it requires a desalination plant or a ludicrously long pipe.

Already, across rich and poor worlds alike, water is flowing uphill to urban users, who can almost always outbid farmers and the rural poor. Water demand for domestic and industrial use is expected to increase by two-thirds by 2025. And in most places, one way or another, that demand will be met. But, equally, money thrown at problems often produces the wrong solution. The World Bank and water engineers said in Johannesburg that it would cost $180 billion to get clean drinking water and basic sanitation to those who don't have it, or about $100 per head. They meant it would cost that much using conventional Western solutions, like large dams, water-treatment works, pipe networks and sewer systems.

That kind of money is unlikely ever to be found, any more than the world's poor farmers will be kitted out with high-tech drip-irrigation systems. But grassroots-aid groups insist that the job can be done at a tenth of the cost with simpler technologies like wells and rainwater harvesting and simple latrines. That must be the strategy.

But if basic human needs for water can be met in most places at most times, what about providing enough water to grow the crops to feed ourselves? That is a far harder nut to crack. The amounts of water involved are much greater. Farmers today get two-thirds of the water taken from the world's rivers and under-ground reserves. But that proportion is sure to decline as urban and industrial customers—including the growers of a handful of cash crops such as cotton—take precedence in the marketplace. Food farming will always be the poor relation when water is in short supply.

By 2025, economists say water scarcity will be cutting global food production by 350 million tonnes a year. That is rather more than the current US grain harvest, and the equivalent of a loaf of bread every week for every person on the planet. For hundreds of millions of people, that disappearing loaf may be the only one they get.

As the rivers run dry, more and more irrigation canals run dry too. And underground reserves cannot make up the difference.

We are already living on borrowed time by mining the aquifers—dipping into the slow, often largely unrenewable water cycle to top up the fast, renewable cycle. We will live to regret this; and if we don't, our children will. Up to a billion people are today eating food grown using underground water that is not being replaced.

Another safety valve is importing "virtual water" in the form of food. Many nations already do this to replace crops they would once have grown for themselves. In the next two decades, water scarcity will shift where the world's food is grown, away from water-poor countries in North Africa, the Middle East and much of Asia. Provided these countries have the money to buy this virtual water, they may get by for a while. But there are limits to this: we cannot all import virtual water, even if we have the money. The real water has to be somewhere for the crops to be grown.

Perhaps the most telling case today is China. Historically, the world's most populous nation has almost always fed itself. But today, increasing water shortages are pushing the country to import food in a big way for the first time. And such is China's size that this is already impacting on world food security. To keep China fed, strategic grain reserves are emptying and world grain prices rising. The agronomist Lester Brown asked in the title of a book on Chinese agriculture a few years ago: *Who will feed China?* But increasingly, as the rivers run dry, we have to ask: who will feed the world?

The good news is that we never destroy water. We may pollute it, irrigate crops with it or flush it down our toilets. We may even encourage it to evaporate into the air by leaving it around in large reservoirs in the hot sun. But somewhere, sometime, it will return, purged and fresh, in the rain clouds over India or Africa or the chalk hills of England. Each day more than a thousand cubic kilometres of water rains onto the Earth. Water is the ultimate renewable resource. And there is, even today, enough to go round. The difficulty is in ensuring that water is always *where* we need it, *when* we need it—for all 6.5 billion of us.

As the late American hydrologist Robert Ambroggi put it three decades ago, "The problem facing mankind is not a lack of fresh water, but a lack of efficient regimes for using the water that is available." The fact that we are so bad at managing water at least shows that the potential for doing better is high. The solution in most cases is not more and bigger engineering schemes. It is not south-to-north projects or river-interlinking projects or giant desert canals or megadams. Such schemes are hugely expensive, and many are the cause of as many problems as they solve. They are, I believe, at the heart of our current inefficiency.

To manage the water cycle better, we have to give up the idea that water has to be extracted from nature and put inside metal or behind concrete before it can be used. We have to treat nature as the ultimate provider of water, rather than its wasteful withholder. We must learn to "ride the water cycle" rather than replace it.

We have to treat water as a precious resource rather than something that just falls from the sky. We have to find the "more efficient regimes" of using the water cycle that Ambroggi spoke of. That certainly means doing better science and investing in a new "blue revolution" to bring the old green revolution crops in line with hydrological realities. But beyond that, we need a new ethos for water: an ethos based not on technical fixes but on managing the water cycle for maximum social benefit rather than narrow self-interest. Access to water, most of the world agrees, is a human right. So water cannot always flow towards money, whether up hill or down dale.

These new priorities will often mean going back to ancient ways, such as harvesting the rain where it falls. There is huge potential for this and it will very often make much more sense than continuing with the twentieth-century obsession with large dams and mass transport of water in pipes and canals. My one technological bet for the twenty-first century is that rainwater harvesting will resume its pre-industrial place in water management in many countries, providing local water to meet local needs.

But the new ethos will also harness modern methods and ideas. It will adopt high-tech irrigation to provide "more crop for every drop," while recognizing the realities of finite water resources inside closed river basins. And it will explore new ways to combine different parts of the water cycle. Why build huge dams when you have natural reservoirs right beneath your feet?

One image of hope is of the disciples of Dada and others in Gujarat pouring monsoon water down their wells. Why not develop this concept on a much larger scale? Proposals for the large-scale diversion of the monsoon floodwaters of the Ganges into the aquifer beneath its plain could make sense. The best way might be to pour river water into unlined irrigation canals and let it seep underground—thus turning conventional notions of irrigation efficiency on their head.

Also underground, we might revert to modern versions of *qanats* as a means of maintaining water tables and reducing pumping. The *qanat* is a classic technology for the communal management of water. It has fallen by the wayside not through any hydrological failing, but because it does not easily fit with the modern vogue for private ownership of resources. We need to relearn some of the old lessons of sharing, if we are to manage water better.

We must realize too that water has to be given back to nature. The environmentalists' case for ensuring "conservation flows" in rivers and on wetlands is unanswerable. This is no optional extra for the "tree-huggers." Nature's free services in maintaining fisheries, protecting against floods and drought, cleaning pollution, delivering free irrigation on flood plains, watering valuable tourists sites and much else are just too valuable to be lost.

The new thinking means going with the grain of nature. To ensure our water supplies and protect ourselves against damaging floods, especially in an uncertain greenhouse world, we will often have to tear down dams and dykes, recharge the underground reservoirs and remake the rivers. We will certainly have to pour less concrete—a twentieth-century solution to a twenty-first-century problem.

The twentieth-century view that the world can only feed itself by artificial irrigation of huge areas of the developing world will also have to go. It is hubris we cannot afford. This kind of irrigation has always been a fantastically expensive and inefficient way of growing crops. It should be a last resort. That is why bodies like the World Bank have virtually stopped funding it. We seem to have forgotten that direct rainfall onto soil is, in Allan's words, "what makes possible well over half the world's crop production." Rain will continue to water most of our crops, and we can recognize that by adopting a global strategy for encouraging rainwater harvesting.

Luckily there are already places where all this is starting, fitfully, to happen. On the plains of India, farmers are taking inspiration from swamis and scientists to capture the monsoon rains on their fields and in their aquifers. In Machakos, similar techniques have turned back the advancing desert, while filling stomachs and swelling granaries. In Los Angeles, they talk of turning the most paved urban area on the planet into a "porous city" that can catch the rain, banish floods and become self-sufficient in water. Similar smaller-scale schemes have begun in European cities. In Iraq, the ancient inhabitants of the Mesopotamian marshes are returning to tear down Saddam's dykes and plug his drainage canals, remaking the wetlands that once gave birth to the story of the Garden of Eden.

Rivers are sacred in most religions. For Buddhists, the gods live at the centre of the universe, where the great rivers of their world—the Ganges, Indus and Brahmaputra—rise. Hindus go on pilgrimage to drink the holy waters of the Ganges and, further downstream thankfully, they cast the bodies of their dead into the same river. Christianity depicts humanity beginning in the Garden of Eden, where fountains fed rivers that watered the world. And, in recognition, Christians baptize the faithful in water. The sources of water are everywhere revered. Aborigines hold the waterholes and billabongs of the Australian outback to be sacred places, physical manifestations of the process of creation itself. The Japanese mark the start of rivers with Shinto temples.

Africans pray at springs in the depths of their sacred groves. Even Europe is peppered with ancient holy wells.

Rivers are symbols of nationhood, too. Like nations themselves, they are always present but always changing. Old man river, he just keeps rolling along. The Yellow River is China's "joy and sorrow." Moses parted the waters of the Nile to save his people. Canadians will trade almost anything except their most abundant resource: water. Russian nationalists in the 1980s rose in anger at the prospect of delivering Siberian water to their fellow socialist republics in Central Asia. The Thames in England and the Murray in Australia, the Loire in France and the Three Gorges in China; trout streams and salmon rivers and even crocodile swamps—all tug at the heartstrings of nations.

But we need new versions of these totems and myths: versions that recognize that the rivers may not be so permanent after all—that without conservation and management they could run dry. Old man river, he just might stop rolling along. It is hard to say how or where these totems might emerge. As hard, perhaps, as predicting the emergence of the Pepsee as a vital irrigation technology. Some things just have to be allowed to happen. But for a start, Spanish opponents of plans to divert the River Ebro were onto something when they called for a "new water ethic" that cherishes water and respects the river.

That is something that Chinese rain harvesters and Indian water priests will understand. So will fishers and environmentalists and the campaigners for "porous cities." It is an ethic that recognizes that rivers are more than just sources of water—more than the feedstock for irrigation canals and hydroelectric power stations. It recognizes that rivers provide fish and silt and recharge for underground reserves; that water purges and purifies; that there is virtue in flood pulses and in the mixing of land and water on a river flood plain.

And it requires us to find ways of storing water without wrecking the environment; of restoring water to rivers and refilling lakes and wetlands without leaving people thirsty; and of sharing waters rather than fighting over them. It requires us to go with the flow. And to do it before the rivers finally run dry.

INDEX